# Happier Hour

'Cassie Holmes is an expert on time, and this
readable, practical book might just make you
rethink how you spend yours'
– Adam Grant, *New York Times* bestselling
author of *Think Again*

'This book is an absolute gem – useful, evidence-based,
and a pleasure to read. Armed with the insights
conveyed in *Happier Hour*, we can all find greater
fulfilment in the time we have'
– Katy Milkman, bestselling author
of *How to Change*

'Terrific advice from one of my favourite
scientists about how to make best use of our
most limited resource: time'
– Angela Duckworth, *New York Times* bestselling
author of *Grit*

'With our schedules overly full, Holmes shares
research and easy strategies for not only how to
manage, but how to tap into deeper meaning.
*Happier Hour* is a joyful guide on how to spend
your hours to live a more satisfying life'
– Eve Rodsky, *New York Times* bestselling
author of *Fair Play*

'A refreshingly novel approach on
how to make your life rich'
– Jonah Berger, *New York Times* bestselling
author of *Contagious*

# Happier Hour

How to Spend Your Time for a Better,
More Meaningful Life

## CASSIE HOLMES

PENGUIN LIFE

AN IMPRINT OF

PENGUIN BOOKS

PENGUIN LIFE

UK | USA | Canada | Ireland | Australia
India | New Zealand | South Africa

Penguin Life is part of the Penguin Random House group of companies
whose addresses can be found at global.penguinrandomhouse.com.

First published in the United States of America by Gallery Books 2022
First published in Great Britain by Penguin Life 2023

001

Interior design by Davina Mock-Maniscalco
All graphics and illustrations by Hannah Sanders
Printed and bound in Great Britain by Clays Ltd, Elcograf S.p.A.

The authorized representative in the EEA is Penguin Random House Ireland,
Morrison Chambers, 32 Nassau Street, Dublin DO2 YH68

A CIP catalogue record for this book is available from the British Library

ISBN: 978-0-241-45895-2

www.greenpenguin.co.uk

*To Rob, Leo, and Lita—*
*For making my hours happier.*

# CONTENTS

Happier
Hour

*One*

# TIME POOR AND TIRED

*This time, like all times, is a very good one,*
*if we but know what to do with it.*

—Ralph Waldo Emerson

In 2013, I was sitting on the late-night train back from New York to Philadelphia and was contemplating quitting . . . everything. Between trying to be a good parent and partner, the incessant pressure to publish and perform at work, the never-ending pile of chores—it was all too much. There simply weren't enough hours in the day to get it all done, let alone to do any of it well. The coordinating and preparing and doing—it seemed to require a zesty superhero's level of energy, and I had run out. I rested my forehead against the chilled window and watched the dark blur of trees and houses whiz by.

I'd given a talk that day at Columbia Business School, sharing my latest research on how the quality of our happiness changes as we grow older. My presentation had been efficiently slotted into lunchtime, flanked by hours of back-to-back meetings, followed by a colleague dinner, throughout which I worked to stay on pace with the guys in witty banter and throwing back beers. Speeding in a taxi to the station, I prayed I wouldn't miss the last train home.

Though my typical days didn't begin in a New York City hotel room, they were similarly jam-packed and no less frenzied. I'd wake at dawn to go for a run and come back for a quick snuggle with my four-month-old, Leo, before racing to get ready and dashing to my office. Inside the bustling halls of Wharton, I'd hurriedly try to get my work done in between seminars and meetings. Then I would dash home to relieve our nanny at 6 p.m. Between putting the groceries away, preparing dinner, and cleaning up, even that precious hour before Leo's bedtime felt rushed. None of these tasks alone took much time, but taken together, these minutes of doing-doing-doing were just too many—especially given how few there were to spare.

I'd felt this way for some time. As the train sped through the darkness, I pulled my coat over me like a blanket. Deeply exhausted, I realized that I needed to truly figure out if doing *all of it* was really sustainable. To accurately assess the feasibility of continuing on this course, I knew I had to account for everything. Not just my routine tasks, but also the unanticipated and extra "exceptions" that in aggregation happened regularly (e.g., haircut, dentist, Leo's doctor's appointment, picking out a gift, getting the car serviced, showing up for jury duty). Plus, I needed to include not just my to-do lists for work and home, but my determination not to flake on going out for my friend's birthday dinner, and my decision to take Leo to his baby music class on Wednesday mornings. "All of it" needed to involve some exercise and a decent amount of sleep, because I'm not nice without either. "All of it" needed to factor in whether I'd still have enough energy to enjoy the moments I shared with Leo and my husband, Rob, at the end of the day.

The real problem I was wrestling with on the train that night was that I *wanted* to do it all. I loved my job. Not every piece of it, but I had worked hard to get to this point and found real fulfillment in conducting research and connecting with people through teaching. I adored my baby and husband, and I could not let either of those relationships suffer. I wanted to stay healthy and be a good friend. And even though I didn't like doing chores, it was important to me that I be a competent contributor to a well-functioning household and society.

I'd felt busy before. In fact, I couldn't remember a time in which I hadn't felt like I was racing against the clock trying to achieve as much as possible during every hour. I am not alone in this. We live in a culture driven toward productivity—so much so that busyness has become a status symbol that is taken to signal an individual's worth. But I knew, both personally and according to my research, that this rushing around does *not feel* fancy.

Yes, having a baby had loaded more onto my plate. I was no longer in charge of just myself and my career. Now I was fully responsible for another person's survival and well-being. But it was even more than the additional to-dos that came with a baby. Seeing him grow made me realize how quickly time was passing. Watching how much Leo had changed in just a few months highlighted how fast everything was flying by. I did not want to miss any of it simply because I was in a rush. I didn't want to speed past his childhood. I didn't want to speed through my life.

I wanted more time, but not just time to get more done. I wanted more so I could *slow down* to actually experience the hours that I spent. When looking at my life, I wanted to feel happy and not only see a blur. With my forehead on the cool window, watching the world outside speeding by, it suddenly seemed that quitting everything and moving to a sunny, slow-paced island somewhere was the optimal solution. I'd invite Leo and Rob to join me.

## The Wisdom of Data

As a social psychologist, I'm constantly looking to data to find answers for whatever questions I'm personally grappling with. (So really, I'm only partially joking when I explain my work by telling people that I conduct "me-search.") And I knew that before charging into my boss's office to tell him I'd decided to leave my dream job as a tenure-track professor, I should carefully consider the realities of living with a whole lot more free time. Before I asked Rob to walk away from his career and pack for the beach, I needed to know whether I'd indeed be happier trading an overflowing to-do list for a blank one. With more available hours in the day, would I actually feel more satisfied with my life?

To empirically guide me through this particular crisis, I recruited a couple of my favorite collaborators, Hal Hershfield and Marissa Sharif. We found a data set to analyze that captured, for tens of thousands of working and nonworking Americans, all of the activities constituting a regular day in their lives, as well as their overall satisfaction with their lives. This treasure trove of data meant that I wouldn't have to rely on advice from any one individual. Instead, we could identify significant trends across a large group of people, which would provide a much more reliable prediction. This data from the American Time Use Survey would help us answer the pressing question: What is the relationship between the amount of discretionary time people have in their daily lives and their overall happiness?

As a first step in our analysis, we calculated the varying amounts of time people had available to spend on discretionary activities—things people *want to do*. This included "doing nothing," relaxing, and watching TV. It also encompassed more active leisure pursuits, like playing sports or going to the movies or sporting events. And it contained purely social activities, like hanging out with friends and family. Importantly, this calculation of available time did *not* incorporate the day's hours spent on obligatory tasks—things people *have to do*. For instance, the litany of work tasks, household chores, dentist and doctor appointments, and errands were all grouped as nondiscretionary activities, counting as time that was unavailable.

We then tested how this calculated amount of discretionary time related to people's satisfaction in life. The results were illuminating. The following graph shows the pattern as an upside-down U-shape—like an arc or a rainbow. This shape is interesting because it points downward toward unhappiness on *both* ends of the spectrum. This means there are not one but two stumbling blocks when it comes to discretionary time. But let's first explore the far left side of this graph, which reflected my particular unhappiness. . . .

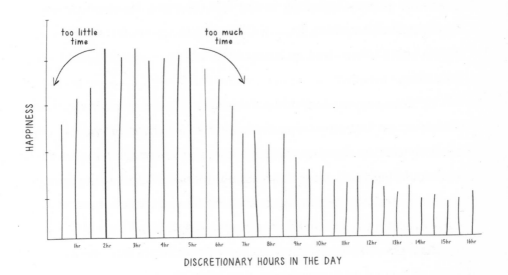

## Too Little

The graph makes clear that happiness is lower with less than approximately two hours of discretionary time in the day. This data confirmed that I indeed had too little time. I was *time poor*—defined as feeling like you have too little time available to do all that you need and want to do. It turns out that those of us who suffer from time poverty are not alone. A nationwide poll shows that nearly half of Americans report they don't have enough time to do what they want to do. Another poll shows that approximately half of Americans say they almost never feel they have time on their hands, and two-thirds say they always or sometimes feel rushed.

Even though moms tend to feel more time poor than dads, and even though working parents tend to feel particularly impoverished, *all* types of people lack for time. And it's not just my fellow Americans. People across the globe—including in the UK, Norway, Germany, Canada, Australia, Brazil, Guinea, Russia, China, Japan, and South Korea—also report being rushed and suffering from a hectic pace of life with too little time.

Validating my distress on the train that night, these results show one of the key reasons why being time poor is such an issue: people with too little time are significantly less happy and less satisfied in life. Studies from other research teams across disciplines (including psychology, sociology, and economics) have similarly shown that being time poor makes us more depressed, more stressed, and more emotionally exhausted. The constant pressure imposed by a culture that reveres busyness and hurries us along carries an emotional toll.

However, there was more to our data's story. The right side of the graph offered an unexpected counterpoint.

## Too Much

In addition to the unhappiness from having too little time, the downward slope on the other side of the arc shows that having more than approximately five hours of discretionary time in a day is also linked to less happiness. It turns out there is such a thing as having too much time!

But *why*? Given how much I longed for more free time, how could having wide-open days make me feel worse? Once I began looking into this, I realized that the story of my friend Ben, passed out in a bed of poison oak in the hills of California's Marin County, offers a clue.

Ben is a brilliant, analytical, and tremendously hardworking guy who ultimately concluded that the grief of office politics involved with running a hedge fund wasn't worth the time away from his wife and four kids. Nor was it worth the stress he carried home each day from the office. Fortunate to have the financial means, Ben decided to retire at the age of thirty-nine. This would give him time to do all the things he had always wanted to do, but had neglected while busy in his job: relaxing with his family, vacationing, reading for pleasure, and doing plenty of exercise.

Yet Ben is goal-oriented. He does not like feeling idle and derives satisfaction from being productive. Despite his intention to chill out, having so much time on his hands made Ben stir-crazy. He needed a goal, so he set one.

Ben decided that he was going to run the upcoming Dipsea. The Dipsea is the oldest trail race in America, stretching from Mill Valley to Stinson Beach in Marin's beautiful headlands. In addition to being known for its scenery, its stairs and steep trails have established the Dipsea's reputation as a grueling, treacherous race.

For months, Ben trained diligently. He closely followed the recommended regimen of hill workouts, long runs, weights, rest days, and diet. On race day, his family gathered with their hand-drawn signs and post-race snacks to greet him at the finish line. He never got there.

Ben had started the race strong and fast, challenging himself to beat the finish time he had calculated as his appropriate target. Yet about four miles in, Ben couldn't catch his breath. His intensity, dehydration, and the hot day had gotten the better of him. The next thing he knew, the paramedics were standing over him strategizing how to get him into an ambulance. Lying in the shrubs, his whole body itched. The toxins of the poison oak that had cushioned his fall had begun to wreak their havoc.

Only after he had reconnected with his terrified family and received the doctor's assurance that he would be okay did Ben laugh at the ridiculous situation he'd gotten himself into. Wired toward achievement, Ben had felt uncomfortable with days spent "doing nothing." Dissatisfied by having nothing to show for his time, he had transformed what was intended to be an enjoyable activity into an extreme goal-directed pursuit. As Ben recovered, he realized the absurdity of just how hard he had pushed himself for this race.

Though Ben is exceptional in many ways, he is not unique in his drive for accomplishment. In a follow-up experiment that Hal, Marissa, and I conducted, we found that lacking a sense of productivity is *why* people with excessive amounts of available time feel less satisfied in their lives. If as a kid you started feeling restless toward the end of a lazy summer, you have experienced something similar. Just like Ben, many people have an aversion to being idle and are oriented toward productivity. There is value to being somewhat busy, because it gives us a sense of purpose in our daily lives.

It is worth pointing out that having a sense of purpose does not require working in a paid job. For one, volunteering (work that is unpaid) often provides a sense of purpose. Additionally, tasks required to produce well-functioning children and households can similarly offer a satisfying sense of accomplishment; and when completed by someone from the household, this work also is not paid. Lastly, some explicitly nonwork activities (e.g., pursuing hobbies and playing sports) are considered by many to be both productive and purposeful. Yet I recognized that in my case, work gives me a significant source of purpose.

In light of the data and Ben's experience after deciding to stop working, I'd become convinced that, for me, quitting everything to spend my days relaxing wasn't the solution.

## Just Right

The pattern in our graph was instructive. It showed that regularly having less than two hours of discretionary time each day is indeed too little. It causes stress and unhappiness, which I knew all too well. On the other hand, from the data I now also knew that regularly having more than five hours of discretionary time in the day is too much, because it undermines one's sense of purpose. Our research suggested that if I quit my job, I would likely feel unhappy as well. With too much time, I would surely find another endeavor to satisfy my drive to feel productive, and this activity too would eventually cause me stress. But whatever I'd end up doing wouldn't utilize the skills I'd spent years developing in a field I truly cared about. Having between two and five hours seems to be about right.

These results didn't merely validate my emotional experience; they offered me hope, and ultimately guided a life decision. The sweet spot for the ideal amount of available daily hours wasn't completely out of reach. It was not unreasonable to commit to having a couple hours each day to spend on what brings me joy. An honest calculation from a typical day showed that I was already pretty close:

- ✦ 15 minutes of morning snuggles with Leo

- ✦ 25 minutes talking to my friend on the phone during my walk home from the office

- ✦ 30 minutes having a glass of wine and dinner with Rob (this would ideally be longer, but Leo's fussing often cut things short)

- ✦ 20 sweet and calming minutes singing Leo to sleep

These were 90 minutes (an hour and a half) in my day that I wouldn't have wanted to spend any other way. Sure, I would have preferred talking to my friend while sitting together over a cup of coffee, and I would have liked not having baby distractions while dining with Rob. But those small imperfections didn't disqualify that time as discretionary, even joyful. It was eye-opening to realize that the target two hours was well within my reach—*without* me having to make any drastic, life-altering changes. Yes, I'd have to be thoughtful and make some tweaks to my schedule to get there. But I could easily implement some small changes to become happier. By protecting work hours from waste and distraction so that I could produce more of what felt purposeful during those hours, by prioritizing time for activities that filled *me* rather than just my schedule, by outsourcing some chores so that I could instead spend that time playing with Leo, by savoring and celebrating day-to-day moments as I shared them with the people I loved . . . maybe I could "do it all." Rob could reserve packing for our next vacation.

## It's About Time

When it came to my happiness, I was right: time has proven to be my greatest challenge. Yet I used to believe that it had to do with quantity: if only I had more hours in the day, I could do everything I wanted, accomplish everything, and feel better. Interestingly, however, the flat portion of the graph between two and five hours suggests that within a pretty wide range, the amount of time people have available is unrelated to their happiness. This is important because it means that, except at the very extremes, to enjoy greater satisfaction in life, it's not so much a question of the amount we have. It's really about how we *spend* what we have.

So the real answer is not about being time rich; it is about *making* the time you have rich. This graph clarified for me what much of my research had been suggesting all along: for greater happiness, time isn't only a challenge, it's the solution. Time is the singular resource that if invested correctly can produce a good, maybe even great, life. If you know how to invest your time *and* are invested in your time, you can make yourself happier. It's about knowing how to allocate the hours you have to achieve outcomes that ultimately matter—the ones that will allow you to look back on your days, years, and life feeling satisfied and fulfilled. And it's about being completely engaged during that time to make those hours happier.

This focus on investing time (as opposed to money) may seem odd coming from someone who has spent her career as a business school professor. In teaching MBAs, success is typically measured by profits. It's about the amount made, and more is better. The very reason that most of my students are getting an MBA and pursuing a career in business is to make money, and, they hope, a lot of it. It's not just my business-minded students, however. In a survey in which my research team asked thousands of people representing a range of occupations and income levels from across the country whether they would prefer more money or more time, the majority chose money. Yet this might not be the right choice.

Automobile mogul Henry Ford is said to have remarked, "Business must be run at a profit, else it will die. But when anyone tries to run a business solely for profit . . . the business must die as well, for it no longer has a reason to exist." This quote applies as much to us as individuals as it does to businesses. Despite the widespread focus on money, the real determinant of success and satisfaction in life isn't so much about the money earned, but the time spent. *Was there a purpose? Was it worth the investment . . . of time?*

Over the years, I have conducted more than a dozen studies testing the effects of focusing on time instead of money as our critical resource. The results are consistent and clear: regardless of how much money or time one has, paying greater attention to time predicts higher levels of happiness. Those who place more value on their time rather than money report feeling more positive in their days and more satisfied about their lives. The benefits of being time-focused accrue from being deliberate and investing in better ways—in activities that are more fun, meaningful, and aligned with one's values. Thus, not straying too far from my business school roots, this book *is* an investment guide. But it's not about money. It's about how to invest your most precious resource.

## Happier Hours

Every one of us has exactly the same number of hours to work with and play with each day. We all have twenty-four hours to allocate the best we can, and the stakes are high. Our hours and days add up to years and decades, and ultimately to our entire lives. How we spend our time defines who we are, the memories we cherish, and how we will be remembered by those we leave behind.

And we all want to be happy. People around the globe consistently rate it among their most important pursuits. This isn't remotely new. Back in the seventeenth century, French philosopher and mathematician Blaise Pascal observed, "All men [and presumably he also meant women] seek happiness. This is without exception. Whatever different means they employ, they all tend to this end."

Happiness (which the psychology literature refers to as subjective well-being and is defined as how positive you feel during your days and how satisfied you feel about your life overall) matters . . . a lot. And it isn't an indulgent or frivolous pursuit. It isn't selfish, nor is it about plastering a smile on your face and pretending everything is swell.

This basic emotion has a tremendous ripple effect. It can make you more resilient, better at your job, and more giving to the people around you. Decades of studies have shown that feeling happy benefits us both in the office and in our relationships (personal and professional). For example, happiness increases motivation, creativity, and adaptive problem-solving—all of which can help us at work and get us through challenging times outside of work. It makes us like people more and be liked by people more. It makes us nicer, more likely to say and do kind things and to help others out.

Happiness is also *good* for us. It boosts our immune functioning, raises our threshold for pain, helps our bodies respond better to physiological stressors, and is a significant predictor of longevity. Altogether, these studies provide undeniable empirical evidence that happiness is key to living longer and better lives. So, not only do we all *want* to be happy, we *should* want to be happy.

This interplay between time and happiness is what has compelled more than a decade of my research, my recent teaching, and now this book. I'm looking to inform the fundamental human question: How can each of us make the absolute most of the time we have?

Since that fateful night on the train, I have continued conducting research and have applied the subsequent findings to guide my own thinking and investments of time. Even though my days are still full, I have finally figured out how to make them fulfilling. Ultimately, I did decide to leave Wharton, but I have not left my career in academia. Though I appreciated my colleagues and the vigor of the school, I took a note from my research and chose happiness. For brighter days, I did eventually ask Rob to move, and it happened to be a place with a beach nearby. But, except when on vacation, we don't spend entire days relaxing. We are now raising Leo and our daughter, Lita, back home in California.

I'm a professor at UCLA's Anderson School of Management. Determined to spend my time more purposefully, I shifted what I taught—now I teach happiness. Inspired by Laurie Santos's Psychology and the Good Life undergraduate course at Yale, and Bill Burnett and Dave Evans's Designing Your Life course at Stanford's design school, I developed a course called Applying the Science of Happiness to Life Design. It shows my MBA students how to optimize their personal and professional lives. I've culled insights from my own research, as well as that of colleagues across the fields of psychology, behavioral economics, marketing, and organizational behavior to help my students craft their time—in their day-to-day and their lives overall—to be happier.

I wrote this book to bring these lessons to you. To highlight how the underlying research—based on hundreds of thousands of data points—relates to you and your life, I'll share anecdotes from my students and my friends, as well as many of my own. These stories are necessarily personal, because our time is personal—it's the substance of our daily existence. And though every experience may not represent your own, I suspect you will see aspects of your life experience in ours. So I invite you to read along and share in this journey, and you can rely on the takeaways following each chapter to cement what you've learned on the way. Perhaps even more useful, I will give you assignments, just as I do for my students. There are more than a dozen exercises throughout the book that I strongly urge you to implement to immediately experience their proven benefits. By doing these exercises, you will essentially be taking my course and, exactly as my students have, you will enjoy greater happiness, meaning, and connection in your life as a result.

In the chapters that follow, I will first boost you out of your scarcity mindset. In chapter 2, I will help you realize that despite *feeling* time poor, you actually have all you need to be able to dedicate hours to what really matters. We'll work on your perceptions and increase your time affluence. I will give you the confidence to decide how you spend your time, which is about what's worthwhile, rather than merely efficient.

In chapter 3, I will lead you through the Time Tracking Exercise. This will help you identify which activities promise *you* the greatest happiness and which ways of spending aren't worth your time—all guiding you how to invest your time more wisely. Noting that there are inevitably some required activities that aren't particularly fun (e.g., chores, work, and commuting), in chapter 4, I will offer some strategies to make these times that threaten to feel like a waste more satisfying.

However, making the most of your time isn't just a question of the activities you spend your time on; it's also about how you engage in that time. It's about how you approach the activity and your mindset as you do it. For instance, even though having a conversation with the love of my life over a cheeseburger and a glass of pinot is among my most joyful activities, if having dinner with Rob becomes so regular that I fail to notice its specialness, or I'm so distracted by the to-do list running through my mind that I fail to hear what he just said, then I've wasted my time (and his). I've missed out on the potential happiness from that hour. So in chapter 5, I will give you strategies to pay more attention, and then, in chapter 6, some techniques to remove distractions—so that you can make the most of *all the time* you spend.

Though you have plenty of time to live a happy life, this is only true if you spend deliberately and don't let it get mindlessly filled. Your daily hours are finite. In chapter 7, I will share the importance of being proactive rather than reactive in your spending—pushing you to prioritize what really matters to you, those ways of spending that bring you joy.

Notably, each hour doesn't stand alone. It's not as straightforward as simply adding your various hours together to sum up to a satisfying week. How your week's activities are pieced together and arranged can have a significant impact on your overall satisfaction. In chapter 8, I will encourage you to view your schedule as a beautiful and colorful mosaic, and yourself as the artist. I will walk you through how to craft your time: selecting, spacing, and sequencing tiles to design an ideal week. This will allow you to increase the influence of your good times and minimize that of your chores. You'll also see that even though it's not possible to do it all and be it all in any given hour, you can do and be everything you want over the course of your weeks and months and years.

Lastly, in chapter 9, we will zoom out from focusing on your hours to consider your years and life overall. Taking this bird's-eye view will help clarify your values, what you truly care about, and what matters to you most. This broader time perspective will guide how to spend today's hours—ensuring that you fill your days with what's fulfilling, so you can look back on your years feeling a sense of meaning, without regrets.

With this empirically based wisdom, you'll learn how to craft the time of your life. It all starts with a happier hour.

## CHAPTER ONE TAKEAWAYS

✦ Time poverty is the prevalent feeling of having too much to do and too little time to do it.

✦ Having *too little* discretionary time (i.e., less than approximately two hours a day) is associated with less happiness because of stress.

✦ Yet having *too much* discretionary time (i.e., more than approximately five hours a day) is also associated with less happiness, because it fosters a sense of lacking purpose.

✦ Except at these extremes, the amount of discretionary time you have available is unrelated to happiness. Instead, happiness depends on how you spend whatever time you have.

✦ Focusing on time (rather than money) increases happiness, because it motivates you to spend more deliberately—in happier and more fulfilling ways.

✦ Feeling happy is a worthy endeavor—benefiting you at work, in your relationships, and in your health, as well as making you more resilient, creative, and kind.

# Two

# ALL THE TIME IN THE WORLD

*You will never "find" time for anything.*
*If you want time, you must make it.*

—Charles Buxton

H ere's a quick thought experiment: When you don't have enough time, what's the first thing that gets cut from your schedule?

I love to go for a run in the morning. I find that running gives me the space and time to myself that I need to think. Plus, it allows me to continue eating my beloved cheeseburgers and gooey chocolatey desserts guilt-free. But at night, as I'm getting into bed and setting my alarm clock, my mind inevitably runs through all that I'll need to do before tomorrow's class: get the kids up and ready for school, their lunches and backpacks packed, and Leo rehearsed for his spelling quiz. I also need to respond to a dozen student emails, and revise and practice my lecture. I need to have breakfast. I need to get *myself* ready, which on a teaching day requires additional time blowing out my hair and choosing a nicer outfit with the right jewelry. And I need plenty of sleep (I know from the research and personal experience that my brain is mush on less than eight hours). Disappointed, I resign myself to the apparent fact: I don't have time to go for a run.

What about you? What do temporal limitations eliminate from your days? I asked a bunch of my friends to complete this sentence: "I don't have time to . . . "

*"I don't have time to exercise."*

*"I don't have time to SLEEP!"*

*"I don't have time to read, write, or think . . . and during COVID, to wash my friggin' hair!"*

*"I don't have time to floss."*

*"I don't have time to read a book, organize my house, or brainstorm about my future."*

*"I don't have time to paint."*

*"I don't have time to learn and play music, read books, or travel to see my friends and family."*

*"I don't have time to work out or play soccer with my son."*

*"I don't have the time (or energy) to deeply connect with my kids and spouse."*

*"I don't have time to go to therapy, or even find a therapist."*

*"I don't have time to myself. And what would I do with that time? Well, I'd go for a long walk, watch inane TV, eat snacks, take a nap, and call someone to just catch up."*

*"I don't have time to meditate."*

*"I don't have time to cook fancy and delicious meals."*

*"I don't have time to create my dream garden."*

*"I don't have time to do it all well."*

The list shows the many healthy and enriching things we wish we could do, but don't—solely due to lacking time. It reveals that without enough time, we fail to care for our bodies by exercising or spending the eight minutes it takes to shower . . . or the one minute it takes to floss. We don't take time for ourselves—to rest, to read, to think, to create. We neglect our interests and what makes us interesting. We stop cultivating important relationships, let alone invest in making new ones. Ironically, the very resource that makes our life possible also seems to constrain it.

Half of the American population and millions of people around the globe feel this way. Author and motivational speaker Brené Brown describes modern culture as one of scarcity—of not having or being enough. Behavioral economists Sendhil Mullainathan and Eldar Shafir wrote an entire book on the perils of existing with scarce resources. I'd argue that in this era of endless access and great expectations, we are more specifically struggling from scarce *time*. Without enough time, we are limited from doing our best and being our best. Not having enough time makes us do less and be less. And as we learned in the previous chapter, it makes us less happy. Being time poor limits the quality of our lives.

## What's Less Isn't More

After surveying my friends, I decided to explore the consequences of being time poor among a broader, more representative population. I searched the academic literature and conducted several experiments myself. These findings proved just as dispiriting as the list. Apparently, having a limited amount of time makes less of *everyone*.

As I walk you through the findings, be prepared because the results will initially seem discouraging. However, knowing how we are prone to skimp will better equip us to combat the limiting effects. And I promise that before the end of the chapter, you'll have some actionable ways to take control of your time and expand it—making more for you and more of your life.

## Less Healthy

My own skimping turns out to be very common: with too little time, people sacrifice getting outside for a run, going to the gym, doing a yoga class, or signing up for a spin session. Irrespective of one's method for getting the body moving, studies show that time stress makes people exercise less in general, and this has a direct negative effect on both physical and emotional well-being. Simply put, by skipping exercise, we are making ourselves less happy.

Time poverty negatively impacts other health-related behaviors too. Too busy to eat fresh foods, get a full night's sleep, or go to the doctor, time-poor people are more likely to be overweight, to suffer hypertension, and to be less healthy overall. If reading these findings feels like looking into a scary crystal ball, don't worry—I'm with you. As confessed, I have often felt too time-crunched to go for a morning run. And I have found that a canned latte and donut *are* faster and easier to consume on the way to work than a fruit salad and egg whites. And though I'll make time to take Leo or Lita to the doctor for wellness checkups or at the slightest sign of illness, I don't do it when I'm the one feeling crummy. Even though these aren't the happiest findings, it's good to know them, because shortly I'll tell you how we can gain from this information.

## Less Kind

Being time poor doesn't just affect how we treat ourselves. When time feels scarce, we become stingy with it—giving less to others. In a rush, we are less likely to take the time to call our friend who just changed jobs, or even hold the door open for a slow trailing stranger. This stinginess has been observed among even the most compassionate people: seminary students. In an experimental classic conducted by John Darley and Daniel Batson in the 1970s, a group of seminary students were tasked with presenting the parable of the Good Samaritan—the Bible story about a stranger who stopped to help a robbed and beaten traveler lying helpless on the side of the road. But here's the catch: before the students headed off one by one to give their presentations, some were told that they were late and didn't have a lot of time. The rest received no such information. In the hallway on the way to give their presentations, each of them encountered a man hunched over, coughing. He was clearly in need of help (actually, he was an actor hired for the study). The researchers tracked which of the seminary students gave up some of their time to stop and help this man (notice the irony here?). The students who were told they had limited time were significantly less likely to spend some time helping.

I also documented this behavior in a simple experiment among college students. For half of my study participants, I conjured the feeling of time scarcity by instructing them to write about a day they felt extremely busy and rushed. I instructed the other half to write about a day they had loads of spare time. A little later, I asked everyone whether they would be willing to stay an extra fifteen minutes to help a needy high school student by editing his college application essay. Compared to those who recalled having lots of time, those who'd been reminded of feeling rushed were significantly less willing to give their time.

Do you see the pattern starting to form? When we feel as though we have too little time, we end up living a smaller life. But I assure you, this is not the only option. After we cover just one more negative consequence of feeling time poor, we will move on to some solutions.

## Less Confident

Not only does feeling time poor make us do less, it also makes us feel less sure of ourselves. Two weeks before their midterm exam, students were asked by a group of researchers to report the grade they expected to get on the test, as well as their level of confidence. Then, on the morning of the exam, the students were again asked to report how they thought they would do. The results of this study showed that when the students had a lot of time to prepare, they were significantly more confident in their exam performance than when they had little time. Unfortunately, the implications of this extend well beyond test-taking. Time scarcity dampens our confidence in achieving all types of goals.

According to a well-established theory proposed by social psychologist Tory Higgins, we have two basic forms of motivation: one focused on achieving positive outcomes (called "promotion focus"), and the other focused on avoiding negative outcomes (called "prevention focus"). Though individuals differ in their general inclination for being more promotion- or prevention-focused, the situation—especially *time*—can also influence the way in which people approach their goals. When we have a lot of time, we tend to be more promotion-focused. Time affluence essentially gives us a confidence boost—making us optimistic and excited about all we believe we can achieve. With enough time, the sky's the limit! But when time is limited (as it so often is), we become pessimistically prevention-focused.

With little time remaining, we get consumed by the possibility of failure and lower our sights to match our lacking confidence. When time poor, we're just trying to get by.

My colleagues Jennifer Aaker and Ginger Pennington and I found evidence for this dynamic in a consumer domain. Among shoppers, we observed that those who still had plenty of time to make a purchase were most attracted to the products that offered "the best" experience and to the ads that promised "the best" deal. However, under a time pressure, shoppers were instead drawn to products that would simply be good enough and were not too expensive. This lowering of expectations with limited time explains why early in January, you will entertain grandiose notions of the very best gift by which you might woo your valentine. With ample time, your goals are set romantically high. But then, when you find yourself shopping on February 13, your aspirations have plummeted. You've become more logistical than romantic in your thinking, and you look for a gift that will merely keep you out of the doghouse.

## Don't Settle for Less

Now it's finally time for some good news! The dismal picture the findings have painted thus far isn't complete. It doesn't include how very busy, time-strapped people can still manage to be confident, healthy, and kind.

The Notorious R.B.G. is one good example. Despite her demanding US Supreme Court schedule of hearing cases and writing opinions that decided (among other issues) the course of the country's women's rights and healthcare system, Justice Ruth Bader Ginsburg still exercised regularly. Well into her eighties, she worked with a personal trainer for a full hour several times a week. Another example and hero of mine is my friend Shaolee. She runs a nonprofit in New York that trains and places women breadwinners in stable jobs in the food services industry, allowing them to put food on their own families' tables. On top of Shaolee's demanding work hours, she shares parenting duties for a five- and seven-year-old with her husband, Scott, who is just as busy in his finance job. Despite having scarce spare moments, Shaolee still finds time to do thoughtful things for people outside her family, her organization, and the many women her organization serves. The other day, I unexpectedly received a book of poetry along with an uplifting note in the mail. It was from Shaolee.

Yes, these women are incredible. Just like the rest of us, however, they only have twenty-four hours a day. They do not *actually* have more time. But they also do *not* cut these worthwhile activities from their days. So, what's going on here?

Here's the reality. Yes, everyone objectively has twenty-four hours each day and sixty minutes in each of those hours. How we perceive an amount of time, however, is surprisingly subjective. How we experience the duration of our days and hours varies dramatically. The amount of time within each objective temporal unit—an hour, a day, a year—can *feel* like all the time in the world, or like no time at all. The reason behind the saying "a watched pot never boils" is that when you're waiting for something, that time you spend anticipating (even if it's actually just ten minutes) feels like an eternity. But when you're hugging your honey goodbye, ten minutes is painfully short. Time does indeed fly faster when you're having fun, and there's even a research paper to prove it.

This relativity is important because how long a minute, an hour, a day, or a decade seems influences whether you view yourself as having "enough." Remember, the definition of time poverty is the *feeling of not having enough time* to do everything you need to and want to do. But notice the subjectivity in both components of this definition: 1) what you want and believe you need to do, and 2) your confidence in being able to accomplish all those things with what you have. Let me unpack this a bit so that you know how to take control of your temporal wealth.

## Limit Your List

The first piece of this puzzle involves the list of activities that you *perceive* could and should make up your day. It's important to note that the content and length of this list is molded, and is thus moldable. A major shaper here is technology. Technological advancements benefit us in so many ways. The smartphones that fit comfortably in our pockets so that we can carry them around with us everywhere are indeed very smart. They place the world at our fingertips. They increase the possibilities of us knowing more and doing more. In general, this is great. But we need to be aware of how this impacts the list of all we *believe* we could and should be doing.

*Social Media.* When people use social media to stay connected within their existing relationships, research shows it promotes well-being. However, the vast majority of time on social media isn't spent messaging loved ones; it's spent watching the carefully curated, smile-filled lives of distant acquaintances and celebrities. Since we are prone to assess how we're doing by comparing ourselves to others, it's this usage that perpetuates feelings of loneliness, depression, and the fear of missing out. In addition to these well-documented hits on emotional well-being, I believe that exposure to social media worsens time poverty. By constantly keeping us apprised of all the desirable things that others are doing and we *could* be doing, social media compiles an unreasonable list of activities for our days.

Given this, one way to increase your available time—subjectively as well as objectively—is to reduce the amount of time you spend scrolling. This will lessen how much you enviously ruminate on all the glamorous (and cherry-picked) ways others are spending their time. It will also free up actual minutes, which, for many, sum up to multiple weekly hours.

*On-Demand Everything.* In addition to greater awareness of what others are doing, smartphones grant us constant access to do more things. Between news articles, TV shows, songs, TED Talks, music lessons, performances, educational seminars, museum tours . . . there are *so many* enticing activities that are readily available to us *all the time.* Of course there aren't enough hours in a day, or even a lifetime, to do it all! It helps to recognize this obvious reality. Managing your expectations here will serve to increase your experienced time affluence.

*Chores.* On top of this overexposure to what we *could* and *want to* be doing, the efficiency afforded by technology also increases expectations for what we *should* be doing. Always having our smartphones on us makes us always feel "on." Even while tackling one task—or, god forbid, taking a moment to relax—there's an incessant pressure to open the phone and use those crucial minutes to check another item off the household's to-dos. Since moms are typically responsible for keeping the list, as well as for completing the majority of these items, this is one of the reasons moms tend to experience greater time poverty than dads.

The critical point here is that your idea of all you could and should be doing is just that: an idea. Including *all* the possibilities is unreasonable. You have a surprising amount of control over what you take on. After you complete the Time Tracking Exercise in chapter 3, you will know exactly which activities are currently filling your time, as well as which tasks are worth your time, which you might outsource, and which are a waste and better to ignore altogether.

### Expand Your Confidence

Now let's turn to the second component of the time poverty definition: confidence. This is about your sense of being able to accomplish all that you set out to do. One of my recent favorite books, Claire Shipman and Katty Kay's *The Confidence Code,* describes the range of factors that shape (and sadly, for women, often undercut) our levels of confidence. A critical takeaway from the book is that your confidence is not set in stone; it too is subject to influence—*your* influence. So, when facing the day's tasks, it's important to understand what you can do to feel less limited so that the time you have feels less limiting. Ever the scientist, of course I have some data to support this. *Self-efficacy* is a term used to describe confidence in being able to achieve all you want to and believe you should do. In a study, we found that when people feel greater self-efficacy, they also report having more time. This is profound, because it means you can consciously and effectively manipulate your time affluence. Remarkably, by implementing ways to increase your confidence, you can make yourself less time poor. So let's now explore proven strategies to expand your sense of self so that you can feel temporally richer.

## To Get Rich, More Is More

### Expand Your Self

The sun was rising, and my breath was flowing in and out in sync with the beat of my sneakers hitting the pavement. I was trucking along, like the song in my headphones. I relished the release. I felt good and clear and ready to take on whatever the day brought. I *could* do it. All of it.

I had previously resigned myself to the apparent fact that I didn't have enough time to go for a run, but I'm so glad I did it anyway. Why did I? Well, nothing about the situation had actually changed. I just decided it was important enough to make the time. I set my alarm for thirty minutes earlier so I'd get back before the kids got up. And I didn't miss out on much sleep, because once I'd committed by setting my alarm, I immediately turned out my light. I didn't waste time watching TV or futzing through more email.

Running up our front steps and kicking off my sneakers, I was in a great mood and eager to tackle the day. By spending that time, I had avoided a typical day's start, which would have involved getting pulled out of bed and right into the hurried and harried day. Out on my run, my sense of constraint had let up a bit. Feeling more confident, I knew I could more swiftly and easily get it all done. Once home, I felt free to slow down and more fully show up for my kids at the breakfast table and at work for my students in the classroom.

Though it's one of the activities that people often sacrifice because they don't have enough time, exercise is proven as an effective means to increase self-esteem. Together with my research, this suggests that spending time exercising might not only be good for your physical health: it could also increase the amount of time you *feel* you have.

Following this empirical thread, in order to boost my students' health, happiness, and time affluence, I assign them to exercise regularly for a week. Now, to help *you* feel healthier, happier, and time wealthier, this is the first exercise that I'll also assign to you.

## Get Moving Exercise

*E*very day this week, exercise for at least thirty minutes. Mark these times in your schedule to carve out, commit to, and ensure that you make the time.

Importantly, your exercise doesn't have to be strenuous. Don't psych yourself out by starting a training regimen that's worthy of the Olympics. You must not let great be the enemy of good. You just need to get up and get moving. You can go outside for a jog, sign up for a spin class, or do a yoga session. It's even enough to walk to work instead of drive or crank up the music for a dance party.

Though I require my students to do this for only one week, I recommend you do it for at least two weeks. This will allow you to really start enjoying the benefits after getting over any initial hump, and it'll be more likely to establish exercise as part of your regular routine. I also suggest that right after a particularly energizing workout, you jot down or leave a voice message for yourself about how you're feeling. This will serve as a reminder the next time you think you don't have enough time. You'll remember that, in fact, you can make the time, and that, in fact, it's worth it.

### Expand to Others

As discussed, one of the other things we typically fail to allocate for when feeling time poor is spending on others. Yet helping another out is an effective (and nice) way to feel personally capable. So, with my colleagues Zoë Chance and Michael Norton, I tested whether giving some time to another might make us feel like we have *more* time.

To start, we conducted an experiment among a bunch of regular people on a regular Saturday. In the morning, we randomly distributed a set of instructions to over a hundred participants. We told some of our subjects, "Sometime before 10 p.m. tonight, please spend thirty minutes doing something for someone else that you weren't already planning to do," and to the others, we instructed, "Sometime before 10 p.m. tonight, please spend thirty minutes doing something for yourself that you weren't already planning to do."

That night, we followed up to find out how everyone spent those thirty minutes, as well as their current level of time affluence. Of those who gave time, some spent it doing something for someone they knew (cooking a special dinner for a spouse, shoveling snow off the neighbor's porch, helping a friend pull up their bathroom tile, writing a letter to a grandmother) while others did something to benefit strangers (picking up litter at the neighborhood park). Of those who kept their time, some spent it pampering themselves (taking a hot bubble bath, getting a pedicure) and others relaxed (reading a chapter in a novel, watching TV).

Notably, cooking a special dinner takes longer than a half hour, and so do most TV shows. Indeed, participants in both experimental conditions went above and beyond our instructions in being kind to others (or themselves). However, our primary interest was to find out not how much time everyone spent, but rather how much time they subsequently felt they had available. For this, we asked everyone to rate on a 7-point scale how limited versus expansive their time feels. We found that people who had given time reported having *more* time than those who had kept their time—irrespective of the number of minutes spent. Fascinating, right?

In another study, we tested this benefit of giving time against an even stricter standard: receiving an unexpected "windfall" of free time. At the end of a one-hour laboratory session, some participants were assigned to stay and give fifteen minutes to help a high school student edit their application essay, while others were allowed to leave the session early, thereby receiving a "bonus fifteen minutes" in their day. Those who had spent the time helping another subsequently reported having more "spare time" than those who had received the fifteen-minute windfall.

Intuition says that keeping minutes for ourselves or receiving a windfall of free time should leave us with more available time. However, given the now-understood role of confidence in the experience of time poverty, as well as the additional data Zoë, Mike, and I gathered confirming that spending time on others increases feelings of self-efficacy, this finding doesn't only make sense but offers an empowering tool to combat feeling time poor.

These results, along with research conducted by Sonja Lyubomirsky that shows the direct effect on happiness of doing kind acts, leads to your next assignment.

## Random Acts of Kindness Exercise

*D*oing good can *feel* really good. Sometime this week, perform two random acts of kindness—one for a friend or acquaintance and another for a stranger. These acts can be large or small, anonymous or identified, planned or spontaneous, sacrifices of time or money; and the act doesn't need to be the same for each recipient.

It is totally up to you what you do, but here are some possibilities to spark your imagination: pay for someone's order at the café; give someone a compliment; help someone (beyond what is normally expected) complete a task; bring someone a tasty beverage or treat of some sort without them asking; leave someone a flower or nice note; throw someone a surprise party. . . .

Whatever it is, you need to do it with the sole purpose of benefiting the other person. Do not think about or anticipate receiving anything in return for your kindness, such as being thanked or appreciated, or engendering a future favor. Devote a little of your time to give, expecting nothing in return.

Before you start doling out *all* of your time, keep an important caveat in mind. You don't want to make the error of giving away *so much* of your time that you cannot be effective in your own life. A follow-up study offers this caution. When we asked people to recount an occasion in which they'd spent "too much time" on another person—such that they were unable to accomplish their own necessary tasks—they subsequently felt less time affluent than had they recalled an occasion in which they'd spent "some time." And they felt just as time poor as people who recounted an occasion in which they had "wasted time." These results corroborate research showing the depleting effects of being a long-term caregiver, where the giving of one's time is an incessant and ongoing obligation. So, to be clear, in order for giving time to give you time, you can't give away so much that you're left with nothing. And it needs to indeed feel like you're voluntarily giving it—not that it's being demanded of you. So before you spend big, do a quick gut check and ask yourself which of these it'd be: Are you kindly *giving* your time, or is it being *taken*?

What we've now learned is that despite the general tendency to be stingy with our time when we feel time poor, if only we'd stop being in such a hurry and spend the half hour to call that friend to check in on her new job, or wait those few seconds to hold open the door (and maybe even offer a compliment as the person passes through), we'd feel not only happier but also more time rich.

## Ultimate Expansion

The ocean has always had a powerful effect on me. Looking out over the Pacific, I feel an ultimate sense of connection. The boundary that defines me as a distinct, separate being seems to dissolve. It's a feeling of being connected not just to another but to *all* others and, well . . . everything. The reason I'm sharing this spiritual (and embarrassingly revealing) experience is because for me, it elicits awe. And finding ways into this kind of feeling can expand your sense of time. In these moments of awe, absolutely nothing feels limiting—certainly not the minutiae of the day's schedule.

Melanie Rudd, Kathleen Vohs, and Jennifer Aaker looked into this phenomenon, testing how feeling awe can influence time affluence. In one study, they showed that compared to reflecting on a happy event, reimagining an awe-inspiring event made people feel less hurried. It also made them behave as though they had more time—making them more willing to volunteer their time for a charity.

I admit that "awe" might seem a little elusive. Yet it has a clear definition: a feeling that is elicited when you're exposed to something so perceptually vast that it alters your understanding of the world, at least for the moment. And according to the study I just described, it *is* achievable. Ninety-eight percent of the participants instructed to recall an awe-inspiring experience from their lives did so without question. Furthermore, the events these people recalled suggest where we too might find it:

### 1. Social Interactions

Awe is fostered by a general sense of connectedness, so a good place to start is to establish a deep connection with another individual. Whether through tender physical intimacy, eye-opening conversation, or cradling a newborn, our interpersonal relationships extend us beyond ourselves—connecting us with other hearts and minds.

### 2. Nature

Whether you're looking out over the ocean's horizon, up into a starry night sky, or taking in the warm colors of changing leaves on a crisp fall day, the enormity of nature puts our day's stresses into perspective. Just being in nature makes us feel happier. It invites us to take longer and deeper breaths.

Therefore, even if you don't live next to a national park or within driving distance of the beach, find ways to get outside. Stroll your neighborhood park. Look up at the moon. Catch the golden-pink glow of dawn or dusk, and you'll feel less rushed.

## 3. Art

Explore the world's wonders represented through a fellow human's creativity. I vividly remember as a Columbia freshman being awestruck by Van Gogh's *Starry Night,* which was on view at New York's MoMA. I'd hurried to the museum and over to the painting, anxious to quickly take the notes I needed for my essay due that Monday.

But then, standing there, peering at the artist's swirling vision, I was enraptured. I was moved beyond concern about time limits. The due date for that assignment, and my other three looming deadlines, was nowhere in my thoughts.

I felt a similar expansiveness more recently, witnessing the joyous Xian Zhang conduct Beethoven's Ninth at the Hollywood Bowl. I had rushed from work through LA's snarled traffic and felt exhausted by the time I arrived to meet my friends at the concert. As the conductor took the stage, I was worriedly scheming how to beat the crowds on the way out so I could get home in time to prep for a morning meeting. But as soon as the orchestra began to play and music filled the summer air, I was released from these pressing concerns. At the closing note, the crowd erupted. I jumped to my feet cheering too, flooded with emotion. It was transcendent.

### 4. Accomplishment

Tremendous inspiration can be found in individual achievement. Witnessing a skillfully executed athletic feat or an illuminating discovery has the potential to open our eyes to the magnificent possibilities born from people's genius and dedication. Indeed, I was awestruck hearing my UCLA colleague Andrea Ghez describe her Nobel Prize–winning discovery of the supermassive black hole that exists at the center of our galaxy. It's truly amazing what people can accomplish. And remember, by spending a bit of time to move your body or help someone out, you'll realize that you too can accomplish significantly more than you had thought.

Finding awe in the world and the people around you will help to lessen feelings of scarcity and increase feelings of plenty. In later chapters, I will give you specific strategies to build these fulfilling experiences into your schedule. These experiences are well worth making the time for, because they promise immediate and lasting effects. They'll stick in your mind and mark your heart, so you can revisit them whenever you're feeling rushed, stressed, and wishing for more time.

## Go Get 'Em!

Like money, time is a scarce resource. But, unlike for money, everyone has the same starting balance—the same number of minutes and hours to spend before the day's end. Still, for so many of us, this just doesn't feel like enough. Not enough to live out the lives we really want. Not enough to be our best selves—to be healthy, kind to the individuals in our homes, offices, and communities, to ourselves and our personal interests, or to feel full and able to do it all well.

Yet from this chapter, you now know that when it comes to being time poor, perception is everything. It fully depends on which tasks you *see* as needing to be on your to-do list, as well as your *feeling* of confidence in being able to do all those things. This sense of self-efficacy isn't just about your belief in what you can accomplish, it directly influences what you accomplish: what you spend your time doing—which then circles back to influence your sense of self-efficacy and the happiness you feel. It's a virtuous cycle. Spending in ways that get your body moving, that connect you to other people, or that make you feel greater connection in general is surprisingly effective in expanding what you feel you're capable of.

Sure, you may have thought of activities like exercise, helping others, or being in nature as beneficial for one reason or another, but you probably didn't realize the effect these activities could have on how you feel about yourself and, therefore, your time. You probably didn't grasp just how much control you have over the amount of time you have. Now, by knowing these factors and knowing how to mold them in ways that boost time affluence, you can make yourself richer. And oddly enough, it's through spending (not cutting) that you can meaningfully increase your experienced wealth.

Until now, the advice offered to combat time poverty has been "Do less." But for those of us who want *more* from life, not *less*, this guidance isn't particularly helpful. Fortunately, the research I've shared allows you to keep your aspirations high, not just to get by. What's similarly encouraging is that you don't have to spend a lot to gain a lot. A smart little investment can pay off big-time.

## CHAPTER TWO TAKEAWAYS

✦ Time poverty has negative consequences, making you less healthy (less likely to exercise), less kind (less likely to help others), and less confident (fearful of failing rather than optimistic about succeeding), as well as less happy.

✦ Yet your time poverty is subjective, and there are things you can do to make yourself feel like you have more time.

✦ To increase your feelings of time affluence, spend time on activities that increase your confidence and overall sense of being able to do all that you set out to do:

  ✦ Get moving: Exercise doesn't only boost self-esteem, it's a direct mood booster too.

  ✦ Practice acts of kindness: Helping others doesn't only make you feel less time poor, it also feels good, and makes others feel good too.

  ✦ Experience awe: Seek awe in social connection, nature, art, and individual accomplishments to expand yourself and your sense of time.

*Three*

# WISER SPENDING

*People are about as happy as they make up their minds to be.*

—Abraham Lincoln

G rowing up, I was referred to as Little Miss Happiness. In fact, I was so perpetually cheery, it was easy to write me off as naïve. But truthfully, I'd always had a lot to be happy about. I was lucky in pretty much every dimension—my inherited temperament as well as the hand life's circumstances had dealt me, including my very own fairy tale.

I cried with joy when my Prince Charming proposed shortly after my twenty-seventh birthday. It all began when we were twelve years old, shyly smiling at each other from across the playground in London, England. When my family's adventure of living abroad ended, this crush could have too. But a decade later, I opened my inbox and saw his name. He had remembered me! And with some pre-Facebook investigative work, he'd found me.

I, of course, responded to his email immediately, and after several months of giddy letter-writing back and forth, we decided to re-meet in person. He drove five hours up from Virginia, I walked several blocks down from Greenwich Village, and, seeing each other for the first time in ten years, we shyly smiled from across a SoHo intersection. Within weeks he moved up to New York, and later we moved together to the Bay Area for graduate school. I was still smiling as I shifted into reverse in our Palo Alto driveway—the car packed with the white dress, outfits for the weekend of festivities, and bathing suits for the honeymoon afterward. I was heading down to San Diego a week early to take care of our final wedding preparations. As I was pulling out, my cell phone rang. "Cassie, I'm not ready to get married."

In that instant, my smiley existence shattered, along with my vision of a perfectly laid future. My fairy tale ended abruptly, and not at all happily. I suddenly found myself heartbroken, humiliated, and saddled with the sad (and costly) task of deconstructing my meticulously planned dream wedding. Not knowing what else to do, I continued backing out of the driveway and drove the seven hours to San Diego. I was sobbing so uncontrollably when I stopped for gas that I felt badly seeing concerned onlookers awkwardly considering whether to offer help. I tried to assure them through my tears that I was fine. For the first time in my life, I wasn't fine. I felt utterly *un*happy.

Though by that point I had begun my PhD studies into happiness, I had never truly questioned my own. But with depression looming those following months, I looked back at the existing literature through a new lens. I wanted to understand what makes us happy, and if there was anything I could do to regain mine. I found answers and promise in Sonja Lyubomirsky's book *The How of Happiness*. From analyzing all the happiness studies up to that point, she concluded that there are three major factors that determine how much happiness we experience in our days and about our lives.

First, a large chunk of our happiness is influenced by personality. You may have already guessed this from having interacted with all sorts of personalities over the years, but studies of twins provided the evidence. Research that examined pairs of people who shared the same DNA suggests we are each born with a natural disposition that ranges in positivity. While some are born with a knack for zeroing in on the emptiness of any partially filled glass, others are inherently equipped to notice the half that is full. Lucky in my genetic draw, I had tended to see the world as wonderfully hydrated. But when my fiancé dumped me, my glass drained out completely. Even my determined cheeriness couldn't save this relationship. Feeling this depth of unhappiness forced me to realize that I shouldn't rely on my disposition to experience happiness going forward.

I was confronted with the harsh reality that bad things happen. To everyone. Perhaps it's somewhat ironic that being abandoned at the altar is what drove this home for me. Here's a circumstance so lousy that Dan Gilbert used it as the example in his book *Stumbling on Happiness* of an event that everyone predicts would irrevocably devastate them. Obviously, this is just one unfortunate example; in the world and in life, there are endless others. Every one of us has been, or will be, faced with situations that bring us to our knees.

But fortune doesn't only dole out bad. The situational circumstances in which we find ourselves can be lucky. Lyubomirsky's analysis indicated that people's life circumstances—including such variables as income level, degree of physical attractiveness, and marital status—do have some influence. However, despite the general belief that having loads of money, being gorgeous, and walking down the aisle are the secrets to living "happily ever after," these circumstantial factors have surprisingly small effects on people's subsequent happiness. In fact, I devote the first two sessions of my course to sharing the many studies demonstrating that such major circumstance-changing events as winning the lottery or getting married actually exert significantly smaller and shorter-lasting effects on overall happiness than people expect.

Though I was comforted to read that the emotional impact of abruptly not getting married wouldn't last forever, I found myself dissatisfied. These inputs suggest that the happiness we feel in our lives is completely vulnerable to chance. Sure, I got the luck of the draw with my inherent positive disposition. But not everyone is so lucky, and now that I'd experienced having my temperament overmatched by the situation, I didn't want to accept that some individuals were naturally stuck feeling this way. Also, I had learned that, like everyone's, my circumstances wouldn't always be cheery. But fortunately, there was one more category of inputs identified in Lyubomirsky's analysis.

Apart from the large influence of our personalities, and the surprisingly small influence of our circumstances, a hefty chunk of our happiness is determined by our intentional thought and behavior. What this means is that our happiness is significantly influenced by what we deliberately think about and *do*. Irrespective of luck or unluckiness, we can purposely spend our time in ways to increase how much happiness we feel in our days and the satisfaction we feel about our lives. We do have some control. Furthermore, knowing *what to do*—and practicing it over and over—is not only how natural grumps can overcome their muted daily enjoyment, but how all of us can get through even the toughest of situations.

When my own happiness was put to the test, it's from this piece that I ended up *even happier* than I was before. I had gained certainty that my perpetual positivity wasn't merely charmed naïveté. I had learned that how I experienced life wasn't only subject to chance events. From this inarguably *un*happy event in my life, I realized that instead of relying on my personality to *be* happy, and instead of expecting the events or circumstances of my life to deliver me happiness, I could *do* happy . . . I made myself happy. And you can too.

Happiness is a choice. How we decide to approach our hours and spend our days determines the happiness we get to enjoy in life. So the question is, how should you spend your waking hours in order to live a better, happier, and more fulfilling life?

## Time Tracking

If I were to ask which of your daily activities you enjoy most, I wouldn't be surprised if you said relaxing in front of the TV. This makes total sense: you're eagerly anticipating this very evening emerging from the day's chaos with a hefty glass of wine in hand and the reward of turning on Netflix. However, if I pinged you at 10:30 p.m. as you're wrapping up your third episode, thirty minutes past your bedtime (two and a half hours into your highly anticipated couch time), you'd probably be annoyed and ignore my ping. You're tired, and you might feel irked by the interruption, anxious to see what happens on the show, or perhaps guilty for wasting yet another evening in front of the TV. Sometimes— even often—our predictions about what makes us happy are not in line with how we actually feel during those moments.

The truth is, simply trusting yourself to know how to plan for pleasure and satisfaction won't always get you the results you desire. Instead, the best way to accurately identify which activities are indeed the happiest is to track how you're spending your time throughout each day for a week or two, as well as how you're feeling during that time. This exercise provides the information you need to take stock of whether what you *think* will make you happy will actually deliver.

## *Time Tracking Exercise*

### Part I: Track Your Time

To track your time, you'll first need to sketch out a timetable on a piece of paper that breaks up your waking hours into half-hour increments. Alternatively, you can just print out the spreadsheet I already made for you from my website: www.cassiemholmes.com. Throughout your days, use this spreadsheet to jot down for each thirty-minute increment 1) what you did, and 2) how you felt. See an example on the following page.

To make this exercise as effective as possible, be as specific as you can be when you note your activity. This will give you more information to work with once you start analyzing your data, and it's easier to later group activities than it is to ungroup them. For instance, instead of just writing the broader category of "work," write, "returning emails" or "drafting presentation" or "staff meeting." Identify the specific task that you're performing. Or instead of writing "family time," write which family member(s) you're with and what you're doing with them.

In addition to how you spend the time, you also want to document *how you feel* during that time. I've added a column for you to quantify this feeling on the spreadsheet. To accurately capture your emotional experience of your various activities, for each activity, rate how happy you're feeling (or you felt) while doing the activity on a 10-point scale (1 = *not at all happy* to 10 = *very happy*).

| | MONDAY | | TUESDAY | | WEDNESDAY | | THURSDAY | | FRIDAY | | SATURDAY | | SUNDAY | |
|---|---|---|---|---|---|---|---|---|---|---|---|---|---|---|
| | ACTIVITY | ☺ | ACTIVITY | ☺ | ACTIVITY | ☺ | ACTIVITY | ☺ | ACTIVITY | ☺ | ACTIVITY | ☺ | ACTIVITY | ☺ |
| 5:30AM | sleep | | sleep | | | | | | | | | | | |
| 6:00AM | go for a run | 8 | | | | | | | | | | | | |
| 6:30AM | | | | | | | | | | | | | | |
| 7:00AM | get ready for work | 4 | get ready for work | 2 | | | | | | | | | | |
| 7:30AM | | | | | | | | | | | | | | |
| 8:00AM | commute | 3 | commute | 2 | | | | | | | | | | |
| 8:30AM | email | 4 | email | 3 | | | | | | | | | | |
| 9:00AM | | | | | | | | | | | | | | |
| 9:30AM | | | client meetings | 5 | | | | | | | | | | |
| 10:00AM | work on slide deck | 6 | | | | | | | | | | | | |
| 10:30AM | | | | | | | | | | | | | | |
| 11:00AM | | | | | | | | | | | | | | |
| 11:30AM | | | | | | | | | | | | | | |
| 12:00PM | lunch w/ colleagues | 6 | lunch at desk | 4 | | | | | | | | | | |
| 12:30PM | | | strategy notes | 3 | | | | | | | | | | |
| 1:00PM | colleague meetings | 5 | colleague meetings | 4 | | | | | | | | | | |
| 1:30PM | | | | | | | | | | | | | | |
| 2:00PM | | | | | | | | | | | | | | |
| 2:30PM | | | | | | | | | | | | | | |
| 3:00PM | work on slide deck | 6 | | | | | | | | | | | | |
| 3:30PM | | | | | | | | | | | | | | |
| 4:00PM | | | work on slide deck | 5 | | | | | | | | | | |
| 4:30PM | email | 5 | | | | | | | | | | | | |
| 5:00PM | | | | | | | | | | | | | | |
| 5:30PM | commute | 3 | | | | | | | | | | | | |
| 6:00PM | grocery shopping & errands | 6 | commute | 4 | | | | | | | | | | |
| 6:30PM | | | TV | 7 | | | | | | | | | | |
| 7:00PM | cook dinner | 7 | meet friends for dinner | 9 | | | | | | | | | | |
| 7:30PM | eat | 7 | | | | | | | | | | | | |
| 8:00PM | cleanup | 5 | | | | | | | | | | | | |
| 8:30PM | TV | 8 | | | | | | | | | | | | |
| 9:00PM | | 7 | TV | 5 | | | | | | | | | | |
| 9:30PM | | 6 | | | | | | | | | | | | |
| 10:00PM | | 5 | | | | | | | | | | | | |
| 10:30PM | get ready for bed | 4 | get ready for bed | 4 | | | | | | | | | | |
| 11:00PM | sleep | | sleep | | | | | | | | | | | |
| 11:30PM | | | | | | | | | | | | | | |
| 12:00AM | | | | | | | | | | | | | | |
| 12:30AM | | | | | | | | | | | | | | |
| 1:00AM | | | | | | | | | | | | | | |
| 1:30AM | | | | | | | | | | | | | | |

For these ratings, think of "happiness" in its broadest sense—the overall positivity of that activity, including feeling excitedly energized or blissfully serene. Take into account to what extent the activity is engaging, or deepens your sense of connection—whether to another individual or to your community or the world more generally. Or perhaps the activity provides a sense of achievement or confidence. According to positive psychologist Martin Seligman, all of these five elements—positive feelings, engagement, relationships, meaning, and accomplishment—are dimensions of authentic happiness or "flourishing," and you should be open to all of them when rating your happiness during each activity.

Your happiness ratings will simultaneously be monitoring the negative side of the spectrum—identifying activities that make you *unhappy*. These negative feelings can also come in a variety of flavors: anxiety, frustration, sadness, depletion, guilt, or being down on yourself. Don't be discouraged when you find yourself giving low ratings. We all have to participate in activities that we don't enjoy. But learning what these activities are serves as an important step toward crafting your time to be happier. This knowledge will allow you to later dig into and address the underlying sources of negativity, enabling you to alter those activities to make them more enjoyable. This understanding will also help guide your future spending decisions; you might even choose to avoid these activities altogether. The critical thing for your ratings is to be honest. These ratings must reflect how you're *actually* experiencing the activity, *not* your expectations about how you think you'd feel or your general beliefs about whether you "like" that activity.

To ensure more accurate assessments, you'll ideally keep track of your activities in real time as you go about your day. However, don't fret if you're not able to record what you're doing for a few hours. It's okay. (You're busy.) Just catch up as soon as you can, by reflecting back and jotting down how you spent that time and what you were feeling. But keep in mind that the longer you wait to record your spending, the more likely you'll be to impose your general beliefs about the activity, rather than how you actually felt while engaging in it.

Track your time for one or two weeks. Since not every day or every week is typical, this will increase the likelihood that you capture the full range of activities that compose your typical daily life.

## The Research

This method of charting daily hours to identify the happiest activities isn't found only in my course; academic researchers have employed this technique as well. One such researcher is Nobel Prize–winning behavioral economist Daniel Kahneman. He and his team were among the first to track the experienced emotional cadence of people's days in a famous study they conducted among approximately 900 working women. Their results generated a list of sixteen activities that, aside from the present day's social media usage, accurately represents daily life, along with the average enjoyment level for each of these activities. I've translated their findings in the following figure. It shows the list of activities, the relative amount of time spent on each activity (indicated by the size of the circle), and the relative level of enjoyment that each activity generates (indicated by where it lies along the vertical axis labeled "fun"). This is valuable information, because by knowing what activities people actually enjoy while doing them, you can gain insight into your own time usage.

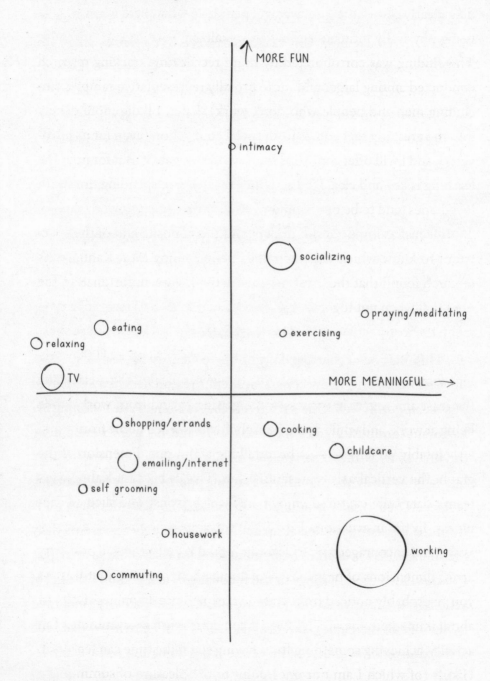

So, what are the most enjoyed activities? The ones that tend to elicit the most positive emotion are those that are socially connecting. The data clearly shows that, on average, people feel happiest when they're being physically intimate and when socializing with friends or family. This finding was corroborated by more recent time tracking research conducted among larger and more broadly representative samples (including men and people who don't work). Later, I'll dig more deeply into the great joy that comes from social connection (even for us introverts), and I will offer some tips for ways to cultivate it. But for now, the learning is key and clear: the activities that involve spending time with loved ones tend to be our happiest.

It is just as important to understand the opposite end of the spectrum: to know which daily activities people enjoy *least*. Kahneman's research found that the most negative activities are, unfortunately, the ones that when put together fill the bulk of our days. In terms of enjoyment, the worst activities tend to be commuting, work, and housework. These findings also are not specific to Kahneman's sample of 900 working women. Across populations, on average people report experiencing the least amount of happiness while getting to and from work, while being at work, and while doing household tasks when home from work.

Notably, so far I've only been talking about one dimension of the graph: the vertical axis representing fun. That is because Kahneman's team's data only captured enjoyment, which is just one slice of happiness. In the instructions I gave you for your time tracking exercise, however, I encouraged you to account for the activity's overall positivity *across* dimensions of happiness—including how meaningful it was. As you've probably noticed from your own experience, happiness isn't just about immediate enjoyment. Even if you don't relish every minute of an activity, achieving something from having spent the time can feel great. Hikers (of which I am not one) point to the pleasure of summiting a mountain as such an example. Or in a less outdoorsy vein, working hard to prepare a presentation might not feel particularly fun, but you're not doing it to feel good right then. You're putting in the time now so that you don't feel like a fool in front of your future audience. And yes, I can tell you that pushing my daughter on her new magenta bike up the hill for the millionth time felt more sweaty than sweet, but watching her eventually find her balance and coast down to a safe stop put a huge heartfelt smile on both of our faces.

Being a goal-driven species, we aren't motivated merely by pleasure itself; we also gain pleasurable satisfaction from our accomplishments. We experience activities that serve a clear purpose as meaningful, and this sense of meaning makes us feel good. Meaning and happiness are indeed closely linked in our experiences. My team, for instance, conducted a study showing that when people are made to feel a greater sense of meaning, they report feeling happier. Since we want to spend our hours in ways that produce greater happiness overall—making us feel more enjoyment *and* more meaning—how should we spend our time?

To investigate this question, a pair of European researchers, Mathew White and Paul Dolan, conducted another time tracking study among 625 adults (including men and women, and those in and outside the labor force). But in addition to measuring how enjoyable each activity felt, the researchers also separately measured how rewarding it felt. I incorporated these results into the graph along with those of Kahneman's team by adding the dimension of meaningfulness. As reflected by the generally upward-sloping pattern of all the dots, we can see that fun activities *tend* to be experienced as more meaningful, and meaningful activities *tend* to be experienced as more fun. Indeed, socializing is both fun and meaningful, and commuting is neither fun nor meaningful.

There are, however, some notable exceptions. While work tends to be experienced as less fun, it does on average feel highly meaningful. And while watching TV tends to feel quite fun initially, it also tends to be experienced as not particularly meaningful (hence your guilty aggravation when I ping you two and a half hours into your comfy couch time). Note that both of these sets of data were collected before the advent of smartphones. Therefore, time spent scrolling social media doesn't show up on this graph. But since social media usage is such a prevalent activity nowadays, it would be helpful to know its associated level of emotion. So I looked to the results from all of my students' time tracking assignment. It turns out that social media usage is similar to watching TV—except it is less fun *and* less meaningful. This is consistent with research that has shown a significant negative relationship between time spent on social media and self-esteem. People who spend more time on social media tend to feel significantly worse about themselves and worse overall.

In sum, the time tracking research points to three classes of activities:

✦ Happy time = both fun and meaningful (e.g., social connection)

✦ Meh time = either fun (e.g., watching TV) or meaningful (e.g., work), but not typically both

✦ Wasted time = neither fun nor meaningful (e.g., commuting... and probably scrolling social media)

This research is wonderfully informative, telling us, for the average person, the average happiness level for the average time doing any given activity. But there is a lot of averaging happening here, and in reality there is quite a bit of between-person and within-person variability.

This is to be expected, of course. Some individuals enjoy certain activities more than others. Even though I enjoy exercising, and going for a run feels like an indulgent treat to me, my son hates the experience of running and views it only as an uncomfortable and inconvenient means to get somewhere faster. Furthermore, a given activity isn't going to be equally fun every time you do it. For instance, preparing dinner feels like an annoying chore when the cook is rushing to get the family fed on a Wednesday. However, at 6 p.m. on a Friday with the music on, a glass of wine in hand, while chatting with your partner, preparing dinner can feel delightful. This is why it's important that you conduct the Time Tracking Exercise. This will help you identify, for yourself, the happiness *you* enjoy from *your* various activities. From this, you will not only get a clear picture of how you're currently spending your time, but you'll also be able to extract the features of given activities that make them more or less positive for you.

## Finding Your Happier Hours

Now we'll return to your Time Tracking Exercise and walk through how to analyze your personal data. This will involve three key steps:

1. Identifying your happiest activities;

2. Identifying your least happy activities; and

3. Looking for the common underlying features of each set.

## Time Tracking Exercise

Part II: Identify Your Most and Least Happy Times

Before you start your analysis, you'll need to gather all of your filled-out time tracker sheets. This is the data you'll be analyzing.

As your first step, skim through all your data and find the three activities that you rated most highly on the 10-point happiness scale. If you find that more than three activities tie for your highest ratings, include them on your list. However, try not to include more than five activities in total because then it will be harder to pinpoint your true sources of happiness.

**Happiest Activities:**

1. _____

2. _____

3. _____

Next, dig into your list of happiest activities and note what aspects made each particularly positive for you. Remember back in first grade when your teacher taught you the definition of a noun? A person, place, or thing. Flip this, and use it as a framework to examine your happiest activities, jotting down their characteristics in terms of:

✦ *Thing:* What type of activity was it? For example, was it professional or personal, active or relaxing, etc.?

✦ *Place:* Where were you? Were you outside or inside? What was the temperature? Was it loud or quiet, bright or dark, clean or chaotic? Were you in nature?

✦ *Person:* What was the interpersonal or social nature of this activity? Namely, were you alone? Who was there? Were there one or two other people, or many other people? How well did you know these people? Was the interaction formal or informal? What was the conversation like—informative or emotionally revealing? What was your role—were you a leader, participant, or observer?

**Happiest Activity #1:**

Thing _____

Place _____

Person _____

**Happiest Activity #2:**

Thing _____

Place _____

Person _____

**Happiest Activity #3:**

Thing _____

Place _____

Person _____

Now, from this list of characteristics, look for commonalities. What features are shared across your happiest activities? Write these down.

**Commonalities across your happiest activities:**

_____

_____

_____

_____

_____

Once you've completed this analysis of your happiest activities, follow the same steps for your least happy activities. Scan through your time tracking data, but this time list the three to five activities you rated as most negative. Then, for each of them, jot down its person, place, and thing characteristics: What type of activity was it? Where did it take place? And with whom? Lastly, look across these characteristics for commonalities, and write them down.

**Least Happy Activities:**

1. _____

2. _____

3. _____

**Least Happy Activity #1:**

Thing _____

Place _____

Person _____

**Least Happy Activity #2:**

Thing _____

Place _____

Person _____

**Least Happy Activity #3:**

Thing _____

Place _____

Person _____

Commonalities across your least happy activities:

_____

_____

_____

_____

_____

From analyzing my own tracked time some time ago, I was struck by two observations. For one, I learned that my cheery mood relies on being in a bright environment. Though this might not seem all that surprising given I grew up in sunny San Diego, it was nonetheless astonishing to notice how consistently true this was even while living in Philadelphia: all of my happiest activities were either outside in open space, near a big window, in a room with light paint, or under my office lamp that pretended to be sunshine. It was partly this recognition that drove my decision to leave my position at the University of Pennsylvania and move to the University of California, Los Angeles—where I could spend more time in *real* sunshine.

Analyzing the "person" feature of my activities was perhaps even more revealing for me. I was extremely happy doing things with other people, but apparently *only when* those activities involved having one-on-one conversations—whether with friends, colleagues, or strangers. If given the opportunity to ask questions and genuinely get to know a person better, I experienced the activity as fun, engaging, connecting, meaningful, *and* worthwhile—earning it a 10+ rating. However, when activities involved only impersonal chitchat, I noticed those times received some of my lowest ratings. As you might imagine, this can be very useful information in guiding my choices about happier ways to invest my time.

So, while it's still fresh for you, note any ahas you gained during this process of analysis. Ask yourself, did any of your observations really resonate as *so true* for you, but which you hadn't really realized before?

Over the years, I've conducted this exercise with countless students. Notwithstanding my own examples, it's remarkable to witness the commonalities across their observations despite time, place, and temperament.

## So Happy Together

Philosophers, scientists, artists, and classic movies like *The Matrix* and books like *Le Petit Prince* have arrived at a similar conclusion, which the Beatles expressed succinctly: "All you need is love."

The Time Tracking Exercise often provides the same answer. Despite their varied backgrounds, professional stages, and life stages, by far the most prevalent commonality identified by my students is that their happiest times are those spent together with loved ones. Loved ones include close friends, partners, kids, parents, and pets.

I bet that if you took a moment now and reflected back on your past two weeks, at least one of your very happiest moments was shared with somebody you really care about. In fact, go ahead and pause right now to relish your memory of this time. So much happiness—anticipated, experienced, and remembered—results from these socially connecting activities, and I want you to savor the happiness from your recent experience.

Investing in our close relationships is the time that proves to be the best spent. We want, even *need*, these relationships in order to be happy. In one of the earlier happiness studies, researchers Ed Diener and Martin Seligman tracked a sample of over 200 undergrads over the course of a school year and compared the people who were very happy (consistently among the top 10 percent on happiness) and those who were very unhappy (consistently among the bottom 10 percent). The results showed that the very happy students did not differ from the least happy students demographically, nor did they experience any more objectively defined good events. They did significantly differ, however, in their degree of social connection. The happiest individuals were more likely to have close friends and stronger family ties, and they were more likely to be in a romantic relationship. These differences reflected how the students spent their time; namely, the happy group spent more time with friends, family, and lovers, and they spent less time (but some time) alone. This data is important because it reveals that although no one variable is sufficient for happiness, close relationships are *necessary* to be happy. That's to say that having friends doesn't guarantee you'll be happy, but to be happy, you need a friend.

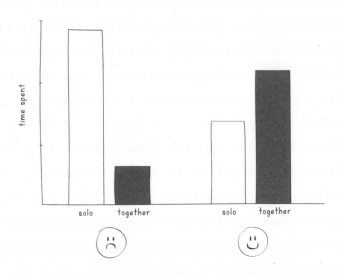

These findings are consistent with classic psychology theories that assert that having strong, authentic connections is essential to well-being. Abraham Maslow argued that love—irrespective of whether it's through friendship, family, or romance—is our most fundamental psychological need. According to Maslow's famous hierarchy of needs, only food, water, and safe shelter are more critical to human survival. And only when we feel a sense of belonging (of loving and being loved) are individual efforts toward personal accomplishment and self-actualization worth pursuing. It's great if you want to climb the career ladder, but only so long as you don't sacrifice your ties to all the people in your life while on your way. It won't be nearly as fulfilling if you have no one to celebrate with when you reach the top rung.

As a species, we rely on the support and care of loved ones throughout our lives. Research has shown that people with close social ties are less vulnerable to premature death, more likely to survive illness, and cope better following intense physiological and financial stressors. Our social nature is so deeply ingrained that we experience interpersonal rejection as actual pain. That's right, social pain shows up in our brain activity exactly like physical pain. When I was pained by my fiancé calling off our wedding, it was the company and comfort of my friends that kept me on my feet. And it was these same friends who, fourteen years later through virtual hangouts, kept each other emotionally sturdy throughout COVID. I'm thus never surprised when I see yet another study showing that having close friends is a strong correlate of experiencing satisfaction in life.

However, these relationships don't just make bad times less bad, they also make good times better. In a 1625 essay, Sir Francis Bacon observed of friendship: "It redoubleth joys, and cutteth griefs in half." Remember: both the researchers' and my students' time tracking results showed that the *happiest hours of the day* tend to be those shared with loved ones.

Learning this, you might find yourself wondering why the hours you spend with others don't always feel the happiest. There's an important distinction within this shared time: simply being with someone doesn't mean you're going to feel greater belonging, friendship, or kinship. As I confessed, though some of my "social activities" received my highest happiness ratings, I rated others quite negatively, and most received ratings hovering around the scale's midpoint. And among my students' happiest activities, I don't think I have ever seen "watching TV" listed—even when with a friend or partner. Instead, the top-three lists typically include things like "evening walk with my wife," "hike with friends," "beating my roommate at Splendor (board game)," "dinner with my sister," or "coffee date with my daughter" (actually, this last one is mine). The key ingredient among these activities isn't the mere presence of another. It is that *spending time with this other person is the primary focus.* Knowing that the quality of the connection during this social time is what makes it a good investment pushes us to further sort out how to make these potentially happy hours happier.

## Connecting through Conversation

One way to enhance the quality of connection during a social activity is by deepening the content of your conversation. A vital feature in the development of close relationships is reciprocal and escalating self-disclosure. Sharing information about yourself (e.g., experiences you've had, thoughts and feelings you're experiencing), as well as actively listening to learn about another's experiences, gives you a good shot at developing a true friendship—being known by and knowing another person.

To help my students make a new friend, I pair them up during class and give them a conversation task to complete with their assigned partner. I provide pairs with three sets of questions. They have two minutes to go through the first set of questions, each partner asking and answering each question. This first list includes basic questions like "What's your name?" and "Where are you from?" I then give them five minutes to talk through the second set of questions, which ask about the person's interests and goals and current experiences (e.g., "What are your hobbies?" and "If you could travel anywhere in the world, where would you go and why?" and "What is one habit you'd like to break?"). Lastly, I give them eight minutes to go through the third set, asking and answering more personal questions like "Is it difficult or easy for you to meet people? Why?"; "Describe the last time you felt lonely"; "What is one of your biggest fears?"; and "What is a recent accomplishment that you're proud of?"

Despite only lasting fifteen minutes, this conversation almost always creates a new friendship. And in cases where the pair already knew each other as classmates (or even as friends) beforehand, this conversation inevitably makes them feel closer. This tool is called the Relationship Closeness Induction Task, and experiments have shown that it helps to make people feel significantly more connected.

A few years ago, there was an odd number of students in one of my classes, so I jumped in to do this exercise with one of them. I quickly learned that my partner—whom I thought of as an outspoken New Yorker—grew up struggling with social anxiety. It turns out that Gaby found herself and a sense of belonging at sleep-away camp, and later volunteered her summers there to mentor other girls as they similarly maneuvered through the challenges of adolescence. Gaby was at UCLA pursuing her MBA for a career in entertainment. She figured that through media, she would be able to reach and help even more people through their emotional life journey. In just fifteen minutes, I developed a fond understanding of Gaby; I later recommended her *as my friend* for her current position at a media company.

So, to your next friend date or dinner date, come prepared to ask (and answer) some more personal questions. For ideas on good questions, you could purchase a set of conversation starter cards. Though seemingly cheesy, their ability to deepen the quality of social gatherings is empirically grounded. I've appreciated the deeper connection they've sparked at my family's dinner table. Hearing each other's answers to the question "What is your happiest early childhood memory?" offered new insight into our family members' personal experiences. That meal was among the most bonding we've had.

Approximately six months after the day of my called-off wedding, I learned the true life-changing power of conversation. I was set up on a blind date and, over a couple of San Pellegrinos at Stanford's Rodin Sculpture Garden, the guy *started* the conversation by asking, "So, what do *you* think are the components of a fulfilling life?" It was as though we were doing the Relationship Closeness Induction Task, but backward—*with the tough questions first!* I'd just met my favorite, lifelong conversation partner. More than a decade later, I'm still happiest when talking with Rob during Friday date nights, Saturday morning runs, vacation wine lunches, and car rides with Leo and Lita asleep in the back seat. This relationship is no fairy tale. It's very real, and absolutely amazing.

## A Breath of Fresh Air

To further direct your pursuit of happiness, let's now turn to the other commonality that my students frequently observe among their happiest activities: being outside. It turns out that simply stepping outdoors to an open sky overhead is a shared source of well-being. Admittedly, this may not sound all that surprising given that I teach my course starting in January in Southern California. So, while tracking their weeks of activities, my students are constantly reminded through news and social media how good they have it. However, this data point isn't just about the weather. Being outside has also been noted as a positive feature during these same winter weeks by students in colder climates, like New York and New Hampshire. (Since I had to conduct my class remotely during COVID, students could attend from anywhere.)

Being outside is a definite mood booster. It is the factor that makes the difference between whether exercise shows up on people's happiest or least happy lists. It predicts whether the post-dinner hour makes the happy list (e.g., "evening walk with my wife") or not ("watching TV with my wife"). Analyzing his list of happiest activities, one of my students, who was residing in Colorado at the time, observed, "All three of my happiest activities involved getting outside, detached from a screen."

My students' observations are consistent with a geolocation study examining the relationship between 20,000 Brits' happiness and their immediate location around the UK. Using a smartphone app, the researchers were able to locate their participants throughout the day, identifying whether they were inside, outside, or in their cars. They could also note the conditions outdoors. At random points, participants would receive a ping through the smartphone app asking them to rate how happy they were feeling at that moment and what they were doing. The results from over a million instances are clear: people are happier outdoors. Furthermore, this boost in happiness doesn't depend on a) the weather (though people *are* happier when it's sunny and warmer), b) what activity they're doing (though some particularly happy activities in the data, like gardening and bird-watching, can only be done out-doors), or c) the environment (though people are happier in nature or green spaces than in urban settings). It's simply about stepping outside. Unfortunately—whether due to choice or obligations—people spend approximately 85 percent of each day indoors.

This is why I'm not into treadmills. Getting *outside* for my morning run has always been key for me. This was equally true in Philadelphia as it's been in LA. (The only difference was that in Philly, I wore more layers and a headband to keep my ears warm.) After moving out of the Palo Alto apartment I had shared with my ex-fiancé, I splurged on an apartment with a slightly higher rent in San Francisco because it was blocks from the bay. In addition to my beloved roommate, being able to get outside every day and exercise with vast views of the Golden Gate Bridge was a major factor in helping me reclaim my happiness.

So, whether it's while exercising or where you choose to take a call, see if there's a way you can move that activity outside. There you'll enjoy a mood boost and some fresh air.

## The Dark Side

As we've discussed, examining our *least* happy activities can also offer great insight for how to invest time better—by clarifying where *not* to spend. Though we often think of ourselves as alone in our grief, the root causes of our unhappiness are shared—humanity is predictable. If an activity thwarts any of the three basic drives of 1) relatedness (feeling interpersonally connected), 2) autonomy (feeling a sense of personal control), or 3) competence (feeling capable), it is likely to make you feel unhappy. Let's look a bit closer at each of these in order to learn which types of activities you might want to avoid.

### Lonely

As we've seen, we humans have an innate need to feel a sense of belonging and connection with others, which explains why socially connecting activities tend to be among our happiest. On the flip side, solo activities tend to be among our least happy. It's important to highlight that being alone or doing activities alone is not necessarily experienced as negative (amid the constant demands of kids and colleagues, I relish my rare pockets of alone time). However, when activities make us *feel* lonely (by watching others' social lives on social media, for instance), that's when we experience an emotional hit. As described by John Cacioppo in his seminal book *Loneliness*, a sense of isolation is the most direct route to depression.

To avoid this feeling, make sure you engage in at least one social activity every day. This can be easy and doesn't require a lot of time. On your phone, for instance, simply close out of that social media app you're in and dial up a friend to actually talk. Or when you go into the office, initiate a genuine conversation with a colleague about what's going on in your lives. If you don't work in a space with others, put yourself in a space with others and strike up a conversation there. Studies show that initiating a conversation with a stranger ends up being way less awkward than you might predict—and it'll ultimately make you *and* the other person feel significantly more connected and happier. I realize that for shy people, putting yourself out there like this might sound horrifying. But trust me, as a fellow introvert, it doesn't have to be. Keep in mind, this is just a small act in service of you choosing greater happiness. Your local coffee shop is a great place to give this brave assignment a shot. Instead of brewing your next cup of joe at home, put your coat on and go strike up a conversation with someone while waiting in the coffee line. When kicking off a conversation with a complete stranger, I don't actually suggest Rob's approach of leading with a tough personal question. That is, don't start with questions from *the end* of the Relationship Closeness Induction Task. Instead, start by cheerily noting something in your shared environment, like the weather or that cute dog that's walking by. Even though it sounds cliché, it's an easy and comfortable way to spark a human connection.

## Obligatory

We want to feel a sense of control in our lives: that we have choice and free will in how we spend our time. We, therefore, do *not* like being told what to do and resent activities we *have* to do. This is why our primary obligations—work and household chores—heavily populate people's least happy activities lists. Indeed, these are two of the three least happy activities identified by the time tracking research. Yet my students' reflections indicated that the unhappiness from work-related activities isn't about work per se. Rather, the parts of their workdays that feel most governed by others and are dictated by others' schedules are the ones that are particularly irksome. On the home front, it is *having to* cook dinner that makes it feel like a chore. In the next chapter, we will unpack how you can turn these activities that you *have* to do into ones you *want* to do, as well as how to decipher which chores you might outsource and not even have to do at all.

## Wasteful

We are driven to feel productive, and we feel good about ourselves when we accomplish our goals and can check items off our to-do lists. Thus, when we spend time on pointless activities—when nothing of value comes out of the activity *and* it isn't even enjoyable—this time feels like a waste. I can attest: realizing that I'd spent hundreds of tedious hours planning a wedding that never ended up happening was excruciating. It was an enormous waste of my time that I could have spent in other more worthwhile ways. Studies show that everyone loathes wasting time—even more so than wasting money. Squandering time feels so painful because, unlike money, lost time can never be regained. It's gone forever. You can never make it back.

Because they viewed this time as a waste, my students experienced these daily activities among their least happy: "unnecessary work meetings," "mindlessly doom scrolling," and "commuting." The Time Tracking Exercise also revealed just *how many* daily hours get wasted. An additional step in analyzing your time tracking data is to tally up the amount of time you spent on your various activities.

*Time Tracking Exercise*

## Part III: Calculate Your Current Expenditures

Using all the data you collected on your time tracker sheets, quantify the amount of time you spent during those weeks on your various activities. To do this, first assign the time you spent to categories: e.g., sleeping, commuting, working, hanging out with friends, hanging out with family, exercising, personal care (e.g., getting ready in the morning and at night), grocery shopping, meal prep, watching TV, scrolling social media, reading, etc. Your goal is to fully capture the ways you spend your time, so use categories that are specific enough to be meaningful for you. For instance, "work" might be too broad a category to be informative about how you are spending these hours. So you may want to break it up into smaller categories reflecting the various types of tasks that make up your workday. My work, for example, can be meaningfully categorized into research-related activities (including book writing), teaching-related activities (including time in the classroom and prepping for class), and other (including a ton of meetings and email). Distinguishing these is helpful because I experience each category very differently.

Next, with all of your activities categorized, go back and calculate the total amount of time you spent on each type of activity. You can do this day by day, or you can collapse across all of your days during those weeks. In addition, by noting the time you woke up and went to bed every day, you can determine your total number of waking hours. Using this as your denominator, you can then calculate the proportion of your waking hours that you spent on each activity.

These calculations will give you a clear picture of how you are actually currently spending your time. With this useful (and sometimes surprising) information, along with the average associated happiness ratings, you can then decide which activities you should allocate more or less time to going forward.

The results of the calculations can be sobering. One of my students who'd left her job and forfeited two years of income to get her MBA was surprised to see that she'd spent the highest proportion of her waking hours watching television (20 percent). This surpassed the 18 percent of her time she spent doing schoolwork and attending class. She regretted this waste, reflecting, "I spend a lot of time watching television! Part of this is because it's my wife's favorite way of winding down after her workday. However, it is shocking and upsetting to see that *so much* of my week goes to sitting in front of a screen."

It's not just TV screens that soak up time. One of my fully employed MBA students with scarce time to spare between his full-time job and classes during evenings and weekends lamented:

> *Over the course of two weeks, I played over twenty-five hours of video games. Before actually tracking my time, I had no idea that I played for that many hours. . . . Although I have fun playing these games, it creates more stress in my life because I tend to play for more hours than I originally intended, despite having an extremely busy schedule.*

Recognizing just how much time you currently waste will help you limit the time you spend on these nonsubstantive activities in the future—thus freeing up hours to spend in other ways that you now know will *actually* make you happier.

## Mood Boosters

There's one more class of activities that I want you to consider when deciding how to spend your time. Even if these activities don't always feel particularly enjoyable while you're doing them, they can have a meaningful impact on how you experience the rest of your day's activities. By giving you a healthy boost of energy, exercise and sleep are very effective mood boosters that have significant carry-over effects. As we learned in chapter 2, these are often the activities that get cut due to time constraints, so it is even more important to consciously make time for them. Doing these activities will help you enjoy all your other time more.

## Exercise

As mentioned, exercising increases happiness. Reviews of research from across the mental health literature show that it reduces anxiety, depression, and negative mood, and it improves self-esteem. Exercise is such an effective mood booster that one study showed it beating out medication for treating depression. Exercise can also make us smarter by improving cognitive and executive functioning (which we use for planning, multitasking, and dealing with ambiguity); and it's correlated with math and reading achievement among school-age kids.

Despite all of these benefits, 74 percent of adults in the United States do not meet the recommended guideline of at least thirty minutes of moderate-intensity physical activity on most days of the week. To nudge you to experience its benefits, I assigned you the Get Moving Exercise in chapter 2. One of my students described it as "life-changing." He told me, "Even though I've heard it over and over again and have always known that I *should* exercise regularly, until I started doing it, I had no idea how much it would improve my approach to each day." So, borrowing Nike's slogan, *just do it.*

## Sleep

Sleep is the other activity that makes us happier and smarter and allows us to enjoy all of our other pursuits more. Research provides plenty of evidence scaring us about the negative effects of sleep deprivation, and wooing us with the invigorating consequences of consistently getting enough. However, if you're anything like me, you don't need science to convince you. After just one night of lousy sleep, my functioning plummets, as do my mood and my civility toward anyone in my path. Yet even though we are aware of needing a sufficient amount of sleep, we often don't make the time. Too frequently, we stay up too late or get up too early trying to get everything done within the limited hours we have. This is why I make it an assignment in my course to go ahead and spend the time needed to get some good nights of sleep. With a portion of their grade on the line, my students become more motivated to hit the hay. And once they've experienced the wonders of being well-rested, they're more likely to continue to regularly spend this time.

### Get Sleep Exercise

One of the reasons we feel burned out by modern life is that we're consistently sleep-deprived. To remedy this malaise, during the next week get *at least* seven hours of sleep (but I'd personally go for eight hours) for at least four nights. Yes, yes, I know—you're super busy this week: there are deadlines to meet, events to attend, errands to run, etc. It's not that I'm not sympathetic . . . but just do it!

Pick four nights this week, note them in your calendar, and enjoy some much-needed sleep. Also, be sure to practice good sleep hygiene: no devices before bed, and try to avoid caffeine in the afternoon and alcohol in the evenings leading into your great nights of sleep.

Each year I invite Dr. Alon Avidan as a guest speaker to give my students some helpful tips on how to get good sleep. An expert on sleep disorders, Professor Avidan is both the vice chair of the Neurology Department at UCLA's Geffen School of Medicine and the director of the university's Sleep Disorders Center. He offers the following advice:

+ Get *at least* seven consecutive hours of good sleep regularly.

+ Your bedroom is for sleep and sex only!—not screens (the blue light suppresses melatonin, tricking your mind into thinking it's daytime).

+ Don't read anything too exciting or anxiety-provoking before bed (i.e., no news or spy novels).

+ Avoid caffeine after 3 p.m.

+ Don't exercise after 3 p.m.

+ Avoid alcohol in the evening (though alcohol can help you fall asleep, it makes your sleep more fragmented and will wake you up more during the night, and in the morning you'll feel less rested).

✦ If you can't fall asleep, get out of bed and go read something boring in the other room.

✦ Regularize your sleep cycle: Wake up at the same time every day and expose yourself to bright light in the morning.

✦ Make your bedroom cold (about 65 degrees), dark, and quiet.

✦ Melatonin, tart cherry juice, warm milk, turkey, and bananas can help to make you sleepy.

✦ A fifteen-minute power nap = 200 mg of caffeine; but when you opt for the power nap, make sure it's in the afternoon (1–3 p.m.) and no longer than thirty minutes.

✦ You *cannot* train yourself to need less sleep!

## Happier Hours Bring Better Days

Lyubomirsky's model taught us that beyond the effects of our inherited temperament or the luck (or unluckiness) of the circumstances in which we find ourselves, we have choice in how happy we feel. Through our intentional action, we can increase the happiness we experience in our days and about our lives. By spending more of our time on activities that deliver happiness and less on those that don't, we can help ourselves to enjoy happier hours, which sum up to brighter days and more fulfilling lives. This chapter tells us which activities those are.

One of the easiest ways to compel yourself to spend in these better ways is simply to become more conscious and *think* about your time. I've conducted studies showing the goodness that follows from focusing on time—instead of staying focused on money—as our primary resource. In one study, I presented Kahneman's list of daily activities to a broad sample of subjects. For each activity listed, I asked to what extent they planned to engage in it over the next twenty-four hours. But before answering these questions, the participants were presented with an (ostensibly) unrelated questionnaire that involved unscrambling a series of sentences. These sentences surreptitiously exposed the participants to either time-related words (e.g., *hours, clock*), money-related words (e.g., *dollars, wallet*), or only neutral words (e.g., *plants, mail*). The results showed that people whose attention had been directed toward time planned to engage more in the activities on the list that we know to be the happiest (i.e., intimacy, socializing), and less in the activities we know to be the least pleasant (commuting and work). Another study showed that it's not just intentions; focusing on time affects *actual* behavior. Upon entering a coffee shop, café patrons were asked to take part in a questionnaire (which again surreptitiously exposed them to time-related words, money-related words, or only neutral words). Unbeknownst to them, these individuals were then observed to see how they spent their time in the café. When exiting, everyone was asked how happy and satisfied they felt. Those who had been led to think about time upon entering the café left feeling happier, because they'd spent a greater proportion of their time socializing. On the other hand, those who had been led to think about money felt less happy, having spent more time doing work.

It is important to remember what these studies demonstrate: happiness isn't about pulling away from work, because (as we know) work can be experienced as meaningful. The point is that *merely thinking about time* pushes us to spend our time in more personally fulfilling ways. Indeed, when I reran that first study among people who find meaning in their work, thinking about time motivated them to work *more*.

The Time Tracking Exercise proposed in this chapter thus provides two major benefits when it comes to your time and happiness. First, the process of tracking how you're currently spending draws attention to this precious resource—making you *really think* about how to spend it. When my students were tracking their time, it made them far more deliberate in their expenditures, nudging them to shift toward better investments. In addition, by rating how you *actually* feel while spending, this exercise informs which investments are indeed better. So, track your time for a week or two. It might seem tedious, but it's definitely worth it. It will motivate you to not waste so much and to invest more in true connection, there finding greater enjoyment and fulfillment.

## CHAPTER THREE TAKEAWAYS

✦ In addition to your situational circumstances and inherent disposition, how you spend your time can have a significant effect on the happiness you feel in your days and about your life.

✦ Therefore, you can choose to be happier by spending your time better.

✦ On average, the happiest ways to spend are socializing with family and friends, and getting outside in nature.

✦ On average, the least happy ways to spend are commuting, doing housework, and doing paid work.

✦ Enjoyment and meaning are closely related, yet there are some activities that are meaningful but not typically fun (e.g., work), and some that are initially fun but not meaningful (e.g., watching TV).

✦ Exercise and getting enough sleep are also great mood boosters, which can make the rest of your day's activities more fun.

✦ The level of happiness generated by activities varies across people, and even across instances of that activity for the same person. To identify which activities and which features of activities make *you* happiest, track your time and the happiness you feel while spending that time.

✦ One truth that persists across people and times is the great happiness that comes from social connection. Having strong relationships and feeling a sense of belonging is critical, so spending to cultivate these relationships is a good investment.

*Four*

# WASTE MANAGEMENT

*There is no greater harm than that of time wasted.*

—Michelangelo

If I asked you to describe a typical day, I bet it would go something like this: Your alarm clock buzzes, and you tiredly get up and ready before heading into the office. If you commute by car, you spend that time scrolling through radio stations, and if you commute by train, you probably spend it scrolling on your phone. Sitting down at your desk, you push off tackling your project list by first trudging through your inbox. By the time you do start in on your "real work," it takes longer than expected, so you stay at your desk, working through lunch to be able to beat the rush-hour traffic home. On your way, you pick up groceries for dinner and your dry cleaning. Then, after making dinner, eating it, and cleaning the dishes, you put in a load of laundry and tidy. Once all your chores are done, you flop onto the couch, mindlessly flipping on the TV or, again, through your phone. Eventually realizing that it is past your bedtime, you drag yourself from the couch to bed, and set your alarm to do it all over again. . . .

Day in and day out, the bulk of our daily waking hours are spent getting to and from work, being at work, and doing housework—and these are the very activities that we just learned make us *least* happy. It's a grind, and no wonder a chunk of the labor force decided not to return to it following COVID. My students' time tracking analyses explained these activities as painful because we *have to* spend this time, and it's often not clear what we have to show for it. These hours are obligatory, a waste, and sometimes both.

Sure, you could join the "Great Resignation" and avoid these activities altogether. But that's not realistic. Most of us need to work. And the majority of jobs are done outside the house, so you need to get there and back. And unless you want a messy home or resentful housemates, everyone has to do some chores. But this is the time of your life, and the current humdrum is no way to spend it. Something *has* to change.

The good news is that it *can* change, and you can be the one to change it. The even better news is that this change doesn't have to involve anything as dramatic as you quitting your job or moving. There are easy, evidence-based alterations you can make to these activities in order to experience them as more worthwhile and like something you *want* to do, rather than *have* to. In this chapter, I will share some surprisingly simple strategies you can implement to make these typically least happy hours significantly more fun.

## Chores Needn't Be a Chore

### Buy Better Time

Despite her husband's insistence, Angela refused to hire someone to clean their apartment. For the $300 it would cost per month, she could instead buy the cute black jumpsuit she'd been eyeing in the store window. Or that money could stay nicely cushioning her bank account for future expenses, or in case she came across other things she wanted to buy. Also, she reasoned, she and her husband could just as well do the cleaning themselves, and she would certainly do a more meticulous job than anyone they might hire.

But after another late Sunday morning argument, when Angela was anxiously nudging her husband and twin boys to leave the park so they could get home in time for her to clean the kitchen and bathroom and for him to wash the floors, she contacted the cleaning service a friend had recommended. Her friend assured her that they would do an excellent job.

So, it was agreed. Every other week, they would pay to have their apartment cleaned. The resulting happiness—for both her and her marriage—was immediate and lasting. That next Saturday afternoon, when they arrived home to a freshly cleaned apartment following a relaxed morning at the farmers market and a picnic lunch at the park, Angela was delighted. Not only did the wood floors glisten, but the sofa cushions had been plumped and flipped, the TV screen had been wiped down, and, even better, she and her husband had the rest of the weekend to enjoy together with their sons.

Not only did they gain more free time, but Angela wouldn't have to spend any of that time or the time leading up to it worrying about getting the cleaning done. She also wouldn't have to spend any of it pestering her husband. Her husband was similarly delighted because he wouldn't get nudged, and they could finally accept their friends' standing invitation to come over to barbecue and watch Sunday night football.

The resistance to and benefits from outsourcing chores are not just Angela's. Researcher Ashley Whillans and her team surveyed thousands of people in the United States, Denmark, and Canada, asking, "In a typical month, do you spend money to outsource tasks (for example, household chores, shopping)?" Less than a third said yes, which means that more than two-thirds don't outsource at all. This isn't simply a case of affordability. Because when Ashley's team asked a group of millionaires the same question, a meaningful portion still said they don't.

Whether people spend money to outsource tasks they dislike is their choice. However, they may not be aware of how much it affects their overall happiness and ability to allocate the reclaimed time to more worthwhile activities. Indeed, Ashley's team also asked people to report their satisfaction in life, and the results showed that, even statistically controlling for other factors (such as respondents' income level, age, gender, marital status, and whether they have kids at home), those who outsource tasks tend to be more satisfied. That is, people who spend money to save time are happier than those who don't.

But what about people who don't have much money to spare? If you are barely making ends meet and all your spending is dedicated to covering basic expenses, this particular strategy may not be for you. However, if there is *any* discretion in your spending, this insight highlights the benefit of choosing to spend money for better time over spending it for more or better "stuff." Research indeed warns that material purchases produce less happiness and less lasting happiness than do experiential purchases. Further, the results of Ashley's team's analysis indicate that the positive effect of outsourcing does not depend on income level. Spending money to buy time can benefit most everyone. Time is similarly precious no matter how much is in your wallet.

Also, this isn't advice to buy out of *all* tasks so that you can luxuriously laze about while others do everything for you. Perhaps you don't mind straightening up your house, whereas washing the floors every two weeks is odious and ruins the entire weekend—every other week. Just having that one chore outsourced might make a big difference for you. Moreover, remember from chapter 1, my research shows that an existence of spending days doing nothing isn't the happiest one. We want to feel at least somewhat productive with our time, because it gives us a sense of purpose.

Yet the most critically relevant piece of this research is that we feel unhappy and dissatisfied with life when our days are consumed by *so many chores* there isn't any time left to spend on what we really care about. If you are spending hours cleaning the house, doing laundry, going grocery shopping, cooking, assembling Ikea furniture, washing the car, dropping off and picking up dry cleaning . . . on top of your eight-hour workday plus commuting, there is nothing left. However, if you were to spend a little money to free up *some* of this time, you could reallocate those hours to what's really important to you. You could spend the time you've bought better—on more fun and meaningful activities. Indeed, Ashley's team's data shows that when people spend the time they save socializing with friends and family, their boost in happiness is even stronger. It also shows that people in couples who spend money on time-saving services spend more quality time together and report greater relationship satisfaction.

Thus, despite her resistance, Angela's decision to have someone clean the house was smart. And it was frugal for the resource that ultimately matters.

So, think about it: Which of your chores could you outsource? Are there clear places you could buy yourself some better time? Fortunately, resourceful entrepreneurs and businesspeople have recognized this pent-up consumer need and have responded by providing a variety of time-saving services and products. As a conscientious outsourcer myself—and someone who loathes cooking and would be fine eating dinners of frozen peas and frozen burritos if there weren't more discerning eaters at my table—I smiled when I opened this week's delivery from our meal service and saw the message, "This box gives you the ingredients for the most precious gift of all—family time, you time, play time . . . Gobble time."

Though cooking weekday dinners counts as a laborious chore for me, it doesn't for Dena. For her, it is an enriching and creative outlet. She designs her family's dinners at the beginning of each week in order to chart out her mornings for procuring ingredients from her favorite specialty stores. Then, tuckered from afternoons of shuttling her three kids from school to their various activities, at five o'clock Dena retreats to the kitchen. This is her time. She skillfully mixes new flavors to create an enriched experience for her family when they sit together for dinner. For her, cooking is meditative. Cooking is Dena's hobby, *not* a chore.

So be careful in identifying what counts as a chore for you. Don't outsource household tasks that your friends might find taxing yet you enjoy. But do recognize that you have the choice. Now that you know your time is ultimately more precious than money, you can choose to spend accordingly.

## Bundle with Fun

For the chores that you don't outsource, you can apply what's called a bundling strategy to make this time less annoying.

In research conducted at the University of Pennsylvania, Katy Milkman and her team demonstrated the benefits of what they call "temptation bundling." The simple (yet powerful) idea is that you can make any activity that you don't naturally enjoy more tempting. Just bundle it with an activity that *is* tempting. For UPenn undergraduates, going to the gym to run on a treadmill is *not* fun (but it is something they *should* do to counteract the greasy effects of late-night Philly cheesesteaks). In one study, Katy's team bundled running on the treadmill with getting to listen to an audiobook of the student's choosing (at that time, *The Hunger Games* was the crowd favorite). When exercise was linked to finding out how Katniss survives her next adventure, these students' gym visits increased by 51 percent, and they ran on the treadmill for significantly longer—voluntarily.

To apply this to chores, simply link the chore you "have" to do to with something you enjoy doing. Take folding laundry: presented with a dryer full of clean clothes, use this as an opportunity to listen to your current audiobook or a podcast, or else give a friend a call and put the phone on speaker, keeping your hands free to fold. Alternatively, you can dump the pile in front of the couch and turn on the latest episode of your favorite show. Soon enough, you'll find your pile perfectly folded, and that you're having too much fun to stop and go put the clothes away in their drawers. Upon learning this strategy, one of my students committed to purchasing a novel item every time he had to go to the grocery store. He'd linked this task with "discovery" and what he described as a delightful culinary adventure. Grocery shopping no longer felt like such a chore.

## Work Can Be Fun

As we've seen, hours spent working are, on average, among people's least happy of the day. Only half of American workers feel satisfied at work, and only one-third feel engaged at work. Many people don't like their jobs and spend their workdays watching the clock, waiting to go home. But when we spend more than half our waking hours working, this is *way* too much of our lives to wait through. And as much as we might try to compartmentalize, our unhappiness at work doesn't stay at work. Research shows that job satisfaction carries over and is a substantial determinant of overall life satisfaction.

Recognizing that work hours make up such a significant portion of our lives, it's imperative we make these hours better. But how?

Let me tell you about Candice Billups. When interviewed by researchers about her work, she said:

*I LOVE patients. I love sick people. I have so much to offer sick people. Because when I don't feel good or when I have had to have surgeries, the one thing that has gotten me through has been work... jokes, just being pleasant, being upbeat, and having a great attitude. And that's what I enjoy the most about being here. It's so upbeat here. In fact, I consider it the "house of hope."*

Can you guess what Candice's job is, what work she does that makes her look forward to coming in every day? Can you imagine where she finds such positivity that it helps her through her own emotional lows and health struggles?

Candice is a janitor at a cancer center. What she describes as the house of hope, an "upbeat" workplace, is actually a place where patients suffering from deadly disease come for chemotherapy treatment. Candice spends her workdays surrounded by people who are very, very sick and their families who are likely worried and scared. And unlike the doctors with whom she works, she doesn't have a fancy job title. Officially, she is responsible for cleaning the rooms and bathrooms on the hospital's first floor and, because of the treatment side effects, this commonly requires wiping up vomit. On the face of it, Candice's job is anything but positive.

Yet somehow Candice enjoys the hours she spends working. More than a decade into a job that typically can't retain workers for even a year, she loves her work. This is because she knows *why* she's doing it. Candice has purpose in her work, and she knows what that purpose is: she helps people by making their days brighter.

The purpose that Candice identified for herself in her work was not part of how the job was pitched to her. In fact, what she does while at work extends well beyond her official job description. In addition to keeping that floor of the hospital clean, she makes the space shine. She jokes with the patients and their families. She makes them feel comfortable, getting them ice, tissues, or a cup of juice. She genuinely cares for them, as well as for the doctors and nurses who are responsible for their treatment. She likes helping these people. She's also good at it. Her humor, warmth, and can-do personality are effective in brightening this space. The ultimate goal that she identified for herself aligns with Candice's values and strengths.

Though this example is extreme and Candice saintly, the benefits of identifying the purpose of one's work are general and far-reaching. A growing body of evidence shows that even if you're not in the perfect job (and let's be real, no job is perfect), aligning your job with your values (what you care about), your strengths (what you're good at), and your passions (what you love doing) makes you more motivated and better at the job—and also more satisfied on the job and with your life overall.

Ideally, you'd be able to have a job with an express purpose that you care about and do well. However, that may not be the case. The story of Candice is especially helpful because it shows that irrespective of the particular job, knowing *why* you're doing what you're doing—and focusing on that—can help make your workdays more enjoyable. Moreover, identifying the purpose of your work can even guide you to reconfigure and tweak your workdays so that those hours are happier.

Organizational behavior researchers Justin Berg, Jane Dutton, and Amy Wrzesniewski developed a tool that leads you through this process, which they call *job crafting*. It involves looking at your job and work tasks in a different way, and shifting how you spend your work hours so that more of them contribute to the ultimate purpose of the work (as identified by *you*). I assign this job crafting exercise to my students—to help them make their work hours happier and this significant amount of time more fulfilling. Having led hundreds of students through this process (and also having done it for my own job), I've found that two elements really drive the benefits: finding purpose and increasing connection. Let's touch on each of these.

## Identify Your Purpose

*Why* do you do the work you do? I don't mean any of your colleagues or a typical person in your profession, I mean *you*. And by work, I mean it in its broadest sense—the domain in which you dedicate your time, effort, and talents. It might be your current job, but it might be your profession, and it doesn't have to be paid. Staying home to raise children is definitely work.

If your immediate answer for "why?" is simply to make money, I urge you to find another, higher-order purpose—a reason that answers an additional layer of why. This is for your sake—for your immediate and long-term well-being. A study that surveyed employees across occupations, levels within occupations, and income levels shows that those who report that their number one goal in their work is to make money are significantly less satisfied—both with their work and with their lives overall.

Knowing your purpose in work (beyond getting a paycheck) will allow you to persist longer and to stay motivated despite the inevitable annoying aspects of the job. Take Candice as an example: Some days on the job are really tough. She struggles when a patient loses the battle against cancer. But Candice is able to carry on and feels even more sure in her work knowing that she'd made that patient's and their family's experience in the hospital more positive.

In a very different profession, Riley is another good example. She's a personal trainer whose job it is to plan and implement an exercise regimen for her clients. Riley views her purpose as much more than that. Her goal is to help people feel good about themselves—to feel stronger and more confident in their lives. When clients come to her explaining all the things they *can't* do, she pushes them to realize all that they *can* do. This is gratifying for her. However, she doesn't love everything about her job. She hates having to market herself and spend time in front of the camera for the workout videos she posts online. But promoting her service and making the videos are necessary to sustain her business. So she motivates herself to do these uncomfortable tasks by reminding herself that they allow her to reach more people—helping more people to become stronger and more confident. It's worth it.

As we've seen, meaning and happiness are linked. Knowing the purpose of your work—the ultimate reason for the hours you put in and the tasks you do (including the unpleasant ones)—will keep you motivated, engaged, fulfilled, and satisfied. Your purpose doesn't need to involve other people, as it does for Candice and Riley. Helping others is a common source of meaning, but there are many other extremely worthy pursuits.

For instance, in his work as a professional photographer, Matt is driven to create. He noted that in other jobs, "Anyone could step in. There wasn't anything unique to me. But the work that I *created* was mine, and something that only I had put into the world." Matt felt strongly that as a young Black man, this established his place in society— his contribution. He explained, "When there was something I envisioned, I couldn't draw it or paint it, but I could see it and then take a picture of it. That's how I could bring it to life."

Now that he is established, Matt is further driven by a desire for social justice. He describes his work's purpose: "To create imagery that reflects stories of people or aspects of life that aren't being told, or that aren't being told properly. These are stories that aren't being told with equity or inclusively." His objective is clear. By doing his work, he "allows more people to see themselves as works of art—more people to see themselves as beautiful, as valuable, as seen"—and for everyone else to see them that way too. Matt's purpose in his work clearly extends well beyond his job description as someone who makes a living by taking pictures, in his case of celebrities and models for magazine editorial spreads and movie promotional materials. By photographing celebrities who are people of color and models who are plus-sized, he finds fulfillment bringing his vision of equity and inclusivity to life. He creates a better reality through his art.

So, when identifying your work's purpose, think beyond the official job description. Also think beyond the way people characterize your occupation. Consider Alex, who is in finance and owns an asset management firm: the description of his job is to invest money for individuals with ultra-high net worth and to handle their savings portfolios so his clients end up with more money. But when you ask Alex what drives him in his work, he talks about his clients' emotional well-being, not their money. He's particularly passionate about his specialty in providing financial advice during divorce proceedings. He explains that other than the loss of a child, divorce is one of the most devastating life events a person endures. Alex identifies his purpose as supporting people through their time of crisis, assuring that they will be okay.

As a university professor, my job description is to conduct research, teach, and do administrative service for the school. Conducting the job crafting exercise led me to question my why for doing this work. My initial answer (borrowed from a colleague) was that my purpose is to create and disseminate knowledge. I viewed my administrative duties, such as serving on committees and being the chair of the marketing area, as peripheral.

After sitting with my answer for a little while, however, I realized that this general goal of academia isn't what really motivates *me*. So I pushed myself to answer another layer of why. *Why* am I driven to create knowledge and share it with students? Yes, I want to help my students be smarter. But more honestly (and you may have guessed), what I really care about is their happiness. I want my students to be smarter in making decisions that will affect the happiness they feel in their days and the satisfaction they feel about their lives. The research projects that keep me up at night (in a good way) and the lectures that I'm excited to present involve, more specifically, knowledge about how to feel happier.

This third layer of asking myself why I do the work that I do led me to identify *my* purpose. Instead of 1) research, 2) teaching, and 3) service, I recognized that my ultimate objectives are to 1) create knowledge about happiness, 2) disseminate knowledge about happiness, and 3) cultivate happiness at UCLA. Not to overstate things, but this exercise led me to realize that I had found my calling. It revealed to me that I am doing work that I deeply care about, and identifying this has, in turn, made my work *feel* more fulfilling and much more fun.

Identifying my purpose has also proven useful by informing how I spend my work hours—the projects and committees I agree to and the ones I decline. If a PhD student comes to me with a research idea I believe could produce a greater understanding about what makes people happy, I'm likely to say yes to advising the project. When there was demand for another section of my happiness course, I agreed right away to teach it. However, when asked to serve as a panelist for a student-run conference on effective social media campaigns (since I'm a marketing professor, this was a reasonable invitation), I confidently declined.

Another benefit of having identified my overarching purpose is that it has led me to reframe how I view particular tasks. Recognizing how tasks contribute to my mission has increased my motivation in doing them, making that time more enjoyable. For instance, I do *not* relish responding to email. However, by reframing emails with my research collaborators as "creating knowledge about happiness" and emails with students as "disseminating knowledge about happiness," I suddenly find writing these emails more worthwhile and satisfying.

It's now your turn. What is your purpose? I realize this is a daunting question, so take a deep breath, pour yourself a stiff drink or a cup of tea, and brainstorm about *why* you do the work you do. When you get to a reasonably compelling answer, ask yourself once more—why is *that* important to you? You might even then ask another why to that, and dig yet another level deeper. It's important to keep in mind during this exercise that what you identify as your purpose ultimately has to matter only to *you*. This ends up being liberating, because it means that your metric for success isn't going to be defined by others. You'll have your own unique ruler, which will keep you intrinsically motivated, and will steer you clear from keeping tabs on how you're doing by comparing yourself to peers.

## Five Whys Exercise

To identify your purpose—what ultimately drives you—ask yourself, "*Why* do I do the work that I do?" First answers typically involve making money or parrot the dictionary definition of your job. But let's be real, *that's* not what gets you out of bed in the morning. That's not what gets you excited to "get to work" and show up again the next day. That's not what makes you feel fulfilled when you realize you've made progress. So, take your first answer and dig a level deeper, asking yourself again: "Why?" Why does doing *that* matter to you? Then, to delve even deeper into your underlying motivation, ask yourself "Why?" for that answer. By the time you answer five layers of why, you likely will have arrived at the heart of *why* you do your work. That's your purpose.

1. Why?

_____

2. Why is *that* important?

_____

3. Why do I care about *that*?

_____

4. And why *that*?

_____

5. Ultimately, what is *my why*?

_____

## Make a Friend

There's a question in a poll conducted by Gallup that, on the face of it, might seem silly: "Do you have a best friend at work?" Despite sounding like something a third grader would ask, it's astute. And people's answer to this question is surprisingly predictive of their happiness. Gallup's analyses revealed that only two out of ten US employees have a work bestie. Yet those who do are more than twice as likely to feel engaged in their jobs, they produce higher-quality work, and they are happier at work. And, as we know, greater happiness at work carries over to increased happiness and satisfaction in life overall.

The time tracking research we covered also connects with this question. Those results showed that while the *least* happy parts of the day tend to be during work hours, the *happiest* are those spent socially connecting. This suggests that if you were to infuse some of your work hours with authentic interpersonal engagement, this time would be more enjoyable and meaningful. So my empirically based advice is this: make a friend at work.

The challenge, however, is that time poverty speeds us through the workday. With so much to get done while at the office, and all the tasks awaiting us at home, we generally feel too rushed to fraternize with colleagues. It might even seem irresponsible to squander minutes joking around the water cooler when you could be spending that time checking items off your to-do list. . . . But as I've said before, when it comes to your time, what matters is what's worthwhile, not just what's efficient.

*Investing in friendship at work is worth the time.* With such a large chunk of our waking lives spent in the office, it would be even more wasteful to spend all those hours miserable. You've also got to rid yourself of the notion that there's no place in your professional sphere for your true personality. Jennifer Aaker and Naomi Bagdonas explain in their book *Humor, Seriously* that bringing your sense of humor into the workplace can actually help you accomplish more, while also cultivating greater connection and fun.

For stay-at-home parents, this equally applies to you. If your workdays involve being on committees at your kids' school, volunteering at the local library or museum, or overseeing your youngster at the playground, make a friend in those places. Regardless of where you spend your nine-to-five, this friend will be there to laugh with you, celebrate wins with you, and give you that gut check or pep talk you need when challenges arise (which they inevitably will).

Jeff, a founder of a Bay Area startup who is in charge of the company's recruitment and retention, recognized the importance of workplace friendships. He told my class during his guest lecture that all of the costly HR programs he'd implemented did little compared to the friendships his employees had forged. Being asked to be in a coworker's wedding or to be the godparent of their child—*that's* what keeps employees from agreeing to go work somewhere else. Having someone you look forward to seeing at the office will motivate you to keep coming back, and that person will help make those hours more enjoyable and fulfilling.

## The Treasured Commute

Rated even lower than working, commuting is consistently found to be the singularly *least* enjoyable of our daily activities. As you probably recall from the graph showing the time tracking research results, commuting was at the *very bottom* of the list. The reason commuting is so hated is that it's a quintessential waste of time: sure, we have to spend these minutes (and in some cases, hours) to get where we're going, but the time itself is empty. And the amount is substantial. The average American spends approximately one hour every day driving to work and back home. For those who take public transit, commuting on buses, trains, or the subway is, on average, no shorter. Throughout this time, we are waiting for it to pass so that we can get on with the rest of the day. And then to get home, we have to do it yet again.

In an ideal world, you would minimize the time you spent commuting. You would select a job that is closer to home or one that requires fewer days trekking into the office. Alternatively, you could choose a home that is closer to your office. That said, these big life decisions about where you work and live happen rarely. Moreover, when you face them, there are myriad other factors in play. The job that requires more time in transit may be exactly the position you'd been hoping for and a career opportunity impossible to pass up. Also, walkable real estate is expensive, and it may not include good schools for your kids. Or you may have a spouse whose job is located on the other side of town, so at least one of you is going to have to suffer hefty travel.

One of the few upsides during the COVID pandemic was that 70 percent of the workforce suddenly didn't have to spend any time at all commuting. With the stay-at-home orders in place, employees were forced (some might say allowed) to work from home. Instead of combating traffic or elbowing fellow subway riders for a seat, we could leisurely amble over to the desk, still getting there in under a minute. The time that used to be wasted commuting had been reclaimed, and those minutes could be reallocated to better uses—to get more work done, exercise, or relax. Perhaps it shouldn't have been so surprising that, realizing the time previously wasted and now free to spend, people refused to return to the office when things reopened.

Not everyone loathes their commute, however. Take Jim. He lives with his wife and two kids in New Jersey—in a community they carefully selected for being tight-knit and having excellent schools. But it happens to be nowhere near his job: a large hospital in Manhattan where he works as a physical therapist. His commute takes two hours— each way. Train to subway to a two-and-a-half-mile walk, and then the same reversed at the end of the day. Surprisingly, he doesn't hate it. In fact, he loves it. He reads spy novels on the train and the newspaper on the subway, and then he picks up a coffee at the bodega outside the station to enjoy on his walk uptown. He notices the seasonal changes in the store windows and the trees. He nods to the dog walkers whose daily sojourns coincide with his. And he mentally prepares for his day of work. Walking that same route home, he sheds the stresses of his patients in stride, and he gets through another chapter of his spy novel on the train. By the time he walks through his front door, he feels refreshed, clearheaded, and eager to give his wife a kiss and start helping the kids with their homework.

What's different about this commute and the typical one that so many experience as excruciating? For Jim, the time is not a waste. The hours he spends getting to and from work are valuable to him. He gets to read. He doesn't indulge in spy novels at home, because there his kids and wife receive his full attention. The walk gives him time outside to move his body, observe the life of the city, and think. This is *his* time, and it's the only time during the day that belongs solely to him. He's not trying to hurry through it simply to get to where he's going (otherwise he'd have taken the subway all the way uptown).

Jim's commute offers an important clue to how to make this typically onerous daily time better. Jim ties his commute to doing something else he values. He applies the same bundling strategy that can make chores more fun. In Jim's case, he bundles his commute time to *his* time—to read, exercise, and think. He turned this time from a waste into a treasure.

Instead of the usual mindless flipping through the radio or your phone, spend your minutes traveling between home and work intentionally. Here are some ideas for other worthwhile activities you might bundle with your commute:

*If you commute by car, you'll need hands-free options that don't require any visual attention:*

- ✦ Listen to audiobooks. One of the activities I often hear people say they wish they had more time for is reading for pleasure. If you dedicated your thirty-minute commute heading into work and back each day to listening to an audiobook, you'd be able to complete a new book every couple of weeks. This might even allow you to finally commit to joining that book club. Keeping up with the reading for a book club can be a challenge; this bundling strategy might help you meet that challenge and enjoy this source of friendship.

  To get yourself excited to get in the car, select a riveting thriller, a novel that carries you into another's experience, a book that gives you good advice, history, biography, or a business book. You decide. *It's your time.*

- ✦ Listen to podcasts. There are so many wonderful ones that can keep you inspired and informed.

- ✦ Learn a foreign language. I've never tried this method of learning a language, but I understand there are some audio language programs that are quite effective. Not only will this allow you to communicate and connect with more people, but you'll be prepared to order yourself delicious meals on a future vacation.

- ✦ Call and catch up with your parents, grown children, or friends. You now know about the deep-rooted happiness that comes from social connection; yet amid busy schedules, it can be hard to find thirty minutes to call and talk. Here's that half hour you've been looking for! You can use this car time to reconnect and stay connected with your loved ones. Since your commute schedule is fairly predictable, you could even establish a standing weekly phone date, allowing you to stay part of each other's day-to-day lives, despite geographic distance.

*Even though it might require headphones and prohibit loud talking, commuting on public transportation affords another host of bundling options, because you can physically look at whatever else it is you're doing:*

+ Read . . . including books with illustrations.

+ Write. Start writing your own novel or start keeping a journal.

+ Check email. Use this time to clear out your inbox so that you don't have to spend the time once you get to your desk or home. Rob admits that he misses his hour-long daily train ride between Philly and New York's Penn Station, because he was able to read the entire newspaper every morning and, in the afternoons, get through all his email and arrive home with an empty inbox and a clear head.

+ Watch TV. With content now streaming to our phones, you can sit on the bus watching the TV shows that no one else in your family enjoys. Watching your shows during this time will cut down on family friction and free up time to spend in other ways once you're off the bus.

*If you're lucky enough to be able to walk or cycle to work, your commute naturally gets bundled with the happiness of being outside and* exercising. While walking to the office, you could add yet another element and listen to audiobooks or podcasts, or call to catch up with someone you love. Of course, you could also savor this time under the open sky and use the time to think. Like Jim, you too can treasure your commute.

## Make Your Less Happy Hours Happier

Don't succumb to the grind. Don't spend the hours of your workweek waiting for them to pass. This is the time of your life, and you can't let it go to waste. Despite what you may have been led to believe, the hours you spend doing housework, working, and commuting are indeed yours. And you have a surprising amount of choice in how you spend them. With a tiny bit of intention, you can turn this time from seeming worthy of the trash bin into a treat. You now have strategies to make what have traditionally been the least happy hours of your day-to-day life significantly more meaningful, connecting, and fun. The changes are little, but the effects are great.

## CHAPTER FOUR TAKEAWAYS

✦ Though, on average, household chores, working, and commuting are the activities associated with the lowest levels of happiness, there are some surprisingly simple strategies you can employ to make these hours happier.

✦ Spend money to buy out of chores, and reinvest this time you've saved in more fulfilling ways (i.e., with loved ones).

✦ Increase your motivation, enjoyment, and satisfaction at work:

  ✦ by identifying your purpose—*why* you do the work you do,

  ✦ and by making a friend.

✦ Bundle your commute with an activity you enjoy (e.g., listening to audiobooks in the car or reading books on the train) so that this time feels like a treat rather than a waste.

## Five

# PAUSE AND SMELL THE ROSES

*Be happy for this moment. This moment is your life.*

—Omar Khayyam

In 2017, four years after my awakening on the train, we'd moved back to California and were living my dream. We'd bought a house next to UCLA's campus, and Leo went to preschool under the shade of eucalyptus trees—four hundred yards from my office. I could walk him there every morning.

One morning we were on our way to school. As usual, it was perfect: The sun was shining, the birds were singing, and four-year-old Leo was skipping along, laughing, a few steps behind me. It was perfect—until you included me in the picture. I was charging ahead, a scowl on my face. It was nearly time for my first meeting of the day. Every few steps, I yelled back at him, "Come on, please hurry."

Then he stopped, "Mama, wait!"

I did not want to wait. "Leo, come. We're late!" I was mentally cycling through my day's to-do list, feeling the mounting panic of not being able to get it all done before picking him up that afternoon.

"But, Mama, look!"

I turned around to see him burying his face in a bush of white roses blooming next to the path.

"Leo," I shouted over my shoulder as I continued walking, "we do *not* have time to stop and smell the roses!"

When I heard those words come out of my mouth, I did stop. As a time and happiness expert, I was horrified at myself, and mortified. It was so wrong, and *so* ridiculously on the nose. Instead of enjoying this walk to school with my son, I was stuck in my head: planning for, preparing for, eager for what was next. I hadn't noticed the perfect temperature, let alone the burst of fragrance I'd just walked past. I wasn't paying attention. I was totally missing it!

Sound familiar? Regrettably, we all share a tendency to miss perfect moments along our daily path. In this chapter, we'll learn why, and more importantly, the ways you can help yourself to notice the good stuff that is right there in front of you. Unlike in chapter 3, this isn't guidance to spend your time on different activities. And unlike in chapter 4, this isn't advice for how to improve your dreaded activities. This is about improving the quality of the time you already spend well.

## We Get Used to Stuff

In the first few months of walking Leo to his new preschool, I noticed the flowers too. The walk captured everything Rob and I had worked so hard for. We were finally back in California and in jobs we loved. By the time I arrived at my office, I'd be elated. I didn't have to thaw after unbundling from layers upon layers. I didn't have to turn on my desk lamp that pretends to be sunlight. Instead, I'd open my office window overlooking the grassy hill where flip-flop-wearing undergraduates would soon be setting up their portable hammocks. I'd take another deep, grateful breath of the dry Southern California air and sit down to start my workday.

But after walking this same path with Leo every day for months, I had become used to it. I had gotten *so* used to it, I stopped noticing. And without noticing, there was no chance for this truly lovely situation to continue having the same positive influence on my mood. Researchers call this *hedonic adaptation*. We humans have a powerful propensity to adapt after continued and repeated exposure. Seeing the same thing, doing the same thing, or being with the same person again and again lowers its impact on our emotional experience. Put simply, we get used to things over time.

Given that the world doesn't only dole out rosy mornings, our capacity to adapt can prove quite useful. After continued exposure to the sound of an annoying vacuum cleaner, for instance, we become less annoyed. This was demonstrated among an unfortunate (but gradually less annoyed) set of experiment participants. Similarly, the water of a cold lake starts feeling less frigid after a few minutes of wading, readying us to take the plunge.

Adaptation helps us survive annoyances and discomforts and also difficult and painful situations. Though there is some loss to which we don't adapt so readily, our ability to emotionally adapt makes us surprisingly resilient.

Take the COVID pandemic as an example. To temper the spread of the novel coronavirus, we were forced to spend much of 2020 confined to our homes—without being able to join friends out at restaurants or see colleagues at the office or walk through the halls of museums or send our kids to school. We had to forgo attending hard-earned graduations or going on the vacations we'd so carefully planned and were looking forward to. And *then*, when we were finally allowed back into shared spaces, our faces were covered by masks, limiting conversation and eliminating friendly smiles.

We adapted to the inconveniences and disappointments. We created new ways to connect and explore. We remained standing on the other side, and even experienced some happiness along the way. Through adaptation, we are able to tolerate adverse circumstances. Research has even shown that prison inmates learn how to cope being isolated in solitary confinement.

Hedonic adaptation is helpful in diminishing the pain of bad experiences. Yet it also diminishes the pleasure of good experiences. Once life's good stuff becomes embedded in the fabric of our day-to-day, we stop noticing it. We experience less enjoyment from the colorful threads running through. We miss out on *a lot* of potential happiness.

You can see this dynamic play out in a tub of ice cream. Conjure in your mind the first spoonful of creamy cold chocolate delicately laced with salted caramel. How does it taste? . . . Divine! The third and fourth bites also taste pretty wonderful. The sixth bite still tastes great. The eighth bite good. By the tenth bite, you're mindlessly eating, thinking more about where you're off to next than the ice cream in your mouth. Your enjoyment gradually declines, and by the twentieth bite, you're over it and probably feeling kind of ill. Hedonic adaptation explains why the first bite always tastes best (and supports my belief that meals should start with dessert).

It's not just about food though. Think of your thrill when you hear your favorite song come on. You sing along, and when it ends, you want it to play again. But after repeating, and repeating again and again, the sound has either blended into the background or has started to grate.

The problem is that hedonic adaptation doesn't just mute our reactions to little pleasures, like ice cream, a favorite song, or a sunny commute. It also leaves us numb to immense joys. Think back to the very first time your partner said, "I love you." Recall this moment as vividly as possible, and remember how you felt. My guess is that you were completely overwhelmed with heart-bursting happiness. You probably felt such joy that it was inconceivable those three words would become shortened to the more efficient "love you" used to wrap up phone calls and announce you're heading out the door each morning. Even something as life-defining as the declaration of love blends into the background.

Research has documented this gradual decline in happiness following even the most extraordinary luck. This includes winning the lottery—a scenario many of us enjoy daydreaming about. Sure, there were probably additional factors at work here, but one study comparing lottery winners and nonwinners who represented similar demographics found that the winners weren't actually that much happier. Since very few of us will ever be so lucky as to win the lottery, what about the effect of receiving a big raise at work? A team of researchers tackled this question by tracking thousands of individuals over sixteen years, measuring their income levels and happiness. Based on changes in these people's happiness following changes in their income, the researchers concluded that a significant raise in income does produce a significant *initial* lift in happiness. But within four years, their happiness returned to baseline levels.

That's for money. What about love? Taking the same longitudinal approach, another set of researchers measured people's happiness levels with respect to a change in marital status. The data revealed a mountain-shaped pattern that peaked on one's wedding day. The data showed an incline in happiness for the two years leading to the big day, and afterward a steady decline to one's baseline happiness. Within two years, individuals went from the excitement of "Just married!" to just being married.

You may find these findings hard to accept, though this reaction is itself a documented psychological phenomenon called *impact bias*. The lack of any lasting effects of such surely happy events is tough to swallow. That's because you're probably imagining how *you'd* feel if you were so lucky as to get a huge raise or find the love of your life. But in your imagination, you're considering *only* the effect of this one, singular event on your happiness. You're not accounting for all the other factors that would soon play into your day-to-day feelings and life assessment.

Say you were indeed so lucky as to find someone amazing enough that you would wholeheartedly vow to spend the rest of your life with this person. You'd be overjoyed by the prospect of getting to wake up next to this person every day. But soon every day would become every-day. Years into your marriage, you would still be waking up next to this person, but a host of other inputs would play into your mood as you opened your eyes. You'd probably have to rush out of bed to get ready for work, and perhaps get your kids ready for school. Then the traffic, the weather, a recent round of feedback from your boss, your son's up-coming parent-teacher conference, a difficult conversation you'd had with a colleague . . . all of these things, among many others, would in-fluence just how satisfied you'd feel. After years of waking up next to someone, it becomes so comfortable that you fail to even notice it, let alone focus on it as a source of incredible luck and joy.

## Time Left

But what if you realized that the love of your life wasn't going to be around forever? Or less dramatically, that your life's circumstances would lessen the moments you would get to spend together? Ulti-mately, your time together will come to an end. But sooner than that, you'll probably just start doing the things you love doing together less frequently. Or when you are able to do those things, some elements will have changed to make those moments a little less perfect. Yes, you and your spouse will continue to wake up in the same bed, but perhaps your conflicting schedules will prevent you from ever getting up at the same time. Or you're groggily tugged out of bed by a hungry toddler before you have the chance to say good morning to your partner. *Or* perhaps even this most basic pleasure of marriage gets traded out for a good night's sleep, relocating the snorer to the couch.

I don't walk Leo to school anymore. He has graduated to elementary school, which is a five-mile drive away. He now carpools, so on the days I do take him to school, he is busy negotiating song choice with his classmate. Had I realized how few mornings I had left of walking with Leo to his preschool, I would have paid more attention. I would have always noticed the flowers.

When do we realize our time left is limited? What prompts us to savor life's little joys?

## Age

Back when I lived in Philadelphia, on my way into work one Monday, I ran into one of our PhD students, Amit. He politely asked how my weekend was, to which I exuberantly blurted, "It was amazing!"

"Wow," he said. "What did you do?"

I stumbled. I actually hadn't done very much of anything, and certainly nothing exciting enough to report at this level of enthusiasm. I described a weekend of strolling the neighborhood with Rob and then-two-year-old Leo. We had tried a new brunch place that had a Bloody Mary cart. We had watched movies. I realized it sounded pretty run-of-the-mill as I described it, but still insisted, "It was all just so fun."

I then asked about his weekend. He had taken the train to New York City to meet up with a crew of buddies from college for an epic night out. They had scored tickets to the year's hottest concert.

"It deserves the hype," he said, beaming. Objectively, there was no question that his weekend was far more exciting than mine. But still glowing from my two days of utter contentment hanging out with my two favorite people, I wondered which of us *was* happier.

By the time Amit and I reached our offices, we'd decided to explore this interesting empirical question together. We realized that nothing in the academic literature on experiential consumption or hedonics could confirm either way.

Looking to pop culture, we found different answers. We recalled Robin Williams's character urging his students in the pivotal scene of *Dead Poets Society*, "Carpe diem! Seize the day, boys. Make your lives extraordinary!" One point for Amit's weekend.

But what about *The Bucket List*? In that movie, Morgan Freeman and Jack Nicholson's characters found out they were terminally ill, which prompted them to set out on amazing adventures—climbing mountains and jumping out of airplanes. But in the end (spoiler alert), they discovered their greatest happiness back at home during quiet moments in the backyard and at the kitchen table with their closest friends and family. One point for mine.

So, which is it? Is it the extraordinary experiences that excite us and push us outside the realm of our daily lives, or is it the ordinary, sweet moments that make up our daily lives? Does the extraordinary or the ordinary contribute more to our happiness?

To answer this question empirically, Amit and I started by questioning hundreds and hundreds of people. These participants represented all genders and a range of ages, income levels, and races. We asked them to tell us about a recent happy experience from their lives. We instructed half of them to tell us about an experience that was *extraordinary*, and the other half to tell us about an experience that was *ordinary*. The experiences people recalled included "I dove the Blue

Hole in Belize"; "Got a yummy Frappuccino! It was perfect that day, as it was really hot and muggy, and the drink was cold and icy"; "I got married!"; "My dog came and cuddled with me on the couch"; "Went out on my back porch to a bright sun shining"; and "Received a text from a good friend." I bet you can guess which type of experience each of these was.

Looking for themes, we found clear differences in the happy experiences people shared:

The extraordinary experiences tended to represent one of three buckets:

1. *life milestone*—graduation, landing a great job, getting married, having a baby, having grandchildren

2. *once-in-a-lifetime vacation*—climbing Machu Picchu, traveling to Paris, diving the Great Blue Hole in Belize

3. *cultural event*—going to a concert, attending a professional sporting event, eating at a world-renowned restaurant

The ordinary experiences fell into a separate set of buckets:

1. *simple moment shared with a loved one (including pets)*— getting a text from a friend, a good-morning kiss from a spouse, a walk with one's son, lounging with one's dog

2. *a treat*—a lovely glass of wine, a delicious sandwich, a warm shower, curling up with a good book, a cold Frappuccino on a hot day

3. *nature*—noticing a sunset, a view, or roses in full bloom

Which was better—the extraordinary or the ordinary experiences? To answer this, we asked participants, in addition to telling us their experiences, to report just *how* happy their experiences made them on a 9-point scale. The answer depended on age. For younger people, extraordinary experiences produced greater happiness than ordinary ones. However, for older people, ordinary experiences produced *as much* happiness as extraordinary experiences. That is, there was not a statistically significant difference in the high amount of happiness enjoyed from extraordinary and ordinary experiences among the older segment.

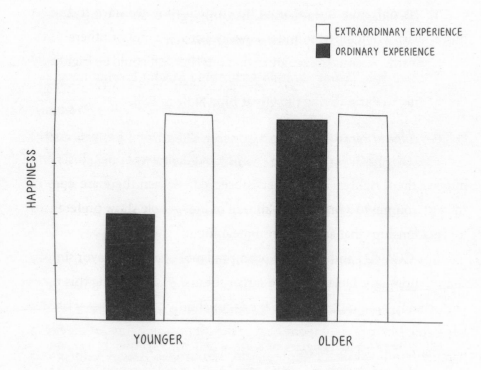

If you're wondering what counts as "younger" versus "older," in this graph it's under versus over thirty-five. But there is nothing magical about this thirty-five-year-old cutoff; it was just the median age among our participants, so we used it to split the data. Really, happiness from ordinary experiences gradually increases with age. As people get older, they naturally start recognizing the limited nature of their time left on earth. Realizing their time is precious, people become more prone to savor even the simplest of moments. These results pointed out that even though I wasn't much older than Amit, I was on my way to life's next phase. And that explained the different composition of our happy weekends.

## Crisis

Age is only one indicator of how much time we have to live. A more heart-wrenching reminder is witnessing the end of others' lives. Seeing death forces us to recognize that our time left could be frightfully short. On September 11, 2001, terrorists killed almost three thousand people in the span of a few hours. Though most of the lives were lost in New York City, people across America and around the globe were confronted with their mortality. They pulled their loved ones closer and hugged them tighter. Researchers observed, "When there are cues in the environment to prime the finitude of life, people show preferences for relationships that are close and meaningful."

The COVID pandemic also prompted more people to savor simple, shared moments. Death loomed larger for many of us during this time, with the TV, radio, and newspapers constantly updating us with the latest toll. Many lost someone they loved. At the same time, while being harshly reminded of the finite nature of our lives, we were forced to pause, ordered to stay home to reduce the virus's spread. Quarantined in our homes, there was nothing to do *but* pay attention to the here and now.

At the time, Leo was in first grade and stuck at home from school.

As an excuse to get us out of the house, we reinstated our daily walks through UCLA's campus, but during these days I had no office to rush to. Aware that life was fragile and time ultimately limited, I was more focused on the present. I was focused on Leo. Together, we slowed to admire the rosebushes.

I wasn't the only one who found some unexpected happiness amid this unquestionably unhappy time. While for some people circumstances got undeniably more difficult, for others things slowed down. One friend described her family's new nightly routine. Their seven-year-old son would set the table for a leisurely family dinner followed by a game of cards: "James definitely comes up with some creative tableaus! He decides on a motif for each evening and goes with it. Last night was a Christmas theme—with rows of holiday candles, red napkins, and special plates." She reflected, "Before, my days were filled, but not with things that were fulfilling. This time has made us closer."

## Life Stage

Of course, we don't need a crisis to realize our days are numbered, nor do we have to be reaching old age. The end of a *life phase* can also push us to make the most of our time.

Sometimes this happens in the face of a pending move. If you've ever left a city, you may have noticed yourself spending more time with your close friends and neighbors just before leaving. You may also have revisited your favorite sites and dined at the restaurants where you felt most welcome. Saying goodbye pushes us to savor the pleasures we enjoy.

You may have become aware of this same soaking up of best-loved activities as college graduation approached. The final days of those golden years likely felt even shinier than the rest. This was shown in an experiment among college seniors. Six weeks before graduation, students were instructed to write about their college experience— reminded either that they had little time left ("graduation is soon") or significant time left ("graduation is far"). A couple weeks later, these students reported their happiness. Those who'd been led to perceive their remaining college life as limited were happier. They were happier because they'd made more of this time. They'd spent it reveling in their favorites—hanging out with their closest friends and visiting their cherished campus spots.

These findings reveal our deep-rooted motivation to make our endings as happy as possible. It also explains why experiment participants tasked with eating a series of chocolates reported the fifth one as tastier if it was presented as their "last" (versus "next") chocolate in the sequence.

## Counting

What can we do to keep remembering that the moments we enjoy in everyday life are, in fact, limited? Regardless of how old we are and where we are in life, how can we offset our tendency to adapt to life's pleasures and joys? Here's an exercise inspired by Tim Urban that provides a nudge toward continuing to notice and enjoy the good stuff. I conduct it among my students each year, guiding them to calculate the proportion of times they have left of an experience they love.

But first, I highlight how measurable and finite our time to live actually is. I present them with a page showing nine rows with ten circles each—a visual depiction of their 90 years of life (assuming they are lucky and outlive the national average). Then I present them with a page showing their life in months (1,080 smaller circles), then weeks (4,680 even smaller circles), and finally in days (32,850 dots). Even though there are a whole lot of dots on this last page, it is notable that *all* of these dots—every single Tuesday or Friday or Sunday—fit quite easily onto a single sheet. This highlights that our days are numbered. Our time is countable.

### YOUR 90-YEAR LIFE IN MONTHS

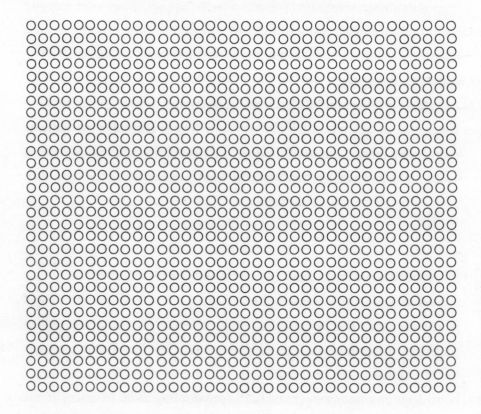

However, the true value of our time doesn't really get captured in temporal units (i.e., a day, a week, a month). The value of our time comes from what fills those days, weeks, and months—the events that we experience over the course of those 32,850 days: the 22 Winter Olympics (assuming none got canceled for wars or pandemics), the 8,212 summer sunsets, the 90 spring seasons, the 4,680 Sunday night dinners, and the 23,400 weekday mornings.

But many events occur during a more limited subset of those ninety years—perhaps because we were not ready for them in our younger years (e.g., sex), or we are not still up for them in our later years (e.g., sex). More critically, since our happiest events tend to involve other people, we have to account for when these people will be available to share in the event. The events that occur every week (like Sunday night dinner with parents) or every weekday (like walking Leo to preschool) only happen for a limited portion of the total number of potential times. I walked Leo to preschool many times. Since we did it almost every day during that period, I thought of it as an everyday activity. Consequently, I adapted to it as if we would continue to do it every day forever. But I hadn't counted. I did not realize that on that very morning I was trying to get Leo to *hurry up*, we had already completed 80 percent of those preschool commutes. We only had 20 percent of our times left to pass the rosebush, walking together through campus.

To urge my students to continue to notice the good stuff, I instruct them to first identify something they enjoy. The vast majority come up with an activity they enjoy doing with someone they care about. One student selected walking his dog on Saturday mornings, another settled on watching sports with his buddy, and another chose eating dinner with her parents.

I then instruct them to calculate approximately how many times they have done this activity in their life thus far.

Next, I ask them to calculate the approximate number of times they are likely to do this activity in the future: how many times they have left. I understand that this seems slightly morbid. Our culture tends to avoid confronting the finite nature of our days. Still, bear with me, because this will increase your enjoyment and satisfaction.

For my students' future calculation, I remind them to account for constraining factors and factors that will likely change. For instance, do they currently, and will they continue to, live in the same place as that person? How would changes in that person's family or work situation influence their availability? How would changes in their own family or work situation influence their own availability? What is the expected longevity of the other person, and of them?

The results of this calculation are always striking. For instance, my student who calculated his Saturday dog walks counted that he had walked his five-year-old dog approximately 230 times (accounting for the fact that he'd adopted his furry companion when the little guy was six months old, and a few weekends were missed for work travel). Assuming that his dog would live another five years (and that he'd have some more work trips during that time), he calculated that they had 52 percent of their Saturday walks left. Realizing that they had already taken approximately half their weekend walks together, with only one-half left, my student committed to himself (and his dog) that he would make the most of their remaining time. That next Saturday, instead of just quickly taking a lap around the block, he loaded up the car and headed with his dog to the beach, which they both loved.

While my student viewed his calculated time left with his furry buddy as woefully limited, it turned out that their remaining Saturdays together were even fewer than he'd expected. This student took another course of mine six months later. He arrived late to his group's final presentation, which was surprising given his conscientiousness. Afterward, he explained that he had just come from the vet where he'd had to put down his dog. When he had done his initial calculation, he didn't know that his dog would be diagnosed with a fast-onset cancer. Though sad, he was grateful to have done the exercise—for the nudge to savor those walks, and to have gone to the beach.

Another student, who calculated the time he had spent on the couch watching sports with his best friend, was embarrassed and shocked (but also a little proud) to learn they had spent approximately 4,700 hours in front of the TV. This included the hours they had spent after school and on weekends throughout their middle and high school years, as well as those since they had each gone off to college, when they dedicated their visits home to making up for lost hours together cheering for their teams. Since moving to different cities after college, with jobs restricting the length of their trips home, they had started visiting each other in their new cities a couple of times each year. But now that my student had a serious girlfriend and his friend was married and had a two-year-old, coordinating these visits had become more difficult. And when they did manage a weekend visit, they weren't free to spend so many hours shooting the breeze while watching sports. Saddened to realize that he only had 5 percent of his overall times left to hang out with his best friend, he called him during the next class break—to say hi, and to set up a guys' trip for the following month.

During the class break, I also overheard the student who'd calculated dinners with her parents giving her folks a call. Before heading off to college, she had eaten dinner with her parents pretty much every night (except for some sleepovers at friends' houses and a summer studying abroad). She noted that their number of dinners together had been drastically reduced while she was at college. She would come home for a few weeks every Christmas and in the summer, and her parents would visit her at school a few weekends each year. This minimal frequency continued during the six years after college while she worked in New York. Wanting to be closer to family, she'd moved back to Southern California for grad school. Since her parents now lived only an hour away, they'd established a routine of Sunday night dinners.

With her parents in their sixties, my student realized they only had a couple decades of weekly dinners remaining. Her calculation determined that she had less than 1 percent of their total dinners together left. She confessed to me that made her feel guilty for the few Sundays she'd canceled due to coursework or events with friends. She also felt sad recognizing that her parents were aging. However, the positive effects of this calculation far outweighed the negative. Going forward, she committed to protecting these evenings—no matter how busy she felt with school or however tempting another social invitation seemed. Later in the quarter, when I checked in with her on how it was going, she said that not only had she spent the time, but she enjoyed the time more. This calculation had caused her to push for more meaningful dinner conversation—learning about her parents' lives before she was born, seeking their advice, and reminiscing about their shared fun and funny memories. She admitted that her mom's comments, which previously might have bugged her, now rolled off her back: "There was no point in wasting these precious moments sweating the small stuff."

## Times Left Exercise

As a way to offset hedonic adaptation and the propensity to stop noticing life's good stuff, count the proportion of a particularly happy activity you have left.

1. Identify an activity you really enjoy. This can be anything: something you do with a particular person, something that you've been putting off . . . Regardless, it should be something that

matters to you (e.g., calling your best friend, reading for plea-sure, having dinner with your parents).

For example, 29-year-old grad student calculating the dinners she has left with her parents.

2. Calculate the total number of times you've done this activity in the past.

Dinners together before college:
18 years x 365 days = 6,570

But then need to subtract two months of dinners while studying abroad (60), and a spattering of sleepovers at friends' houses (20).
So, 6,490 dinners before college.

Dinners together during college:
4 years of 3-week holiday breaks (4 x 21 = 84), plus
4 years of 3-week summer visits (4 x 21 = 84), plus
4 years of 3 parent weekend visits (4 x 9 = 36).
So, 204 dinners during college.

Dinners together during years of living in NYC:
6 years of 1-week holiday breaks (6 x 7 = 42), plus
6 years of 1-week summer visits (6 x 7 = 42).
So, 84 dinners during NY stint post-college.

Dinners together since moving back to California:
1 year of Sunday dinners (52), minus
some cancels because other things came up (6).
So, 46 dinners in the past year.

Altogether (6,490 + 204 + 84 + 46), have had 6,824 dinners with parents in the past.

3. Calculate the number of times you have left to do this activity in the future—in the way you enjoy doing it and, if relevant, with the person you enjoy sharing it. When making your future projections, account for constraining factors and factors that will likely change. For instance, if your activity involves a particular person, consider whether that person currently lives and will continue to live near you. Also, how might changes in their family and work situation, or changes in your family and work situation, influence their and your own interest and availability to do this activity? What is their expected longevity, and what is yours?

With 65-year-old parents, could assume that they will live to 90, giving 25 years of weekly dinners left (25 x 52), which would be 1,300.

However, to be more cautious, might want to use the average life expectancy (~76 for men and ~81 for women).

This would give 11 years of weekly dinners with both parents (11 x 52), which is 572 dinners together left, and this is assuming that none are skipped.

4. Calculate the percentage of the total times you have left to do this activity. Is your remaining time more limited than you thought?

Of the total number of dinners (6,824 + 572 = 7,396), only have around 8 percent with parents left.

$$\frac{572}{7,396} \times 100$$

Recognizing that what might seem like an everyday activity won't go on forever will make you take notice. This calculation will help you decide to prioritize and protect this time, and to make the most of these moments—savoring and cherishing them more.

Recognizing that your time left is ultimately scarce will make the time you spend happier. Though it might be unnerving to note that your time is so limited, you'll pay more attention and become more apt to notice simple joys. Knowing that "this too shall pass" doesn't only help get you through hard times, it reminds you to pause so that you don't miss out on the good ones along the way.

## Turn Routine into Ritual

Here's another way to offset hedonic adaptation. Rather than simply paying more attention to the ordinary, you can turn the ordinary into something extraordinary.

By the time Leo's little sister started in the preschool on UCLA's campus, I knew our commutes together wouldn't last, so I had to make the most of them while they did. That realization prompted the creation of Lita's and my standing *Thursday Morning Coffee Date*. I italicize the name because this event is *that* important and held in *that* high a regard. Our *Thursday Morning Coffee Date* is a momentous occasion highly anticipated by both Lita and me. It is respected and slightly envied by brother and dad. It is fiercely protected in my calendar. It is well-memorialized in photos (taken on my phone). And it is known from afar: Lita's teachers and friends and my students have heard about it. It's a thing.

After every Thursday morning carpool, as soon as the big kids tumble out of the car at Leo's school, our date begins. It starts with song. "Hey, Siri, play . . ." Though you wouldn't want to hear me singing my selection of Bob Marley's "Three Little Birds," Lita's renditions of Cyndi Lauper's "Girls Just Want to Have Fun" and Whitney Houston's "Higher Love" are inspired. Upon arrival at our local coffee shop, Profeta, the baristas welcome us with a smile (in itself a sought-after and hard-earned achievement). Even though we wreck the place's vibe, they have come to like us and appreciate our weekly ritual. And despite the long line, once we reach the counter, they patiently wait as Lita shyly builds up the courage to place her order: "May I please have a hot chocolate in a small mug and a plain croissant?" They know I'd like a nonfat flat white. Lita is particularly thrilled when Max is pouring, because he takes extra care in crafting heart flowers in the milk foam on top. Sipping our warm drinks and covering the table with croissant flakes, Lita and I celebrate our morning. It's our treasured time, just the two of us.

We transformed what would otherwise have been a routine caffeine stop. We turned this habit into a cherished, ritualized tradition. We gave it a name. We established implicit and explicit codes of conduct. We took pictures. Thanks to all of these deliberate features, we can talk about it, we know what to expect, and we have documentation to help hold it in our memories. We made it special. Whereas habits serve to help get us through the day without extra thought, traditions imbue these passing moments with greater meaning. Traditions serve to connect us to each other and across time. They give us a sense of belonging.

To offset hedonic adaptation, name the event. Instead of just scheduling evenings for you and your partner (or you and your friend) to go out to dinner, call it "a date." Even that simple reframing makes it more significant. Put extra thought and care into the components of the event, like seven-year-old James did when setting his family's dinner table with special plates to match the evening's motif. Or use different utensils. One experiment showed that participants instructed to eat their popcorn using chopsticks (instead of their fingers as usual) enjoyed the popcorn and their overall snack time more. Special touches don't have to be fancy. Yes, you could pull out the crystal and silver you received as wedding gifts to amp up a dinner date at home. But you could also simply put a frond from your backyard in a jar to create a centerpiece. Or try arranging your place settings on your front stoop, so that you can honestly tell your children (and yourselves) that you're "going out" for your weekly Dinner Date (especially useful during the COVID stay-at-home period).

Within your relationships, call out an enjoyed piece of your shared routine as a ritual. Refer to it as your tradition. This could apply to anything—an afternoon coffee run with a colleague, a movie night with a roommate, or going out to dinner with your partner. One couple I know kicks off every dinner out together with a shot of tequila. I once joined them in this tradition and can attest that it certainly anoints the evening as a celebration! There is value in having shared rituals. Research has shown that in the context of romantic relationships, for instance, having explicit shared rituals increases relationship satisfaction and commitment.

The benefit of having established traditions doesn't just pertain to ordinary events. By connecting us to each other and to other times, traditions help get us through funerals, they make weddings more meaningful, and they enrich the experience of annual holidays. A study showed that families who have holiday traditions are more likely to gather during these times of year. Not only are these families more likely to spend this time together but they enjoy it more. So, state your family's traditions. And if you don't already have them, make them. There is no good reason why my family eats fondue every Christmas Eve other than "that's what we do" . . . and dipping bread in melted cheese is ridiculously delicious.

All of this is about celebrating these moments such that you *can't help* but notice them. It's about sanctifying this time, making it more meaningful.

## Give It a Break

How can you make sure these cherished rituals don't revert to routine events?

Let's go back to that tub of ice cream to illustrate this next strategy. If you took a break after the eighth bite—you put your spoon in the dishwasher and the tub back in the freezer—the next (ninth) bite would likely taste just as divine as the first. Studies have indeed shown renewed enjoyment after taking a break from getting a massage, watching a TV show, and eating chocolate. In the chocolate experiment, for instance, the researchers instructed a portion of their chocolate-loving participants to refrain from eating any chocolate for an entire week. Another group was instructed to eat as much chocolate as they comfortably could, and the rest weren't given any chocolate-related instructions. A week later, all participants were invited back to the lab to eat a piece of chocolate. Those who had abstained ate the chocolate more slowly and happily. They savored it more than the other two groups.

The happiness that follows from taking a breather doesn't happen only for little indulgences, like TV and chocolate. Let me tell you about Cat. She'd always get frustrated when movies depicting love stories ended on the wedding day. She thought this wrongly promised that simply getting married meant living "happily ever after." Cat, however, knew about the peaked-mountain data pattern of marriage that I described earlier. She knew that after the wedding day and honeymoon period ended, the vast majority of couples' happiness slowly declined, eventually returning to each partner's individual baseline. So, when it was her turn to get married, she was determined to set a different course.

She made sure of their lasting happiness by making the choice to get married every day. That is, instead of looking into each other's eyes to make their lifelong commitment to each other just once on their official wedding day, she and her new husband would restate their vows every morning—while putting on their wedding rings. To be clear, this never involved a whole long speech. They each just stated that they were choosing each other for today and for the rest of their lives, and they did this every day. If every day was like their wedding day, their happiness levels would surely stay at the wedding day peak.

Not quite. After a decade of marriage, even this romantic and deeply meaningful ritual turned into a habit. It became a mindless part of their morning routine. It lost its specialness. So they took a break. Not from each other or their marriage, but from putting rings on each other's fingers after brushing their teeth.

A few months into the break, one morning Cat's husband picked up her ring from the little tray next to her toothbrush and again asked for her hand in marriage. Her heart filled with joy, just like before. She was reminded how lucky she was to have this wonderful, smart, good man in her life, and "Yes!" . . . of course she would spend the rest of her life with him!

It's good to have a break from even the best things. Taking a breather from those pieces of everyday life you enjoy helps offset adapting to them.

## Add Some Variety

Finally, let's touch back to that morning of Leo's and my walk to his preschool. What if rather than living in Southern California, where it's sunny and warm the entire year, we'd been back on the East Coast, where there are seasons and varying temperatures across the year? If it had been the first warm day of spring, I'd have noticed the perfectness of that morning.

Hedonic adaptation occurs because we stop noticing when the same good thing happens again and again. Change, however, makes us pause and pay attention. For instance, if you swapped in a spoonful of mint ice cream after your eighth bite of chocolate-caramel, you'd notice. Jordan Etkin and I conducted research showing that greater variety among good stuff keeps us engaged—and therefore happier. In fact, simply focusing on the variation of what's already there works too. In one study, we asked some of our participants to tell us about all the *different* things they had done over the course of their week, while we asked the others to tell us about all the *similar* things they had done during that time. The participants who focused on variety reported being happier and more satisfied. In another experiment, we actually told people how to spend the day. We instructed half the participants to spend their day doing many different things, while we instructed the other half to spend their day doing many similar things. At the end of their days, those who had done a variety of activities were happier and more satisfied.

Variety can spice up relationships too. Studies conducted by the famous relationship researcher Arthur Aron and his colleagues showed that married couples who do more novel activities together end up less bored in their relationships and thus happier with their spouses. So, if you do have a standing date night with your partner, make an effort to go out and try a variety of activities. I know a couple who invented a tradition of Wandering Wednesdays. Every Wednesday evening after work, they tried something new. Sometimes they would visit a restaurant they had never been to, once they joined a pottery painting class, they attended a variety of concerts and performances, and on nights when they couldn't come up with anything novel, they would order something they had never tried before from the menu at their corner wine bar. Years later, they are still wandering together through life, hand in hand.

## CHAPTER FIVE TAKEAWAYS

✦ Hedonic adaptation is our psychological tendency to get used to stuff over time, such that we stop noticing it as much.

✦ Hedonic adaptation is helpful in getting us through negative events.

✦ From a happiness perspective, however, hedonic adaptation can hurt because it causes us to overlook life's pleasures—little and big.

✦ To continue savoring life's joys:

  ✦ Recognize that your remaining time is limited and thus precious.

    ✦ This happens naturally as you age, when faced with crisis, and at the end of a life phase.

    ✦ You can also actively remind yourself by counting your times left doing something you love (likely with someone you love).

  ✦ Turn a routine activity into a celebrated and sacred ritual.

  ✦ Take an occasional break from what it is you enjoy doing.

  ✦ Incorporate a variety of activities across your days and weeks.

*Six*

# DRIVEN TO DISTRACTION

*Live the actual moment.*

—Thích Nhất Hạnh

Kate keeps a running to-do list that she carries with her everywhere. During (sometimes tedious) work meetings, she reviews her list and often jots down personal tasks alongside her work ones:

✦ get gift for Connor's birthday party

✦ make reservations for dinner with the Schwartzes

✦ email soccer parents about snack duty

✦ finalize slide deck for tomorrow's meeting

✦ call Maria with project updates

✦ attend research seminar

During one research seminar, the speaker shared his lab's terrifying findings on a danger of technology usage: drivers distracted on their mobile phones are even more deadly on the road than drunk drivers. Yet this shocking presentation was no match for the list that gripped Kate's attention. She was cycling through her to-dos and strategizing about which task to tackle next. Then, nodding as though she were paying attention, she discreetly picked up her phone and ordered Connor's birthday present, along with a card and festive wrapping.

Kate's list of to-dos absorbs and compels her. Even while working on one task, she's in her head planning and coordinating others. As the seminar wrapped up, Kate felt satisfaction as she crossed two items off her list. More tasks completed. A gratifying sense of accomplishment.

Yet how does this constant management and tracking of her to-dos influence Kate's experience *while doing* the activities on her list? Did she hear anything the speaker said? While busy on her phone selecting the optimal wrapping paper motif for a seven-year-old, did she miss the fact that car crashes are among the world's leading cause of death year after year? When the weekend comes around, does she spend her son's soccer game on her phone, anxiously working through the list instead of watching him play? Rushing from activity to activity, all the while busying herself by coordinating future activities, Kate is rarely present.

Research shows that many of us are like Kate and perpetually oriented toward productivity. But does this drive toward *doing* distract us from ever just *being*? And is there anything we can *do* to spend less time planning for what's next and more time living in the moment? Lastly, would this make us any happier?

## Distracted

To assess how distracted we really are, two Harvard psychologists, Matt Killingsworth and Dan Gilbert, conducted a study examining how often our thoughts wander off to other places and times instead of staying focused on the here and now.

Killingsworth and Gilbert used an app to check in with people via their smartphones at random moments throughout the day. At each of these check-ins, participants were asked a) What are you doing? b) Are you thinking about something other than what you are currently doing? and c) How good do you currently feel? With thousands of adults participating over several months, the researchers were able to capture almost a quarter of a million moments. This data confirms that Kate isn't the only one prone to distraction. Everyone's mind wanders—*often*. In fact, people are *not* focused on what they are doing approximately half of the time (47 percent, to be exact).

Moreover, it is not just sitting in a meeting that propels the mind elsewhere. It turns out that what people were doing didn't have a significant impact on whether or not they were paying attention. Except while in the throes of making love, people were just as likely to be distracted whether they were exercising, getting dressed, commuting, working, doing housework, relaxing, watching TV, reading a book, taking care of children, or talking with a friend.

This is shocking because, though it's fine to be in our heads planning out the day as we get ready in the morning, I think you'd agree that we should be paying attention to our friends when they are talking to us. We certainly don't want caregivers to be inattentive to our children. We want teachers to be paying attention, and doctors.

Traveling in our minds to other places and times isn't always bad. Mind-wandering is actually an incredible cognitive feat unique to us humans. It frees our minds from being stuck when in bad situations. It allows us to imagine solutions. It lets us prepare for the future and reminisce about the past. It gives us the capacity to envision other people and what they're doing without having to be there with them. But with our minds somewhere else half the time, we risk mentally missing half of our lives.

Indeed, Killingsworth and Gilbert's data warns that when our minds wander, our current moment suffers. Remember, in addition to asking their participants to report what they were doing and whether they were thinking about what they were doing, the researchers also asked how they were feeling at the time. The results were definitive: people are less happy when distracted. This is terribly important if we are distracted almost 50 percent of the time.

There's one more lesson in these findings. Killingsworth and Gilbert show that *whether* people were focused on what they were doing had a bigger impact on their happiness than *what* they were doing. This suggests that paying attention to your present activity could be a greater determinant of your happiness than the activity itself. It also warns all of us doers about the unhappy consequences of constantly being distracted.

Still, in our go-go-go culture, slowing down to truly focus and be present can be a challenge. We all need concrete tools to know when and how to shift from doing mode to being mode, so we can make the most of our time. Here are four empirically based strategies to try:

## #1: Treat Your Weekend Like a Vacation

When was the last time you woke up in the morning without rushing out of bed to get ready for something? When did you last linger cuddling under the covers, or chatting over breakfast, or with a cup of coffee and the morning paper splayed out on the table in front of you? Can you recall a time you were sitting at a restaurant with friends, your brunch plates empty, and you ordered another round of mimosas because, well, why not? You had nowhere to get to and nothing pressing to get done. Assuming you're able to conjure such a state, it was probably while you were on vacation.

Vacations are glorious. Research verifies their gloriousness, showing that taking a vacation has positive effects on satisfaction, health, creativity, and even job performance. From analyzing the data of hundreds of thousands of Americans surveyed in Gallup's US Daily Poll, Colin West, Sanford DeVoe, and I documented the happiness from vacations. There's a question in the poll that asks people how often they "make time for trips or vacation with friends and family." Our analyses show that those who prioritize time for vacation enjoy more positive emotion and less negative emotion in their daily lives, as well as greater life satisfaction overall.

One key reason for this boost in well-being is that vacation blocks out time for taking a break—a break from the rushed routine of day-to-day life. Unfortunately, however, we get so busy tackling our to-do lists that we too often don't take these needed breaks. We fail to make time for vacation.

It turns out that Americans are particularly bad at taking vacations. The United States is the only industrialized nation without vacation legally mandated. While European countries such as France, England, and Germany give their workers between twenty and thirty paid days off for vacation each year, one out of four working Americans doesn't get a single one. The issue, however, isn't just about policy. It's also about personal decision-making. Even when vacation days are given, more than half of Americans don't take them. One reason is money. The other primary reason is *time*. People feel like there's too much to do, and they just don't have enough time to get away.

Fortunately, some breaks are already baked into our regular routines. At the end of every workweek, for instance, comes the weekend. The majority of workers get (and take) Saturdays and Sundays off from work. But then the question is, why doesn't the weekend *feel* like a break? Why aren't we all lingering in bed or relaxing over brunch on Saturday morning? It's because, like Kate, we carry our to-do lists over from our workdays into our weekends. We continue to be distracted by focusing on what needs to get done.

So, what if you were to treat the weekend like a vacation? Would it feel more like the break you need? I'm not necessarily talking about getting out of town. Perhaps you don't need to wake up in a Hawaiian hotel room to relax in bed a bit longer. And maybe you don't even have to take any additional days off from work in order to enjoy another round of brunchy beverages. If you simply treated your weekend like a vacation, maybe you'd enjoy this time off more and would return to work happier.

Colin, Sanford, and I tested this idea. Over regular weekends, we conducted experiments among full-time employees. On the Friday going into the weekend, we gave our participants a simple set of instructions. We told half, "Treat this weekend like a vacation. That is, to the extent possible, think in ways and behave in ways as though you were on vacation." For comparison, we instructed the other half, "Treat this weekend like a regular weekend. That is, to the extent possible, think in ways and behave in ways you normally would on a weekend."

Leaving our participants to interpret and apply these instructions however they pleased, we reconnected with everyone after the weekend to see how they were feeling on Monday, when they were back at work. Our idea proved correct. Those who'd treated their weekend like a vacation ended up happier, less stressed, and more satisfied. They were also happier throughout the weekend, enjoying Saturday and Sunday more.

Even though we had predicted it, we were a bit surprised and very excited by these results, because the implications were significant. It suggests that something as simple as reframing our time can make us happier during it and afterward. Colin, Sanford, and I wanted to understand *how*.

We first looked at how our participants spent their time during the weekend. It turns out, those who were treating their weekend like a vacation behaved kind of like they were on vacation: They spent less time working and on housework. They also reported spending more time "engaging in intimate relations"—so they did linger in bed a bit longer. And they spent more time eating, so probably did chill at the brunch table longer. These results show that the "vacationers" allocated less time to what we know are the least happy activities, and more time to happier activities. Interestingly, however, it wasn't the amount of time they'd spent across these activities that ultimately drove their happiness when they returned to work.

The variable that *did* drive the vacationers' increased happiness on Monday was their *increased attention* throughout the weekend. They were less distracted while doing their weekend activities, and this made them happier during that time, as well as afterward.

Kate would benefit from treating her weekend like a vacation. Though she'd still attend her son's soccer game and take him to Connor's birthday party, this slight mental shift might lead her to approach these activities differently and enjoy the time more. As an illustration, on a regular weekend, in her typical hyperfocused drive to get things done, she'd yell like a drill sergeant to hurry her family to fill water bottles, wrestle on shin guards, and hustle out the door to get to the field. She'd then spend most of the game on her phone—texting to coordinate playdates, placing lunch orders, buying supplies on Amazon. Distracted by these tasks, she'd miss seeing her son's save at the goal. She'd later huff about having to drive him to the birthday party—a chore she'd try to get through as efficiently as possible, so she could get on with her looming list of to-dos.

*However*, if she were to instead treat the weekend like a vacation, her family would likely arrive at the game without getting barked at. Maybe she'd kick back in her folding chair on the sideline, happily soaking in that hour of fresh air and sunshine with her family. She might chat with the other parents, and when her son made the save, she'd be watching and jump up excitedly and proudly cheer. Later that afternoon, on their way to the birthday party, she'd relish the opportunity to spend time with her kid, just the two of them. They'd roll down the windows, crank up the tunes, and together belt out some karaoke.

Our experiments show that part of the benefit of vacation is a change in *mindset*. When we give ourselves a break, we shift from doing mode and allow ourselves some moments of simply being. And as a consequence, we feel happier—even without having to get on a plane or pay for a fancy hotel room.

Though Colin, Sanford, and I tested and observed these benefits in the context of weekends, you could apply the vacation mindset to any time you have off during the week. You could, for example, treat your Wednesday afternoon or Thursday evening when you get home from work like a vacation. Instead of tackling your to-do list, you could chill out, turn on some tunes, and linger at the dinner table. It is that simple. I encourage you to give it a try. Give yourself a break during the breaks you already have. For the upcoming weekend, treat it like a vacation. Close your laptop, slow down, and enjoy the view.

## #2: Practice by Meditating

Even if practice doesn't always make perfect, it can certainly help make you better. Meditation is the *practice* of ignoring distractions and bringing your attention to the present moment. It increases mindfulness, which is defined as a "state of being attentive to and aware of what is taking place in the present." You're probably familiar with this term because, though it has a long history in Buddhist tradition, mindfulness has now become popularized in the West.

Even though some view mindfulness as a little hokey, it has been well-researched, and its far-reaching benefits have been scientifically validated. Studies have shown that mindfulness is linked to improved mental health, physical health, behavioral regulation, and interpersonal relationships. For instance, whether individuals are naturally inclined or are otherwise encouraged, those who practice mindfulness report feeling happier in the moment and more satisfied with life overall. Mounting evidence shows that in addition to making us happier, mindfulness meditation can also make us smarter (increasing our executive functioning) and nicer (increasing feelings of connection).

Through the practice of bringing your thoughts to the present, meditation quells worrying thoughts about the future. It quiets concerns about being able to get everything done. Meditation is therefore an effective method to treat anxiety—an all too pervasive feeling in our time-poor culture. Anxiety disorders are documented as the most prevalent mental health issue in the United States and around the world, with women twice as likely to be affected as men, and diagnoses increasing threefold during the COVID pandemic. So if you are someone who suffers from anxiety, meditation might be a good tool for you.

So, how do you do it? The main objective is to direct your attention to a single reference point in your present environment. Your breath is a good option for this focal point, because it is readily available and continual, and makes you feel calm as you settle your thoughts on each deep, long inhale and exhale.

How long should you do it? Well, the research has typically studied the effects of meditating for ten minutes daily. However, sitting still and quiet for ten minutes can feel uncomfortably long for beginners. Since your goal is simply to do it, don't deter your practice by setting the bar too high. I suggest starting with a three-minute or five-minute session and working your way up from there.

Given our many years of practice in rushing about, it can be truly challenging to slow down and stay focused. The practice of meditation itself requires some practice. To begin, I'd encourage you to find a guide. Fortunately, there are many available to choose from. For instance, UCLA's Mindful Awareness Research Center offers free guided meditations in person and online in multiple languages. There are also apps such as Headspace and Calm, which provide guided meditations spanning a variety of durations, themes, and voices. It's important you find your right fit, because if the meditation is too long or the person's voice grates on you, you're less likely to do it again.

In my course, the final assignment requires students to design and implement (for three weeks) a "life hack" that they predict will improve their well-being. Over the years, I've noticed that meditating is among the most common of these projects. These meditation practices have proven effective at decreasing anxiety and increasing happiness—so long as my students were able to identify a guide whose voice and style they liked, a duration that suited them, and a placement in their schedule that made them likely to do it (e.g., first thing in the morning sitting at the foot of the bed, in bed right before going to sleep, in the car for five minutes before entering work).

Despite knowing about the benefits, I am too fidgety and impatient, and I find sitting still to meditate extremely difficult. For those of you who are like me and could use more remedial steps, I'll share a simple meditation practice that I like. You can do it alone or involve others. I do it with my kids during walks around the block.

## Five Senses Meditation Exercise

*F*ocus your attention on your immediate environment using each of your five senses.

Within your surroundings, identify:

- ✦ 5 things you can see

- ✦ 4 things you can touch

- ✦ 3 things you can hear

- ✦ 2 things you can smell

- ✦ 1 thing you can taste

You can do this meditation alone or with others. If you do it with others, go ahead and share out loud the things you're noticing with each of your five senses.

In meditation, you *practice* being mindful. It is an exercise of not letting yourself get distracted—a method to stay focused on the present moment. But the ultimate goal is to apply the muscle you've strengthened by meditating to your day's activities. Your goal is to pay attention *while* doing whatever it is you're currently doing and to be more present throughout your daily hours.

### #3: Shut the Door

No matter how practiced at mindfulness you are, a kid requesting a snack, a phone ringing, or a colleague stopping by your desk *is* going to distract you. Though meditation can help keep your mind from wandering, you still need to set up your physical space to protect yourself from other interruptions. This is particularly important if your immediate pursuit requires deep or creative thinking—if you're hoping to get into "the zone."

The zone is also referred to as being in a state of "flow," which is a transcendent state of energized focus studied by Mihaly Csikszentmihalyi. This Hungarian-American psychologist spent his career interviewing and observing thousands of individuals around the world—including monks, mountain climbers, professional athletes, world-renowned musicians, university students, and regular people during their regular working lives—to identify and understand their most fulfilled moments. In his seminal work *Flow: The Psychology of Optimal Experience*, Csikszentmihalyi argues that people are happiest while in flow.

When you're in flow, you're so fully immersed in what you're doing that you lose track of time. And when you emerge (and only once you emerge, because during the activity you're too absorbed to consider how you're feeling), you realize how *great* it felt. This is most likely to happen during activities that you intrinsically enjoy and that require skills you have.

Ask yourself—when were you last in a flow state? If you're able to identify a time, you probably think of it fondly (because you felt at your best) and wistfully (because it's so hard to access amid your frenetic daily life). Recalling this experience, you know you want to be able to get there again.

Athletes usually recall experiencing flow during competition or out on the trail as "runner's high." However, for the majority of people, flow states occur during work. Depending on the type of work you do (and which professional tasks you're particularly good at and enjoy doing), you may have experienced flow while coding, or perhaps while writing, or maybe when designing a presentation. To be productive, you *need* this time. And to be fulfilled, you *want* this time. It is in these moments that you create. But it only happens in the right environment, and it doesn't happen so often even then.

To set up the appropriate conditions to get into flow, you need to remove all distractions. Here are some tips, using the work setting as an example. But feel free to adapt as necessary to create your own zone:

1.  **Clear your space of threads for other tasks on your to-do list.**

    Since important tasks usually require extra effort, it's tempting to procrastinate (while still feeling productive) by tackling smaller, more accessible tasks. Research shows that we often get diverted from important tasks by seemingly urgent yet unimportant ones. Clean off your desk to avoid this temptation. Move the piles pertaining to other projects out of sight. Maybe even move your desk plants out of view. The three little potted succulents on my desk receive far too much care. Especially when I am gearing up to do important work, I too often busy myself fussing over the dampness of their soil and pruning their dead leaves.

2.  **Clear your schedule for at least several hours.**

    Research shows that transitioning between tasks is costly because it keeps you from getting into the groove on any one task. For instance, I know that for me, meetings require a particular social energy, and it then takes me a while to settle back into my own thinking. I therefore try to reserve bigger blocks of time for writing, and I consolidate meetings on certain days or in the late afternoon. Since flow involves losing track of time, it's important that you don't need to monitor the clock to make sure you're not late for what's next.

3. **Create this space during the time of day when you're most alert.**

Sleep experts say that despite best efforts to shift our internal clocks, some people are inherent larks (wake up early and are energized in the morning) and others are night owls (stay up late and think best when everyone else has gone to bed). I'm definitely a lark and know that I do my best thinking before lunch. Therefore, I protect my morning hours for my deep-thinking work and hold off on email, meetings, and other tasks until later in the day. Depending on whether you're a lark or a night owl, carve out your temporal space accordingly. If you don't have the luxury to control when you work, manage your caffeine so you can turn on your brain when you have the space and time.

4. **Shut the door.**

It is so simple, yet so effective. Close the door to your office to communicate to your colleagues (or if you work from home, family members) that you're not to be bothered. Though it's important I'm accessible to my colleagues and students, even a "quick question" derails my focus. I have to protect these few precious hours for my intense work, so that I can truly be available when my door *is* open. If your workspace has an open floor plan and there isn't a door to close, try reserving a conference room that does have a door.

**5. Put in earplugs or put on headphones.**

Listening to conversation, the TV, or the sound of construction next door inevitably draws your attention away from what you're doing. To minimize these audible distractions, use a pair of earplugs or put on headphones playing white noise or background music. (And if you are in an open-plan office, this also serves as a great cue to colleagues that your door is effectively closed.)

**6. Close out of email.**

Despite our best efforts, we are not *actually* able to multi-task. Research found that people trying to do multiple non-automatic tasks at once couldn't do them simultaneously, but rather alternated between them—doing one at a time. One study, for instance, showed that students listening to a class lecture learned and remembered less if they also had their laptops open (which is why I have a "no laptop or tablet" policy in my class). It is also why I advise you to close out of email when you're trying to work. Not only will this avert the temptation of quickly responding in order to check a few easy items off your to-dos (and you getting sucked into clearing out your entire inbox), but it will also protect you from glancing over at the sound of every new ping.

**7. Put your phone away.**

Don't just put your phone on vibrate or facedown on your desk. Put it all the way away, completely out of sight. More on this next. . . .

Though entering a state of flow is rare, it's worth striving for. It is a time when you are at your best—using your skills to fully engage in doing something, creating something. Once you reemerge, you'll realize those hours were indeed happy ones.

### #4: Put Your Phone Away

These days, the primary culprit for us being so distracted is our phones. A recent study shows that Americans pick up their smartphones at least ninety-six times per day—that's once every ten minutes. Eighteen-to-twenty-four-year-olds check their phones twice as often. This frequency means no activity is spared, even ones as sacred as dinner dates and church. Meetings, outings with kids to the park, and gatherings with family and friends are all susceptible to disruption.

In addition to being a serious driving hazard, this distraction proves costly—both personally and interpersonally. We already learned about the hit on your happiness from being distracted, but every time you check your phone, you are also signaling to those around you that your attention is elsewhere. It communicates that they aren't worth your complete attention. By making us less present, the mere presence of phones threatens to undermine social connection—the very thing that could make us happiest.

This was simply yet vividly demonstrated in an experiment conducted by social psychologist Elizabeth Dunn and her research team.

They recruited small groups of friends to have a meal together at a café. Using a cover story to prevent participants guessing what was being tested, the researchers assigned some of the diners to put their phones away. For comparison, they allowed the others to keep their cell phones out on the table (as they usually do). The results showed that those without their phones enjoyed their dining experience more. Those whose phones were in plain sight enjoyed their meal less, because they were more distracted.

The takeaway here is simple: put your phone away.

The very first assignment in my course is to do exactly this—except, instead of just their phones and just for a meal, I instruct my students to disconnect from all of their digital devices for a full six hours. This assignment is, without fail, met with resistance. My students don't believe they can do it—and they also don't believe it will be in any way beneficial. Still, I insist, and link it to 5 percent of their final course grade.

## Digital Detox Exercise

*C*arve out a six-hour period during your waking life to be "offline"—this means no phone, email, social media, TV, or any form of internet during this time. (Streaming music or reading a book on a Kindle is fine, because the digital component is the mode, not the activity.) Afterward, write a brief reflection piece on the impact of this digitally disconnected time on your emotions, thoughts, and behavior.

Since we, and everyone around us, are habituated to constantly being on our phones, it's easy to believe that we *need* our phones, so we never put them away. The reflection piece serves as a useful personal reminder to read later on of just how transformative this time offline was. The reflection piece also allows me to gauge whether my students actually did the assignment and (selfishly) delight in reading about their resulting happiness.

Even though everyone has their own lightbulb moment, there is a shared cadence to how this exercise is experienced. First comes trepidation. People are nervous that they are going to miss out on people reaching them, and they're frustrated at me for limiting their ability to get things done during these hours. This aggravation continues for about the first hour, during which they habitually reach for where they usually keep their phone. In this early stretch, some describe feeling uncomfortable in social settings, wishing to avoid awkwardness by looking occupied while waiting—at an event, in a café line, or in a classroom before class starts.

But soon enough, a shift occurs. People settle into what they're doing in the moment and whoever they're with at that time. Disconnecting from all the more distant goings-on and fully connecting with the present brings calm and fulfillment. They realize that, in reality, people aren't trying to reach them. And even if they are, it's okay to wait a few hours to respond.* They learn that without such easy means to procrastinate,

---

*There are always exceptions. One of my students emerged from her digital detox to an angry mother and group of friends. If you have people in your life who expect an immediate response (your boss might fall into this category), you should provide these individuals forewarning that you will be offline for this period of time. Others' expectations, however, shouldn't keep you from giving yourself times to disconnect. In these cases, it's all the more important—to reconnect with yourself. These others will learn that this brief separation doesn't detract from your relationship (or productivity) overall, and might even improve it. My husband's work team, for instance, has come to expect that he will log off at 6 p.m. on Fridays and log back on Sunday evening after putting the kids to bed—rejuvenated and excited to dig back in.

they're more apt to do the important tasks they'd been putting off. So, counter to their initial fear of not being able to get anything done, they often end up being *more* productive during this time.

The benefits of this exercise extend to the social sphere as well. Without their phones as an escape valve, my students are more likely to strike up a conversation with a stranger, which we learned can be surprisingly enjoyable and connecting. But it's not just strangers. Liberated from the distraction of phones, my students forge deeper connections with each other. One student described the contrast between dining with a classmate before doing this exercise and dining with the same classmate while doing it. During their pre-detox meal, both scrolled through their Instagram feeds, only interacting when one arrived at something funny to show the other. All of us have either experienced or observed this dining dynamic. She recounted their later meal during the digital detox as drastically different. With her phone put away, he put his away too. Even though they'd dined together before, this time they actually got to know each other, talking and laughing. During this undistracted meal, two classmates became friends.

Another student noted—like Tiffany Shlain in her book *24/6: The Power of Unplugging One Day a Week*—that this is exactly what his family and Jewish community have been doing every week from sundown on Friday to sundown on Saturday. Attributing his closeness with his family and friends to their observation of Shabbat, he was excited to share in this tradition with his classmates.

Despite the initial resistance and period of withdrawal, many students find this time disconnected from their digital devices so wonderfully connecting that they go on to voluntarily implement it in their regular routines—albeit for shorter durations. But this still works, because the benefits of being offline kick in more quickly and can be enjoyed for even brief periods, once you've detoxed before.

## A Caveat

In this chapter, I've explained the detrimental effects of being distracted and have offered ways to minimize distractions to help you get more out of the time you spend. However, we sometimes *want* a distraction. When the current situation is truly awful, it can help to divert our attention away, for at least some of the time. This need to mentally escape is evident in research showing an increased preference for reading lighter books and watching funnier movies during darker economic times.

Also, I must warn that removing distractions will reveal the reality of your current situation. During the COVID quarantine, without being able to busy themselves otherwise, some people found themselves stuck at home in bad relationships or unspeakably lonely. During this time, along with increased anxiety, rates of depression and domestic violence went up. Without distraction, we are forced to reckon with the underlying fabric of our lives and in ourselves. My hope is that by removing distractions, we can focus on the changes we might need to make. And my greater hope is that everyone has the means and strength to make those corrections.

## CHAPTER SIX TAKEAWAYS

✦ We are often distracted by our minds wandering, and this decreases happiness in the present. Therefore, to increase your happiness, strategically remove distractions and focus on the here and now.

✦ Taking time for vacation increases happiness, along with creativity and performance at work.

✦ Even treating the weekend like a vacation can increase happiness by making you more engaged during this time off.

✦ Implementing a meditation practice helps you learn to be mindful of the present, and it can help quell anxious thoughts about the future.

✦ Set up your environment to protect yourself from outside distractions, increasing your likelihood of entering a flow state.

✦ The mere presence of smartphones can be distracting, so put yours away for a happier time.

*Seven*

# THE TIME JAR

*Time is the coin of your life. It is the only coin you have,*
*and only you can determine how it will be spent.*
*Be careful lest you let other people spend it for you.*

—Carl Sandburg

A professor walks into his classroom, every seat filled, and he places a large clear jar on the front desk. He unloads a big bag onto the desk chair. Out of the bag he pulls a box of golf balls and empties all the golf balls into the jar. He asks the students, "Is the jar full?" With the top golf balls reaching the jar's opening, the whole class nods and answers, "Yes."

The professor seems to agree. But then he reaches into his bag again, and he pulls out a container of small pebbles. He pours them into the jar. The little rocks tumble over and around the golf balls, filling up the crevices, and the professor asks his students, "Is it full now?" Again, the class nods and answers, "Yes."

Next, out of the bag comes a container of sand, which the professor pours into the jar. The sand covers the golf balls and pebbles, filling the remaining holes. The professor shakes the jar slightly and, with the help of gravity, the sand settles to the bottom of the jar. "What about now? Is the jar full?" The students are now smiling as they nod, seeing his point.

It appears the demonstration is over because there's no more room in the jar. But then the professor pulls out two bottles of Corona. At this, the whole class starts to laugh. Using a bottle opener from his pocket, he opens both bottles. He pours one of the beers over the golf balls, pebbles, and sand, and takes a sip of the other.

Holding his beer, the professor walks around to the front of the desk, perching himself next to the jar. He explains, "This jar represents your life. The golf balls are the important things: your family, your friends, your health, and your passions. The pebbles are the other important things: . . . your job, your home. And the sand is everything else; it's just the small stuff. Now, if you put the sand in the jar first, you won't have room for the pebbles and the golf balls. The same is true of life. If you spend all your energy and time on the small stuff, you won't have time for all the really important things that matter to you. . . . Place your golf balls first. Set your priorities, because everything else is just sand."

One of the students then raises his hand and asks, "Professor, what does the beer represent?" The professor chuckles, "Glad you asked. It goes to show that no matter how full your life may seem, there's always room for a couple of beers with a friend."

This short film by Meir Kay, which I play during the first day of my course, reminds us that we need to be deliberate in allocating our hours. We each have a jar representing the time of our life, and we have to be thoughtful in deciding which activities we let into and put into our jars—which activities get space in our lives.

It's a useful analogy for time that I often use when making my own time-spending decisions: Do I start watching another episode? Do I agree to give a talk? Do I accept a social invitation? Do I serve on a school committee . . . or as a room parent . . . or as Lita's soccer coach? Do I take a quick peek at my inbox to see if there's anything in urgent need of a response? Do Rob and I go away for the weekend?

This little film makes a big point. It is about prioritization. If the professor had let the sand fill the jar first, there wouldn't have been enough space for the most important activities—the golf balls. If you spend all your time on the little stuff, it is the equivalent of sand filling up your jar, and you won't have any time left for *your* golf balls—the activities that are most important to you. You will find yourself suffering from time poverty, with your days full of activities that don't really matter to you.

Only if you identify what really does matter can you carve out and protect the time. It is about putting your golf balls in first. Once these important activities have their secured space in your week's schedule, then you can allow your hours to get filled by other to-dos, new requests, or vegging out.

Like space in the jar, our hours are finite. There are twenty-four hours in the day, one-third of which are spent asleep. This leaves only sixteen hours. At first, this might seem ample. However, now consider that for every workday, half of those hours are spent at the office, one is likely spent commuting to the office (thirty minutes there and thirty minutes home), and it takes an hour to get ready in the morning. This leaves only six total hours—just one-quarter of the day—to do everything else.

"Everything else" includes all the things you *have to do* (walk the dog, grocery shopping, prepare dinner, wash the dishes, take the kids to school, pick the kids up from school, put the kids to bed, get the car washed, do laundry, clean the house, buy a new pair of shoes, pay that darn parking ticket, get a haircut), all the things you *really want to do* (go for a run, watch your daughter's dance class, sit down for a relaxed family dinner, read the kids a bedtime story, have an unhurried glass of wine with your partner), and all the things you *would really like to do* (meet up with an old friend for a drink, meet up with a new friend for a drink, finish the book for book club, get your nails done, read the article your partner has so thoughtfully put aside knowing you'd find it interesting, clean out your sock drawer). Clearly not everything is going to fit into your six available daily hours. In fact, your weekly schedule only has room for a select few of these activities. You need to be choosy.

## Sand Traps

Cheryl is insanely busy. She works full-time as a healthcare administrator and dedicates her nights and weekends to working toward her MBA. Cheryl completed the Time Tracking Exercise from chapter 3. Looking over her time use data for those two weeks, she tallied up the number of hours she'd spent on her various activities (e.g., working at the hospital, attending class, doing her coursework). The calculation that really shocked her was the amount of time she had spent on social media:

> I tracked 12½ hours my first week and 10½ hours the second week on social media. Even though this is a huge amount of time considering everything else I have on my plate, I sadly know these numbers are not even a true reflection of my full usage. I am literally never off my phone all day long every day. If I have even a small break in my day, I am instantly checking social media. Or if I am bored, I do it too. Even though I think it will be just a quick check, I always stay on longer than I intend, and apparently, these minutes really add up. Also, my time on social media makes me take longer doing other things, like getting ready in the morning. I get lost in checking it, writing someone, or reading replies to my posts.

Screen time proves to be a major sand trap for many of us. As Cheryl observed, what's intended to be a couple minutes of scrolling here and there can all too swiftly turn into a significant number of weekly hours. Or as we saw from Cheryl's classmate in chapter 3, what's thought to be an easy way to unwind with one's partner at the end of the workday can inadvertently turn into 20 percent of the entire week in front of the TV.

Cheryl's social media usage isn't unique, nor are people's zoned-out evenings on the couch. Surveys show that, on average, Americans spend three hours every day on their smartphones. And this isn't just phone-addicted youth. Yes, millennials do spend more time per day on their phones (average of 3.7 hours) than Gen Xers (average of 3.0 hours), but not by much. Baby boomers also spend multiple daily hours (average of 2.5 hours) on their tiny screens. Statistics further indicate that, on average, adults across generations spend approximately five hours watching

TV every day. This means that it wouldn't be uncommon for someone to spend a couple dozen hours week after week in passive screen time.

Clearly, not all TV viewing or smartphone usage is wasted time. Indeed, there's a difference between hours that get mindlessly soaked up versus deliberately spent. A nonprofit organization that educates around safe media usage, Common Sense Media, is definitive: not all screen time is created equal. When there's an opportunity for education, storytelling that heightens empathy, or active engagement with loved ones, screens (big or little) provide a portal for good. But still, there's the issue of time.

If time wasn't limited, the hours Cheryl spent scrolling wouldn't be so problematic. But as the jar parable highlights, time *is* limited. Cheryl laments that, given her busy work and school schedule, she "doesn't have time" to socialize with friends or her sister. However, if she were to cut down on the hours she spent on social media (an activity she rated as a mediocre 5 on her 10-point happiness scale), she'd have that time to see friends (which she gave an average rating of 7.5) or grab dinner with her sister (a 10).

What is your sand? What unintentionally fills your hours such that you look back feeling pangs of regret, realizing that you wish you had spent that time better?

My email inbox is my major sand trap. Responding to email swallows my work hours and home hours alike. I've all too often found myself at the end of a workday having accomplished nothing of substance because of the time consumed responding to email. In fact, this very page has taken me a full day to complete, because I keep getting interrupted by "urgent" emails! I'd never be able to write a chapter (much less a whole book), or complete a research paper, or prepare a lecture if I stayed up-to-date on my inbox.

Email doesn't only threaten my productivity, it threatens time for true enjoyment. After dinner, I feel the compulsion to get back online to make sure I'm caught up. The thing is, there's *always* another request, another question, another email in need of a response. It is a never-ending task that fills up all the time I give it. And this time given over to email lessens the hours I might otherwise spend enjoying a glass of wine with Rob, an evening walk with my neighbor, reading for pleasure, watching a movie, or calling my brother to hear how he and the kids are doing.

Whether they arrive in the form of email or not, incoming requests that aren't ruthlessly managed can very quickly fill our entire jar. It's relentless, and can feel suffocating. Will you serve on this committee? Will you do me a favor? Can I pick your brain, and how about over a cup of coffee? Can you drive the kids? Will you speak on this panel? Will you bring the snacks? Will you arrange the gift from us? Can you coordinate the event? . . . Often you don't even notice you're being buried until it's too late—you're overcommitted, overwhelmed, and not sure what (if any of it) is worthwhile.

Part of the conundrum is that when asked, it just feels easier to say yes. We agree to speak on the panel, to bring the snacks. Even though there's not a second to spare now, surely there will be then. But then, on the day of the panel or the snack-needing event, why do we inevitably find ourselves frantically rushing about wondering what the heck we were thinking when we said yes?

Researchers Gal Zauberman and John Lynch conducted experiments explaining the psychology behind our tendency to overcommit. In one study, they asked participants to think about the activities they have today and their available spare time. They then asked these same participants to think about their activities and available spare time for the same day of the week a month from now. After this vivid envisioning of their current and future busyness, participants rated their available time on a 10-point scale ranging from 1 = *much more time available today* to 10 = *much more time available next month*. Gal and John's results reveal a consistent belief everyone holds: we will have significantly more time available next month than we have today.

Of course, this is ridiculous. In reality, today is like any other, including the one a month from now. Just like today, there will only be twenty-four hours, and we will have overcommitted ourselves by previously having said yes to requests. However, it's exactly because we expect that we will have more time available in the future that we say yes now. Gal and John appropriately refer to this finding as the "Yes . . . Damn! Effect."

Fortunately, there's an easy solution. By knowing the underlying psychology, you can counteract the effect. The strategy to combat this sand trap is to only say yes to requests that you would be happy to spend the time on *today*.

Another thorny part of the problem is the difficulty in saying no—and women are significantly worse at this than men. Though empirically demonstrated in academia, this same dynamic plays out across contexts. Sara Mitchell and Vicki Hesli conducted a survey of over 1,000 faculty in political science departments. They found that female professors are significantly more likely to be asked to serve on committees and do other nonprestigious, non-career-advancing service tasks than their male colleagues. But it's not just that they are being asked more often; they *say yes* more often.

Agreeing to frequent requests to do administrative work crowds out time for research. Yet research is the primary reason many pursue careers in academia in the first place: it's fulfilling. Moreover, research forms the basis of evaluation when going up for promotion, which might explain why female faculty are less likely to advance through the academic ranks. Notably, while 36 percent of assistant professors are female, only 19 percent of tenured full professors are. The reluctance to say no thus proves costly—both emotionally and professionally. These results are important in warning against always saying yes to incoming requests. Though it might seem easier in the moment, the downsides are serious.

Now, clearly you will sometimes be presented with requests that are worth accepting and that you will *want* to say yes to. Recognizing the finite space in your time jar is helpful here. It encourages you to apply strict filters to sift out the sand. These filters should be based on your personal purpose (to make your hours meaningful) and the activities that offer greatest happiness (to make your hours fun).

## Purpose Filter

I explained in chapter 4 the value of identifying your purpose in your work: *why* you do the work that you do. Knowing your purpose is critical because it helps you focus on the tasks that are key to meeting your objectives, and it also increases your enjoyment and motivation in doing these tasks. However, the value of identifying your purpose extends well beyond the professional realm. There is value in identifying your purpose more generally: *why* you do what you do. What drives you? What is your ultimate goal?

In conversations over the years, I've heard individuals articulate their purpose in a variety of ways:

*"To give a voice to those who don't have one."*

*"To make the future I see a reality."*

*"To be a good father."*

*"To entertain."*

*"To build things that improve lives."*

*"To stay sober."*

*"To make friends."*

*"To leave the world a better place."*

*"To be helpful."*

Knowing your purpose will help you sift out the sand and determine the activities that feel meaningful and worth your time. Like the plastic beach toy my little Lita uses to gather seashells, your higher-order "why" works as an effective sieve, separating the worthwhile activities from everything else. It will help clarify which activities to prioritize: which to spend time on and which to let pass.

Using myself as an example, by now you've heard that my goal is to disseminate happiness. This is closely related to my professional purpose I shared in chapter 4: to create and disseminate knowledge about what makes people happy. With this, I can more accurately predict what activities will feel fun and meaningful. When asked to speak on a panel, I say yes or no depending on whether it would help spread the understanding of emotional well-being. Or if I'm asked to serve on a committee, I decide based on whether it would better the well-being of those I care about: my kids, their community, or my community of colleagues and students. This filter reduces the emotional tax and time I spend responding to requests, because the right answer is obvious.

### Happiness Filter

From the Time Tracking Exercise in chapter 3, you identified the specific activities in your daily life and their common features that actually provide you happiness. This knowledge can serve as your filter to sift out which activities will likely bring you joy from those that threaten to mindlessly fill your jar.

I will again offer myself as an example. When analyzing my time tracking data, I identified that one commonality among my preferred activities was doing things *with* my kids (as opposed to some of my less fun activities, which involved doing things *for* my kids). Knowing that I derive a great amount of happiness doing things with Leo and Lita is helpful, because I can use this as a filter for kid-related spending. For instance, when I was asked to serve on their school's gala committee, it was an easy and quick no. None of this work would have involved me spending any time with either Lita or Leo. However, when asked to serve as the room parent for Lita's class, I agreed. Sure, it would involve sending some parent emails and coordinating classroom events, but I would get to help create a positive experience for my daughter's class community that year. More importantly, I'd get to be with her in her classroom for those events. And when I was asked to chaperone Leo's class's field trip to the Grammy Museum, I also said yes. Taking off from work to join Leo and his friends while learning about the creation and performance of recorded music was absolutely worth my time. I got to spend the day with my son.

So many of us are time poor. We are stressed out by having too much to do with overly committed schedules and not enough time to do it all. However, by sifting out the sand, you *can* create space in your time jar for what matters most.

## Your Golf Balls

Your purpose and happiness filters will help you in reacting to incoming requests. However, you ultimately want to become more proactive in deciding how to spend your time. You need to put your golf balls into your time jar first. Prioritize them. The next chapter will guide you in how to optimally place your golf balls within your week's schedule. But first, you need to determine what they are. What are your most important activities—the ones that truly make you the happiest?

The Time Tracking Exercise in chapter 3 is a data-driven approach to identifying your golf balls. I highly suggest you do that exercise, because the results can be surprising. However, you can select your golf balls even without doing the complete exercise. Reflecting back over your past two weeks, ask yourself: *What are the activities that sparked the greatest joy?*

This is very much like tidying guru Marie Kondo's advice for how to declutter your house. She says to hold up each article of clothing and ask yourself whether it speaks to your heart and "sparks joy." If not, thank it for its service and then let it go. However, this is not just about your old T-shirts. You can employ this same question to determine how to spend your most precious resource.

When my husband scanned his weeks to identify the activities that sparked joy for him, he realized that reading *Harry Potter* with Leo gave him tremendous happiness. With the lights turned down, sitting next to Leo on his bed in the evenings, Rob found contentment. In this quiet space, his son's and his energy aligned, and their minds traveled together to a fantastical world of endless possibilities. Despite his relentless workload and our family's frenzied evening routine, Rob realized that this thirty minutes of reading with Leo is worth protecting every day. It is a priority.

When my sister-in-law, Christina, looked back on her previous two weeks, she found her joy on a weekend hike with a friend. She liked the physical activity. But even more than feeling good in her body, she liked being outside and socializing. With an open sky above her and no tasks within reach, she relished the space to listen and to share. This sense of connection and happiness didn't require an extreme full-day trek. In fact, it was as simple as getting outside and going for a walk with any person she enjoys.

For me, date night with Rob is one of my greatest joy sparkers. When the two of us go out for dinner, we step away from our routine and wrangling of logistics, away from kitchen cleanup, and our primary focus is each other. Even during COVID, when we couldn't go out to restaurants, we'd order delivery and eat at a little table I'd set up with candles and music on our front stoop—*outside* our front door. After our workweeks of living and working alongside one another, this is when we turn and face each other for actual conversation. This time ensures that we don't lose touch amid the busyness of the day-to-day, so it *has to be* a priority.

## Joyful Activities Exercise

Looking over your past two weeks, what activities "sparked joy" for you?

1. _____

2. _____

3. _____

4. _____

5. _____

## Time to Think

In addition to the moments you've found for yourself, let me suggest another golf ball for you to prioritize: a "Shultz Hour." *New York Times* writer David Leonhardt describes how former US secretary of state George Shultz would protect one hour each week for quiet reflection:

> *He sat down in his office with a pad of paper and pen, closed the door and told his secretary to interrupt him only if one of two people called: "My wife or the president," Shultz recalled.*
>
> *Shultz . . . told me that his hour of solitude was the only way he could find time to think about the strategic aspects of his job. Otherwise, he would be constantly pulled into moment-to-moment tactical issues, never able to focus on larger questions of the national interest. And the only way to do great work, in any field, is to find time to consider the larger questions.*

I'm not advocating for Shultz's foreign policies. I am, however, advocating for his thoughtful practice. Try it. Carve out some time for quiet reflection. It doesn't even have to be an hour—start with half an hour or even fifteen minutes dedicated to letting your mind brim with thoughts.

For your Shultz Hour (or quarter hour), clear yourself of ordinary distractions, including people, emails, texts, phone calls, the radio, and the TV. Just as you do to create space for flow, for this time close the door and hide your phone. Or you might get away from your desk and go outside for a walk.

The value of your Shultz Hour exceeds the enjoyment from removing distraction, which we've already discussed. It's during this time that you can more deeply process, more limitlessly create, and more ably strategize about the important decisions awaiting your attention: Do you take the next step in your relationship? Do you take the really hard step of ending your relationship? Should you go ahead and move neighborhoods/across the country/across the world? Should you put in your two weeks' notice even though you don't have another job lined up? Do you go back to school? What traditions do you want to cultivate for your family? Should you try for another kid? Should you give in to your kids' pleas for a puppy? Is it finally time to have that tough talk with your friend?

These decisions all deserve their own space in your time jar. You shouldn't hurry through them. Leonhardt observed, "If you spend all your time collecting new information, you won't leave enough time to make sense of it." Prioritize space for thinking.

## Prioritize Your Priorities

Dianna and Justin received a supreme wedding gift: two nights at the San Ysidro Ranch. It's an idyllic hideaway nestled in the foothills of Santa Barbara, California. The vine-covered cottages, each with a private, exquisitely landscaped garden, are perfect for couples to spend leisurely mornings relaxing on fine linens, munching on warm croissants delivered in a basket along with homemade jams. Here, windows are left wide open to invite in aromas of jasmine and orange blossoms and the cheery sound of buzzing hummingbirds and honeybees. This place is so perfect for romantic getaways that American royals John and Jackie Kennedy honeymooned here, and Hollywood stars Laurence Olivier and Vivien Leigh exchanged vows under its canopy of trees. Though it's quaint, staying at the San Ysidro Ranch carries a hefty price tag. Needless to say, it was a *very* nice gift, and Dianna and Justin couldn't wait to enjoy it.

Ten years later, they had not yet redeemed the present. They were still married, and very happily. Yet a decade on, they still hadn't taken the time to get away, just the two of them. This wasn't because they didn't enjoy each other's company, or because the siren song of tranquil mornings eating warm croissants had waned. And clearly, cost wasn't the barrier because it was a gift. The singular reason that Dianna and Justin hadn't yet stayed at the San Ysidro Ranch was because something else had always come up. They had booked a cottage on several occasions, but a cousin's birthday, a kid's soccer game, or pressure at work interfered, and they had ended up canceling their trip each time. Despite it being a priority, they had never prioritized it.

In my field of behavioral decision-making, most researchers tackle issues associated with people being myopic or nearsighted—succumbing to the temptation of what's close and easy. This means that people choose immediately enjoyable options and ignore the negative consequences these options will impose in the future. Indeed, the bulk of the research has focused on how to nudge individuals to choose "shoulds" over "wants," and virtues over vices. Drawing on the huge number of studies and decades of research, there are some wonderful books, including Katy Milkman's *How to Change*, that offer tactics to help people improve their self-control: to behave in ways that may not be fun right now but are healthier and smarter in the long run. Having witnessed the severe costs suffered by individuals who consistently fail to exert self-control in their eating habits or financial decisions, I agree this is incredibly important work.

However, I've just as often noticed people suffering from the opposite problem. There are people who constantly sacrifice immediate enjoyment to avoid the guilt from not achieving the best outcome later. In our highly competitive school system and professional environments, there's a great compulsion to work rather than play, to get things done rather than relax. In this camp, I admit that my most challenging New Year's resolution wasn't to go to the gym every day, it was to *not work* during the weekends.

Researchers Anat Keinan and Ran Kivetz observed this phenomenon as well. They cleverly called it *hyperopia*: the tendency to be excessively farsighted, always choosing the future over the present. It is an issue of being overly self-controlled. They note that, yes, it's healthier to choose an apple over a piece of chocolate cake for a snack; however, if you choose the apple-type option every single time, you'll never get to experience the pleasure of chocolatey goodness. If you *always* choose shoulds over wants, there is *never* an opportunity for enjoyment. And after years and years of making only should-driven decisions, you may look back and feel intense regret at missing out on the happiness that life has to offer, including croissant flakes on white linen sheets.

Keinan and Kivetz conducted several experiments demonstrating this point. In one study, they asked people to recall a situation that occurred years prior in which they were deliberating between spending time on work or pleasure, and then ultimately chose either work or pleasure. Compared to those who chose pleasure, those who had chosen work reported feeling significantly greater regret and as if they had missed out. In a separate study, Keinan and Kivetz asked college students to reflect back on their winter break from the year before.

Thinking back to how they'd spent their time, students were significantly more likely to agree with the statement "I should have traveled more" than with the statement "I should have worked more."

To avoid this regret, you have the chance to prioritize your activities. It's important not only to identify your golf balls, but to actually put them in your time jar. It wasn't enough for Dianna and Justin to make a reservation at the San Ysidro Ranch; they needed to actually *go*.

Admittedly, there are Friday afternoons when I haven't finished the work I'd intended to, and I feel like I should stay in to get it done. It would be extremely easy to cancel date night. Rob appreciates all that I'm juggling. Plus, he wouldn't mind relaxing after his busy workweek in front of the TV. Shouldn't we just push it off to a later time? *No.* Precisely because this time is so easy *not* to spend, it's especially important to commit to spending it.

To ensure that we actually follow through and go out for date night, we have implemented what behavioral economists refer to as a *commitment device*. A commitment device is a way to lock yourself in to follow through on your goal, and you do this by imposing a cost on yourself if you don't follow through. For instance, Dianna and Justin could have made a noncancelable reservation at the San Ysidro Ranch, so that they would have to forfeit the price of their stay if they decided not to go. As a commitment device for our date nights, Rob and I have scheduled and committed to paying a babysitter for every Friday night. Not only does this eliminate the task of finding (or the excuse of not finding) a sitter, but having this trusted adult invariably show up at our house on Fridays at 6 p.m. compels us to get out the door. And inevitably, once we're out and removed from the other pulls of life, Rob and I have no regrets.

In addition to such commitment devices and the scheduling strategies I will share in the next chapter, simply realizing your time as limited can help motivate you to go ahead and spend this important time. Much as the Times Left Exercise in chapter 5 reminds you to make more of the times that bring you joy, the time jar analogy will remind you to prioritize the times that bring you joy.

I saw Dianna a couple days after she returned from her and Justin's stay at San Ysidro Ranch, and she looked radiant. Justin was taking my course and had seen the film about the time jar. They had devoted their time to what ultimately mattered.

## Make the Time

I hope that you will touch back to the jar analogy as a reminder of how limited your time is when making your own spending decisions. There are finite hours for you to allocate. If you let the sand—whatever "stuff" is thrown at you or asked of you or lures you into mindlessness—fill those hours, there won't be enough time in your days for the really fun and meaningful activities. You won't have any time left for what is truly worthwhile. You've got to be deliberate in how you spend your hours. Be proactive, rather than reactive, in determining where your time goes. You need to put in the golf balls first and commit to that time, regardless of whether you're in the mood or sand washes in.

## CHAPTER SEVEN TAKEAWAYS

✦ We are prone to letting our days get mindlessly filled with activities that are unfulfilling.

✦ One reason is that we too frequently say yes to incoming requests, because we (incorrectly) believe we will have more spare time in the future.

✦ Another reason is that we often choose future rewards over current enjoyment.

✦ However, always putting off enjoyable activities for later can lead to greater feelings of regret.

✦ So, identify, commit to, and prioritize space in your finite time jar for the activities that bring you joy.

# Eight

# TIME CRAFTING

*You can't stop the waves, but you can learn to surf.*

—Jon Kabat-Zinn

N ow that you know the science, it's time for you to create art. I will help you piece together your hours to design an ideal week, like piecing together the tiles of a mosaic. I like to think of this process as time crafting.

As you craft your time, think of your activities as the tiles. Varying in color and size, some are inherently more appealing than others. At this point in the book, you know which the prettiest tiles are: which are the most fun and meaningful for you, which activities "spark joy." But you also know that you can change your perspective to brighten any tile. And you have strategies to amplify the beauty of already pretty tiles by offsetting hedonic adaptation and eliminating distractions. You even have strategies to make the least pretty tiles (housework, work, and commuting) shinier.

In this chapter, I will help you figure out how best to piece all of these tiles together to craft a magnificent mosaic—one that reflects your purpose, inspires you, and is sustainable. I will guide you in how to optimally place and sequence your tiles among those that are already set. In this process, you will increase the impact of your favorites and minimize the impact of your least favorites.

Though your mosaic will look intricate, the steps of time crafting are basic, and the suggestions are practical. Throughout the chapter, I will remind you of concepts we have previously covered, and I'll suggest simple ways to apply them in designing your optimal week. This is really an exercise in scheduling, but unlike the way you've tackled your calendar before, now you are informed by science and equipped with your personal priorities and purpose. You will be deliberate and mindful in deciding which tiles you're going to place and where—ultimately crafting the time of your life.

## Your Canvas

The following blank week schedule is your canvas onto which you will place your tiles. I suggest you print this out from my website, www.cassiemholmes.com, and follow the steps, sketching your design in pencil. Have an eraser handy, because you'll probably want to revise and revisit your decisions along the way.

Since it's useful to have a concrete example to follow, I will show you how I crafted one of my own weeks. However, please remember that the activities you engage in and how you place them must be specific to you. It's about what is fun and meaningful to *you*—what brings *you* joy. Also note that your week will be subject to your own logistical realities and family structure, as well as your work, and the flexibility of that work. For instance, because I have young kids, all of my hours outside of their school hours must be coordinated with the kids, their childcare, and Rob. If you don't have young kids, you'll likely have greater autonomy in designing your schedule. On the other hand, as an academic, I have more control than most professionals over how I spend my work hours. Though some of my teaching responsibilities have set hours in the classroom, the bulk of my work is self-determined.

I decide what projects I do and when I work on them. In this respect, I am my own boss. Therefore, several of the design elements that apply to my work hours will only be relevant to those who have similarly flexible work schedules.

Recognizing that many professions don't have this flexibility in their workdays, I will also share the example of my sister-in-law, Christina. As the program director for a school that helps young children with special needs, she is required to be at her office throughout school hours. In addition to her "day job," Christina conducts in-home sessions to support students with special needs individually, and those sessions happen at the same times each week throughout the school year. Christina's workdays are therefore highly structured, and she has minimal control over the hours she works. She provides a good example of someone who is particularly motivated to craft her after-work hours and weekends to make the very most of this available time.

Though particular time crafting strategies will be more relevant for some people than others, the basic steps are the same for everyone. So print out your canvas, grab a pencil, and follow along.

## Your Canvas

| | MONDAY | TUESDAY | WEDNESDAY | THURSDAY | FRIDAY | SATURDAY | SUNDAY |
|---|---|---|---|---|---|---|---|
| 6AM | | | | | | | |
| NOON | | | | | | | |
| 6PM | | | | | | | |
| 11PM | | | | | | | |

## Step 1: Set Your Already Set Tiles

You likely have some required activities each week with set times. It's helpful to have a clear sense of what these are before you start making decisions. Penciling out these tiles will let you know exactly what hours you have available to craft.

On your canvas, enter these set activities first. Frame out these times and label them. Don't block out these times completely, because there may be opportunities later in the crafting process to make more of them. For instance, you might decide that you want to bundle one of these activities with another, more enjoyable activity. Or you might benefit from breaking up or consolidating these times to manage their overall impact.

What your set activities are should be clear to you. However, it's not quite as simple as just marking down whatever you currently do every week. You should only count those activities for which *you have no choice about whether you do them, nor about when you do them.* For instance, if you have a job outside your home with defined work hours, you should place this work and the associated commute as set tiles. Or if you are responsible for taking your kids to school and picking them up at specified times each day, or you have a standing weekly meeting or required appointment that you'd only cancel in an emergency, you should include these as your set tiles.

Christina, for instance, has to be at her school in Manhattan from 8 a.m. to 3:30 p.m., Monday through Friday. She lives in the New York suburbs and has a one-hour commute each way. Additionally, on Mondays, Wednesdays, and Thursdays, she travels to students' homes for one-on-one sessions, and on these nights she gets home at 7 p.m. Her set tiles therefore include her commute and her work hours.

## Christina's Time Crafting: Set Tiles

| | MONDAY | TUESDAY | WEDNESDAY | THURSDAY | FRIDAY | SATURDAY | SUNDAY |
|---|---|---|---|---|---|---|---|
| 6AM | | | | | | | |
| | COMMUTE | COMMUTE | COMMUTE | COMMUTE | COMMUTE | | |
| | WORK | WORK | WORK | WORK | WORK | | |
| NOON | | | | | | | |
| | | COMMUTE | | | COMMUTE | | |
| | IN-HOME SESSIONS | | IN-HOME SESSIONS | IN-HOME SESSIONS | | | |
| 6PM | COMMUTE | | COMMUTE | COMMUTE | | | |
| 11PM | | | | | | | |

In my example, I was crafting a week during a month while teaching at UCLA. I must be in front of the class on Wednesday 1–4 p.m., Wednesday 7–10 p.m., and Thursday 8:30–11:30 a.m. I like to arrive at my classroom thirty minutes before class starts in order to be available to students for questions, and I usually stick around a little afterward. I therefore placed these class tiles on my canvas at their set times. In addition, every Friday morning and through lunchtime, I have mandatory faculty meetings and seminars. I placed these as set as well. Of course, between preparing lectures for class, research, and administrative duties, I work dozens more hours throughout the week; however, because exactly when I do this work is flexible, I don't include these hours among my set tiles.

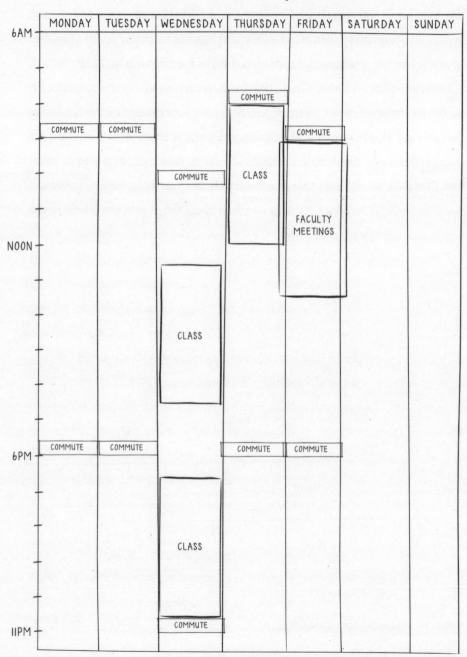

Cassie's Time Crafting: Set Tiles

### Step 2: Place Your Joyful Tiles First

With your set tiles in place, you can see what hours you have available to craft. This next step is the most important in the process: *Place your joyful tiles first.*

The previous chapter highlighted the importance of prioritizing activities that truly matter to you. This step is analogous to putting your golf balls in your time jar first. A difference here is that you are specifying where within the jar your golf balls should go. In crafting your time, you want to dedicate your best hours to your most meaningful activities. You'll also want to block out these times completely. This will help protect these prized hours from other obligations, requests, and mindless screen time.

For this step, you'll first need to gather these key tiles: your activities that "spark joy." These are the pursuits you want to ensure you dedicate time to, because they are truly fun and meaningful. To identify these tiles, go back and look at what you wrote for the Joyful Activities Exercise in chapter 7 and your Happiest Activities in Part II of the Time Tracking Exercise in chapter 3.

## Time Crafting Strategy 1

### Protect time for social connection.

As we learned in chapter 3, some of your joyful tiles likely involve social connection. If you're an introvert (like me), you're probably happiest when connecting with your favorite people, and if you're an extrovert (like my Leo), you're happy connecting with any and all people.

But busy schedules tend to crowd out the time we devote to others.

Our days get so packed that it's easy to neglect the simple act of picking up the phone for the joy of saying hi to a friend or family member. Hours feel so hurried we often fail to slow down and revel in the company of those around us. To ensure that no more of your weeks pass without building and enjoying these relationships, place these tiles on your canvas first. Block out and protect these times in your week's schedule.

*Date Night.* As you know, my conversations with Rob provide me a deep sense of connection and give me immense joy. It might be assumed that because we live under the same roof, we could talk any night of the week, so there's no need to make a thing of it. Yet it's precisely because it seems so easy that it's dangerously easy to push off. And in reality, our kids absorb our attention when we aren't each otherwise absorbed in work. So we *need* to block out this time together. We do this by scheduling a weekly Date Night.

In addition to making the time, it's important to place this tile in an ideal spot. Friday nights are perfect. This location on my canvas establishes these evenings as special. Date night gives us something to look forward to throughout the workweek, and with good wine and tasty food, it creates a celebratory way to kick off every weekend. Also, since we don't have to wake up early and be productive the next morning, our enjoyment isn't dampened by work-related worries.

With this tile in place, Rob and I schedule work dinners or nights out with friends on other nights of the week, and we schedule social engagements that include the kids during other parts of the weekend.

*Time Crafting Strategy 2*

Protect the times that really matter to you from distraction by making them a "no phone zone."

As we know, the presence of our smartphones distracts us from what we are doing and reduces our enjoyment. Since you certainly don't want to be distracted during the activities that bring you greatest joy, protect these times during the week as "no phone zones." Put your phone away, out of sight. Without peeking at email and social media feeds, you will experience a deeper connection.

*Family Dinner.* Despite his work never being finished, he would leave his office every evening at 6:30 p.m. sharp in order to make it home in time to sit down for dinner with his wife, mother-in-law, and two daughters. For those next two hours, until he tucked Sasha and Malia into bed, his staff knew not to disturb him. President Barack Obama did not focus on concerns of the nation or the future of the world. He was completely focused on his girls. He engaged in their tales of playground drama, what they'd learned in school, what songs were hot—exactly the conversations that float across most dinner tables. The former United States president described these routine family dinners as his lifeline.

I also value the grounding and sense of connection that comes from dinnertime. So at 5:30 p.m. (except on nights I'm teaching), whether or not I'm at a reasonable stopping place with my work, I head home. Rob does the same. Our routine kicks off at 6 p.m., when the music turns on.

The next two hours are protected as a no phone zone, so Rob and I leave ours by the front door. In her time crafting, Christina found reserving evenings as no phone zones to be perhaps the most powerful of the strategies. She described it as "life-changing," and said she got to know her kids better. By removing this distraction for just a couple of hours, she felt like she was making up for years of lost time.

## Time Crafting Strategy 3

### Maximize times of joy by outsourcing chores.

In our house, it takes about fifteen minutes to get dinner on the table. Since there's so little time between getting home from work and Leo and Lita's bedtime, I've prioritized spending this time *with them* rather than separately going grocery shopping and laboring over a recipe. We therefore pay for a meal service that delivers delicious and healthy dinners to our door. This way, I can get a hot meal on the table in the time it takes the kids to set the table.

## Time Crafting Strategy 4

### Assign time to focus on what's good.

Like the Obamas, our dinner conversation provides an opportunity for us to hear about each other's days and to stay in tune with each other's lives. I additionally use it as an opportunity to focus us on happy happenings. Studies have shown that people who regularly reflect back over their days and write down what they are grateful for end up happier during their days and more satisfied with their lives overall.

Keeping a gratitude journal is effective because it trains us to direct our attention to what is good in our lives and in the world, of which there is plenty. This practice can actually shift natural "glass half-empty" types into perpetually more cheery people, and helps all of us to offset hedonic adaptation and continue to notice simple pleasures. I don't require my family members to keep gratitude journals, but while we eat, I ask everyone to share their favorite part of the day or something good that happened. Telling these positively focused stories helps pull us into each other's experiences while also increasing our happiness from those experiences.

My friend instituted a similar and sweet practice with her kids, which they do during their car rides home from school. Once everyone is buckled up, she asks each to share their rose (something good that happened), their thorn (something bad that happened, which is helpful because it opens the conversation for problem-solving), and their bud (something they are excited about). This practice isn't only for kids. One of my students told me she does something similar with her best friend. At the start of their weekly phone dates, they each share what they are grateful for from the week. This practice also needn't involve others. You could assign a few minutes during any routine activity—perhaps while brushing your teeth before bed— to reflect on what's good. Whenever and however you do it, you will enjoy greater satisfaction by inserting time to focus on the positive.

## Time Crafting Strategy 5

### Establish a tradition of regularly getting together.

As we learned in chapter 5, families who have holiday traditions are more likely to get together to celebrate, and they enjoy this time more. One reason is that these traditions let everyone know what to expect. Everyone can then plan for it and look forward to it. Also, by setting the intention that folks will gather again next time, these traditions maintain a sense of connection across time and increase belonging. Are there traditions that you can establish with your family members or friends? Are there events that you can schedule at the same time each week to ritualize this special time?

*Thursday Morning Coffee Date.* In chapter 5, I described Lita's and my tradition of a Thursday Morning Coffee Date. After dropping off Leo's school carpool on Thursday mornings, Lita and I would stop at Profeta on our way to her preschool and my office. But when Lita started kindergarten and would get dropped off with Leo, she and I needed to find another time dedicated to just the two of us. Saturday mornings wouldn't work because we were frequently rushed getting to soccer games or birthday parties. But being the family's early risers, we decided we could let Leo and Dad sleep in and have our date on Sunday mornings. So now, at 7:30 a.m., we pull on sweatshirts and flip-flops and sneak out the front door. We hold hands chatting on our half-mile walk to the coffee shop. We're the first in line when their door opens at 8 a.m.

## Time Crafting Strategy 6
### Dedicate time to foster friendship.

Shortly after I arrived at Wharton as an assistant professor, I asked a senior female colleague (whom I admired) for advice: "How have you managed to do it all?" Not only was she a highly respected researcher and star teacher but she was happily married and had great relationships with her two now grown children. Furthermore, when she'd started out, there were even fewer women professors in business schools, which meant that she had faced even more challenges. Yet she had maneuvered her career with finesse, so I wanted to learn from her success.

Her response to my question was as matter-of-fact as she is: "I just did it." I knew from others that her "just doing it" included teaching a classroom full of (mostly male) MBAs just five days after giving birth. Fortunately, policies had been updated to make my version of just doing it more doable. Though her pragmatism was informative, what she said next struck me and has influenced how I invest my time since: "Cassie, I didn't manage to do it all. I missed out on having female friendships."

This resonated with me because I could easily imagine myself twenty years on in that very same situation. Between the kids and Rob and work subsuming so much of my time and emotional energy, there's very little left. Plus, I know that establishing and cultivating good friendships requires a lot of both time and emotional energy. Yet, heeding my admired colleague's warning and recognizing the energy I gain from spending time with women I like and respect, I make it a priority.

*Lita's Dance Class.* I leave my office at 2 p.m. on Thursday afternoons to pick Lita up from school and take her to dance class. It's cute to watch her and her friends leap about. However, the real reason I dedicate this time is for the opportunity to get to know and cultivate friendships with the other moms.

*Book Club.* I go to my book club on the first Thursday evening of every month. I like having this motivation to read for pleasure. However, again, my true motive behind spending this time is connecting with women I enjoy and can learn from.

Now, I admit that my current form of hanging out "with the girls" might cause you to pause ("Isn't Lita's dance class just an excuse to spend more time with your daughter?") or yawn ("I'm sorry, but girls' nights should really include shots and dancing"). However, these days I find these ways of spending time with friends absolutely delightful.

Placing these tiles on Thursday is ideal because by this point in the week, I'm done teaching, so I feel less stressed and more open. Also,

Friday evenings are already saved for Rob, and weekends are reserved for Rob and the kids.

## Time Crafting Strategy 7

### To make sure you do it, bundle an activity you want to do with an activity you have to do.

In chapter 4, we learned the value of bundling activities to increase our motivation to get through chores. Here, I suggest bundling as a way to ensure that you dedicate time to tasks you enjoy. By linking an activity you *want* to do (e.g., talking to a friend) to an activity you *have* to do (e.g., commuting), you'll be more likely to spend the time to do what you want to do. Better yet, if you link two activities you *want* to do (e.g., talking to a friend and getting outside for a run), you're more likely to view it as time you absolutely must spend, so you do. To be clear, time crafting is an exercise in being intentional to spend time on what's worthwhile, and not merely efficient. This, however, is a case in which you can do both: be efficient in spending your time in worthwhile ways.

*Phone Dates.* I live far away from some of my closest friends. To stay part of each other's lives, we schedule phone dates. Yet, because we are all busy juggling careers and families, we have few spare minutes to stop and talk on the phone. I therefore try to schedule calls for when I'm in transit: during my walk home from the office, for instance.

*Run with a Friend.* In the last chapter, I described one of Christina's golf balls. When she looked back over her previous weeks, Christina realized that she felt great joy when she was out on a hike with a friend. She loved being active and healthy outside, as well as the time to socialize. This led her to devise a way she could more regularly bundle exercise with seeing friends. Now, on Tuesday and Thursday mornings before getting ready for work, Christina and a friend meet up for an early-morning run. It is worth the 5:30 a.m. alarm. She starts these days with joy.

## Time Crafting Strategy 8

### Protect time without distractions to pursue your purpose.

By contributing to your sense of purpose, some work activities can be experienced as meaningful and satisfying. For your ideal week, identify the work (whether it's paid or unpaid) that contributes to your higher-order goals. You can flip back to the Five Whys Exercise in chapter 4 to help figure out what these activities are for you. In your schedule, protect hours for this work during the portions of your week when you have the greatest mental energy and when you're best able to minimize outside distractions. To help you identify your prime work hours, observe when you feel most alert during the day (without the aid of caffeine) and are best able to close yourself off from disturbance.

## Time Crafting Strategy 9

### Schedule the times you need to be alert during times you're naturally alert.

Consider the optimal placement for these key tiles on your canvas. Even though you have sixteen waking hours each day and seven days available, you're not at your best across all of them. When do you have the most mental energy? During which hours are you most productive? Dedicate these hours to the activities that demand your best.

*Happy Work.* I am a morning person and am most alert at the day's start. I pretty much wrote my entire PhD dissertation during dawn hours. Right when I woke up, I'd pull my laptop into bed and write until I needed breakfast. But now that I have kids who need breakfast, I can't reasonably stay in bed working from 5 a.m. until noon. However, once my kids are off to school and I'm in my office, I still protect the day's start for work that requires my best thinking.

On every weekday possible, I block off 9 a.m. to 1 p.m. for research and writing—the work that contributes to my purpose: my "Happy Work."

## Time Crafting Strategy 10

For times you want to be productive, remove distractions and set up conditions conducive to entering flow.

I block this time off in my schedule and block myself off from all distractions. Following the tips in chapter 6, I set up the appropriate conditions to get into flow. For these hours, I close out of email, turn off the ringer on my phone, and shut my office door. I even pack my lunch so that I can continue working when I get hungry. Though it'd be nice to eat with my colleagues each day, for me to be able to make progress on my research without cutting into evenings and weekends with Rob and the kids, I need to protect my productive hours. Then in the afternoons—when I have less mental energy—I open my door and my schedule for "Worky Work," including meetings, tackling the requisite email inbox, and administrative tasks.

## Cassie's Time Crafting: Joyful Tiles

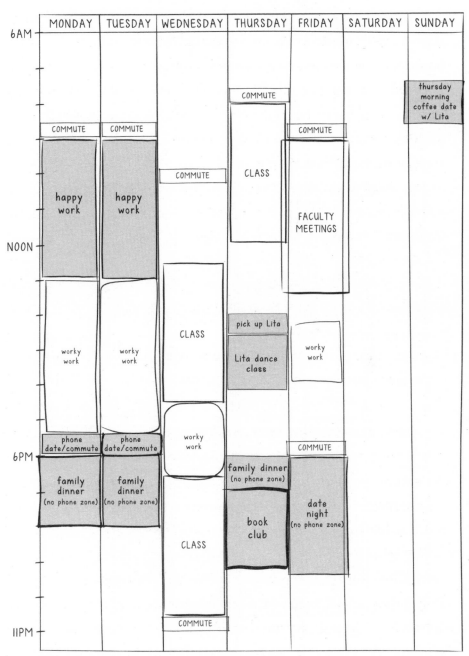

## Christina's Time Crafting: Joyful Tiles

### Step 3: Some Space

Artists are deliberate in how they incorporate space amid color. Sometimes they will leave portions of the canvas unfilled in order to increase the visual impact of the rest. Likewise, when crafting your time, you should consider leaving portions of your week unfilled. However, to protect these spaces from getting covered by color (or filled with sand), you might need to actually schedule this time—for yourself to rest, to reflect, and to be spontaneous.

## Time Crafting Strategy 11

### Carve out time for you to spend however *you* want.

As a parent of young children, you are in constant demand. Between feeding and bathing and brushing teeth and dressing and helping with homework and filling backpacks and preparing lunches and scheduling and playing and teaching and staying engaged (and off screens) and ensuring the home is clean and the fridge is stocked with food, there is rarely a moment of rest. There is rarely a moment not spent addressing someone else's needs. If you work outside the home as well, there are even fewer unfilled moments. Even when you're not currently being asked to do something, your mind buzzes with a mental list of all the tasks you know still need your attention. The open portions of your canvas are never free.

This is why parents of young children are the most time poor in the population—and moms even more than dads. Research shows that among couples with children where both partners work outside the home, mothers tend to assume more of the child-rearing and domestic responsibilities than fathers. It's perhaps not surprising then that moms' careers suffered the most during the COVID pandemic—with disproportionately more dropping out and staying out of the labor force when children were stuck home from school. Ashley Whillans and her colleagues collected time-use data from over 30,000 people around the world during this period. The results showed that when everyone was home in the pandemic, moms spent significantly more time doing household chores and assumed more of the childcare responsibilities than dads did. Also, moms were significantly less happy.

*Mornings Off.* Once I had kids, the times I missed most were weekday mornings. That's when I have the most energy and long to get outside for a run and am eager to do my purposeful work. I was not happy when the frantic scurry of getting the kids up and ready and to school every morning replaced my own productive mornings. Trying to be an equal contributor, Rob was around to help on the days he wasn't traveling. But reflective of the statistics, I was the one who was ultimately responsible, which he knew, and I wished I wasn't.

So Rob and I devised a scheduling solution. Instead of us both being on duty to get the kids ready *every* morning, we divvyed up the days. We assigned each of us mornings so that one of us is "on" with the kids and fully responsible for their day's kickoff, and the other is "off" duty and can kick off their own day however they chose (go for a run, start work early, meet a friend for coffee, whatever).

The thing we (really, I) *cannot* do on an "off" morning is intervene with how the other parent is handling the kids. If Lita's hair isn't brushed the way I'd like or Leo's clothes don't match, I've got to be fine with it. There's no "maternal gatekeeping," as Sheryl Sandberg describes it. We follow Eve Rodsky's rules of fair play about how to divide domestic work between couples. Rob and I agreed that delegating these times means full and complete delegation. I know that Rob is capable and the kids will be fine. Moreover, the benefits of this solution far outweigh the cost of Leo occasionally going to school with mismatching socks.

It is important to find the space in your week that you can protect as your own. For instance, Christina found that going to a Saturday morning yoga class was ideal time for herself. After a serene hour and a half, she returns home feeling refreshed and excited to spend the rest of the weekend with her family and friends. For your time, you can spend it however you please. You might pursue a personal hobby, like signing up for a painting class or joining a tennis clinic. Or maybe take an hour to yourself to walk through town and window-shop. Or maybe you nestle into your favorite chair and read a book.

This time to take care of your own needs and develop your own interests is particularly important for women who often get consumed taking care of others. Don't feel guilty about taking time for yourself. Remember that only by taking care of yourself can you wholly and fully take care of the people you love. The analogy of oxygen masks on airplanes is apt: In emergencies, adults are instructed to put on their own masks first.

## Time Crafting Strategy 12

### Carve out time to think.

*Shultz Hour.* In chapter 7, I described the value of a "Shultz Hour": an hour protected for quiet reflection. Amid all the rushing to get things done, this is time to stop and think—deeply and broadly and creatively. Assign space on your canvas for a Shultz Hour (but it's fine if you can only manage a half hour or fifteen minutes).

On Monday mornings (my first "off" morning each week), I go for a run. As I described in chapter 2, this is the time I feel most confident that I can accomplish what I set out to do. It's when I feel least time poor. I bundle my Shultz Hour with my Monday morning run so that as I'm thinking through my more consequential life and work decisions, I approach them with optimism. This empowers me to weigh my various options according to their desirability, rather than merely their feasibility. On these particular runs, I don't listen to music or podcasts. I dedicate this time to thinking through questions I'm currently grappling with, like what should I title this book? Or I just let my mind wander.

Place your Shultz Hour during a pocket of time in which you're least likely to be objectively or subjectively hurried. Christina assigned hers to Friday afternoon when she gets home from work. Before getting swept up by the kids and their weekend fun, she puts their dog, Slash, on a leash and sets out for a half-hour walk. As Slash gets his exercise, Christina reflects on her week and strategizes for the year. Alternatively, you could place this space as its namesake, George Shultz, did: in your office with the door closed, a pad of paper in front of you, and your phone's ringer turned off. Whether you bundle it with another activity or assign it its own tile, give yourself time in your week to think.

## Time Crafting Strategy 13

### Protect time to do nothing.

As you know, we are prone to overschedule ourselves. We are reluctant to say no, and we say yes to far too many future commitments, because we think we'll have more time then. Plus, we are driven to be productive *and* social. Without intention, our time jars quickly fill up. Even with intention, our canvases get covered.

But this can wear you out. And it leaves no space for spontaneity. It doesn't allow room for you to live in the moment. To save time for being present, you may need to schedule time to keep unscheduled.

The value from clearing our calendars became evident during the COVID pandemic. By not being pulled away to our individual activities, many couples and families became closer. Without the pressure to get somewhere, we were all forced to slow down. Without outside entertainment, we had to figure out how to entertain ourselves. We became more creative. Our hours were open to do whatever the moment suggested—whether it be playing a game of Monopoly, taking a nap, or doing nothing at all. Despite experiencing the relief of open calendars, as soon as restrictions were lifted and normal activities could resume, we filled our calendars right back up.

*Nothing.* To maintain the presence my family enjoyed from those open hours together, we reserve Sunday afternoons to remain unscheduled. This is time for us to do anything we feel like or nothing at all. We also make this time a no phone zone to ensure that it doesn't get mindlessly filled and wasted.

## Cassie's Time Crafting: Reserved Space

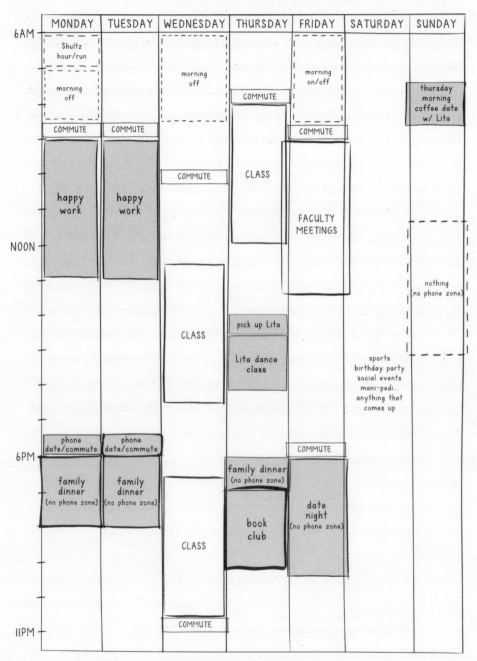

### Step 4: Sequence Your Tiles

Once you've identified your set tiles, joyful tiles, tiles for space, and those for the other activities you have to and want to do during the week, the next step is to piece them all together. It's now time to sequence your tiles on the canvas with the goal of maximizing the impact of the good times and minimizing the impact of those that feel like a chore. This will produce a week that you experience as happier and more satisfying overall.

*Time Crafting Strategy 14*

## Break up and spread out the activities you enjoy.

In chapter 5, I described how hedonic adaptation plays out over years, influencing your emotional response to such major events as getting married. The same pattern plays out within the week, and even within hours for such ordinary activities as watching TV.

Because we get used to things over time, we are particularly sensitive at the start of an activity. This is when we're paying most attention and will experience the activity most intensely. Therefore, to leverage hedonic adaptation, you should break up the activities you enjoy— creating more beginnings and warding off the onset of boredom. This spreading out of the good stuff will also give you more occasions to look forward to.

TV watching provides a clear example here. Because of hedonic adaptation, watching TV is an activity that, though enjoyable, tends to produce less overall happiness than expected. During those initial moments of viewing, you feel fully engaged and genuinely delighted. Yet as you sit on the couch longer, you start to zone out and enjoy watching less. If it weren't for the skill of Hollywood writers and their knack for ending episodes with cliffhangers, you probably wouldn't start the next.

However, if you were to apply this strategy and instead of watching five hours in one sitting, you broke up your TV time to five one-hour sittings across the week, you would enjoy more of those five hours more. In fact, one study showed that by essentially creating more beginnings, commercial breaks lead people to enjoy watching the show more.

If you'd like yet another strategy to escape the grips of Hollywood writers, you can employ a trick my friend uses. She turns off the TV ten minutes before the episode ends. Not only can this head off entire evenings getting filled by bingeing, but when you begin your next viewing session, you will start with a super-exciting cliffhanger and immediately get to see how it resolves.

As you employ Time Crafting Strategy 14, consider the optimal amount of time needed to get the most out of a given activity. There are some activities that require a bit of time to settle into, and you wouldn't want to break them up. You wouldn't want to interrupt a flow state by segmenting that activity into smaller increments, for instance. You wouldn't want to pause a date just as you're shifting into deeper conversation. In research I conducted with Jordan Etkin on the happiness derived from variety, we found that when people try to do too many different activities within hours, they end up *less* happy. The ping-ponging between activities leaves people feeling like they are never actually able to complete anything. However, incorporating a variety of activities *across* the week keeps people feeling interested and engaged, and happier.

## Time Crafting Strategy 15

### Consolidate the activities you don't enjoy.

As for activities you don't particularly like to do but must, this same psychology advises to bunch these times into a single session. This will give you fewer beginnings to dread and intensely feel.

Take your chores. Even if you followed my suggestion to outsource, you will still likely have some jobs that you need to do. Someone once told me that if I did just a little bit each day, it wouldn't be so bad. However, because of hedonic adaptation, this was not great advice. It would sprinkle the annoyance of starting up on chores across the entire week, and it would subject me to dreading having to do them throughout the week. Instead, here's some evidence-based advice: consolidate all your chores. This way you can efficiently get them out of the way . . . and really, because of hedonic adaptation, they won't be *so* bad once you get started.

*Chores.* Christina applied this strategy by setting aside Wednesday evening to do laundry and clean the house. Instead of these household tasks piling up and waiting for her on Sunday night, her consolidation and thoughtful placement of this tile keeps these loathed deeds from looming in her mind throughout the weekend. I'm even more anxious to get my household tasks out of the way, and assign Monday evenings to plow through my to-dos.

## Time Crafting Strategy 16

### Bundle an activity you enjoy doing with your chores.

To make her Wednesday chores less onerous, Christina applied the bundling strategy from chapter 4. For a long time, she'd been wanting to listen to podcasts. Her coworkers and friends had been telling her about some really great ones they knew she'd enjoy. This was her opportunity to devote some time to expand her mind. So she queued up her friends' suggestions, and listened while cleaning and folding. It was a success: she had recrafted this time, turning it from a drag into a delight.

## Time Crafting Strategy 17

### Schedule a positive activity directly following a negative activity.

The happiness or unhappiness you experience from a particular activity can extend well beyond the time you spend actually doing it. Recognizing this, you can thoughtfully sequence your tiles to optimally manage these carry-over effects.

For instance, you know going into particular activities that you're likely to exit them feeling crummy. Unfortunately, those negative feelings— whether stress, anger, or sadness—tend to stick around and color the rest of your day, and maybe even the rest of your week. To lessen these lasting effects, you can schedule an activity that you know will boost your mood directly following the predictably lousy one. Not only will this shorten the duration of the subsequent bad feeling, but knowing that something good is waiting on the other side of the foreboding event will help motivate you to attend and get through it.

*Boba Walk.* All-school faculty meetings tend to stress me out. Though I genuinely enjoy my colleagues one-on-one, for some reason the broader group dynamic provokes anxiety in me. Given this, when I see an all-school faculty meeting on my calendar, I go ahead and schedule a walk to get bubble tea with one of my colleagues afterward. The stress from the meeting is quickly erased as I connect with a friend, walking across the beautiful campus we share.

*Time Crafting Strategy 18*

## Continue to mentally revisit your positive experiences.

As you've learned, a large body of research shows that experiences produce greater immediate and lasting happiness than do material goods. One reason for this is that while we adapt to the possessions that clutter our shelves, we can continue to revisit experiences in our minds, and we feel them anew every time. So, when noting your sources of gratitude, count these blessings. Having already invested the time, think about these joyous tiles often.

This strategy is critical. It allows the impact of the quality of the time we spend to outweigh that of the quantity of time we spend in determining our satisfaction. This is crucial for all of us who are time poor, wanting more hours. Yes, I wish I had more time with Rob and the kids and friends; however, I feel a deep sense of connection from Date Night, Lita's and my Thursday Morning Coffee Date on Sunday mornings, Book Club discussions, and the minutes I spend singing to Leo at bedtime. These feelings pervade my mood throughout the week—particularly when I revisit them in my thoughts. If at other times I find myself feeling down or stressed, I can guide my mind to wander back to these joyful ones.

## Cassie's Time Crafting: Ideal Week

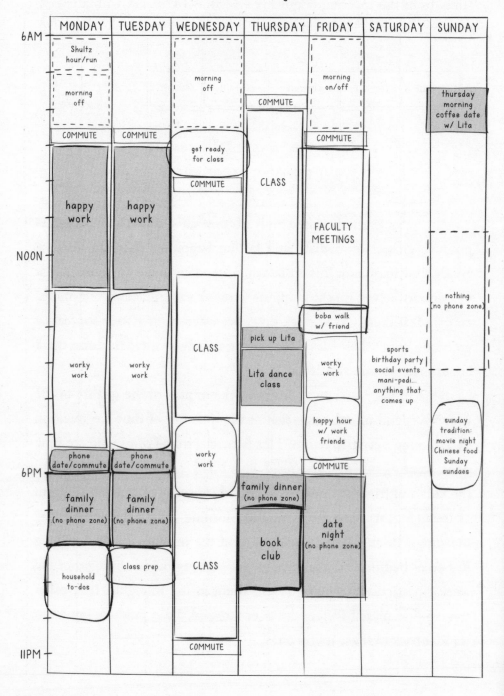

## Christina's Time Crafting: Ideal Week

| | MONDAY | TUESDAY | WEDNESDAY | THURSDAY | FRIDAY | SATURDAY | SUNDAY |
|---|---|---|---|---|---|---|---|
| 6AM | | run w/ friend | | run w/ friend | | | |
| | COMMUTE | COMMUTE | COMMUTE | COMMUTE | COMMUTE | | |
| | | | | | | | gym w/ friends |
| | | | | | | yoga | |
| | WORK | WORK | WORK | WORK | WORK | | watch PJ play soccer |
| NOON | | | | | | | |
| | | COMMUTE | | | COMMUTE | social time | |
| | IN-HOME SESSIONS | walk w/ one of the kids | IN-HOME SESSIONS | IN-HOME SESSIONS | Shultz half-hour/ walk the dog | | |
| 6PM | COMMUTE | | COMMUTE | COMMUTE | | | |
| | no phone zone | no phone zone | chores/listen to podcasts | no phone zone | fun dinner & tv night w/ Sam (no phone zone) | | |
| 11PM | | | | | | | |

## The Beauty of the Mosaic

Up close, any tile can be pretty or not. But tiles aren't set alone. You don't live just one moment. You live many moments. It's the piecing together of those many moments that creates the texture of your days, the pattern of your weeks, and the mosaic of your life. Not until you step back and see the colorful complexity can you appreciate the real beauty of your hours.

Unfortunately, we often don't step back. Our attention gets stuck on the singular tile that's immediately in front of us. We get preoccupied by imminent concerns, feeling the pressure of minutes passing. We get lost within our hours, not thinking about how those hours are part of something bigger or how they fit together to form something greater.

This myopic view frames questions of how to spend the time we have as all-or-nothing decisions, causing conflict and guilt and regret. Regardless of whether you choose to invest in something you *want* to do or something you *should* do, you wind up feeling regret from not having spent on the other. If you choose to stay at the office instead of meeting up with your friend for dinner, you feel guilty for being a bad friend and for missing that opportunity to connect. And if you choose to stop working when you're not yet finished with your project so that you can meet up with your friend, you feel guilty for not being serious about your job. There's no winning.

However, if you take a step back and look at your mosaic, you can see these moments as pieces in the bigger picture. As you look across all the hours of your week (and the weeks of your year, and the years of your life), your spending decisions shift from questions of *whether* to questions of *when.* You no longer feel conflict about what to do in *this* hour, because you have the opportunity to decide *which* hours you are going to assign to what you genuinely care about. You get to choose *when* you are going to do all the activities that bring you joy. If having dinner with your friend is a source of joy, you carve out and spend that time. You also don't feel bad about it, because you can immediately look across your week at all the other undisturbed hours you've protected for the work that matters to you. You're reassured knowing that you will spend that time too. Yet if that dinner feels like an obligation that won't contribute to your sense of connection, it's now more evident that it's not worth space on your canvas.

Viewing your time as a mosaic helps to clarify that a singular hour isn't a verdict on your values—or your life. A singular hour doesn't define who you are. It's the combination of hours that represents *all* that you value and *all* the dimensions of yourself. It's possible to have multiple priorities, multiple sources of joy. Those Date Nights, Family Dinners, Runs with Friends, Happy Work, and Mornings Off radiate a spectrum of pleasure. You don't have to pick just one color. You don't have to choose between being a good parent and having a career. Answering questions of *when* instead of *whether* allows you to cultivate deep connections in your life *and* produce work that feels purposeful. So when you leave the office at 3 p.m. to pick up your kid from school, this is not a conflicted, guilt-laden, personally defining decision. You just look at your mosaic and can easily see the many hours you diligently devote to your work alongside those spent with your child. Your canvas is full, and it's fulfilling.

This perspective was the answer I was looking for on the train that fateful night. Yes, I cannot do it all and be it all in any given hour. But I *can* across the hours of my week. I *can* across the years of my life. And you can too.

This perspective offers yet another benefit: it allows you to spend each hour with more presence. In their purposeful placement within your mosaic, individual tiles can shine brighter. Seeing the other tiles alongside reduces the worry of *whether* you'll be able to get it all done, because you know *when* you will. You no longer have to rush through your hours trying to be done faster, because that's the time you've set for that activity. You can slow down and focus on and enjoy what you're currently doing. You make your time worthwhile by allocating it for what's worthwhile. Unlike other approaches to time management, time crafting is not compelled by efficiency. It's about the joy you experience during your time, spending on what matters to you most.

What's more, here, you are the artist. You're not just an observer, subject to passive viewing. This is *your time*. You pick and place the tiles. You decide how best to sequence them over the week. The mosaic you create is the magnificent life that *you* get to live.

## CHAPTER EIGHT TAKEAWAYS

✦ Craft your time, ideally using a visual aid. Like an artist creating a mosaic, select, space, and sequence your activities to create an ideal week.

✦ You can schedule your activities to increase the impact of the good times and minimize the impact of your chores.

✦ Block out times for your most important activities (i.e., your most connecting activities, activities that help you fulfill your purpose, time to think, time to do nothing, time for yourself).

✦ Apply "no phone zones" to these times, so you're not distracted during them.

✦ To make sure you spend on what you want, bundle these activities you *want* to do with other activities you *have* to do.

✦ To make your chores more enjoyable, bundle these activities you *have* to do with other activities you *want* to do.

✦ Spread out your happy activities to intensify the enjoyment you experience while doing them and to give you more good times to look forward to.

✦ Consolidate your less happy activities to minimize the amount of time that feels intensely onerous and that you spend dreading these chores.

✦ Looking across the hours of your week can reduce conflict and guilt by reframing your time-spending decisions from questions of *whether* to questions of *when*.

## Nine

# THE TIME OF YOUR LIFE

*Time is too slow for those who wait,*
*Too swift for those who fear,*
*Too long for those who grieve,*
*Too short for those who rejoice;*
*But for those who love, time is eternity.*

—Henry van Dyke

Gathering together to celebrate a life, we were reminded how good one can be. Shaking slightly and full of emotion, the speaker approached the front of the room. She pulled out a piece of paper and rested it on the podium.

*As we stand here today to remember Nicole, I want to be clear that this funeral is going against her wishes. In her final days, she said, "I know you'll throw me a fancy shmancy funeral, but I hate being the center of attention. Just get me in the ground . . . oh, and make sure everyone is well fed . . . maybe little tins of homemade granola as party favors?"*

*That was Nicole. She enjoyed living a life under the radar where she found fulfillment in small moments of joy and by surrounding herself with people she loved. She was a hands-on, loving mother, but* always careful not to smother her children. When her eldest son said, "I don't want to go to college," she simply shrugged and said, "Fine by me . . . I have a small sum of money I saved for your college fund. Come back to me with a plan for being happy and self-sufficient, and it's yours to spend however you like." And, as you know, both of her children are happy, self-sufficient, and thriving.

Nicole was a loving wife and sparked quite the frenzy with an essay in her book "Ideas, Reconsidered" in which she pioneered the idea of the 5-day-a-week marriage, explaining how everyone benefits from 2 days a week of separation. With their savings, she and her husband bought a small condo they alternated enjoying to themselves. It seems to have worked for them, happily married for 45 years! She was always questioning the way things are done. "Why do we trap animals in our homes, isolate them from their families and arrange our entire schedules based on their urinary habits?" she wrote in her essay about the absurdity of having pets. She questioned, "Why do people get married before having children? Why don't they decide to have a child—which effectively bonds them together more than marriage ever could—and then after 15–18 years of that, consider whether they want to spend the second half of their lives together?" "Ideas, Reconsidered" is a great example of the legacy Nicole leaves behind. She encouraged people around her to think differently about ordinary ideas we accept as normal.

Nicole was also committed to a life of doing good for others and enabling them to do good for themselves. The charity she started, Cooking with Elders, connected young people who wanted to learn how to cook with older people who had no source of income. At its core, the elders made money by teaching young people dishes they had mastered. However, Nicole designed the program to make the benefits far-reaching: It provided companionship for lonely senior

*citizens as well as gave them a sense of dignity in earning an income
in their own home. It brought together the community over food,
and it was no accident that over half of the elders were foreign born,
infusing a sense of tolerance and appreciation for other ethnicities.*

*We will miss Nicole, but her legacy lives on in her children,
"Ideas, Reconsidered," Cooking with Elders and the beautiful fruit
and vegetable garden she tended to so diligently. In her memory, I
hope you try to change your mind about something you have always
taken for granted as "the way things are done." Oh, and don't forget
your tin of homemade granola.*

Commemorating Nicole's life reminded us to make the most of ours. But how? How do you live a fulfilling life? How can you spend your time to experience it as meaningful? What legacy do you want to leave? What choices will make you happy in the end? These are the big life questions we will grapple with in this chapter, and which underlie the intention of this entire book. It is by zooming out to consider your life overall that you can gain clarity on how to make the most of each hour, and each day.

## Taking a Bird's-Eye View

So far in this book, we've been focusing on hours. We have covered which activities you should spend them on, and how to be mindful while spending them. We have also learned how to optimally schedule these hours across the week. Now we are going to take a broader view, thinking in terms of years and decades. I will push you to consider your life as a whole. The goal is to make you happier, and I have data (of course) suggesting that this zooming-out tactic can work.

Tayler Bergstrom, Joey Reiff, Hal Hershfield, and I conducted surveys asking hundreds of people how they think about their time. We found that those who often employ a broader perspective are happier. Our results showed that irrespective of their age and other relevant demographic variables, the individuals who took a bird's-eye view of time reported feeling more positive and less negative emotion in their days. They also reported greater overall life satisfaction, and greater meaning in life. We identified these people as those who very much agreed with the following statements:

+ *"I take a bird's-eye view of my time, looking down and seeing all of the moments in my life at once."*

+ *"I tend to view my time as if I am looking down on a calendar, seeing all of my days and weeks and months laid out."*

+ *"I try to take a broad view of my time, thinking in terms of years instead of hours."*

+ *"I make decisions thinking about my whole life span."*

## Your Mosaic

There are multiple reasons for the heightened happiness caused by taking a broader time perspective. One is the beauty of the mosaic. At the end of the previous chapter, I described the benefit of looking across all the hours of your week as a combination of tiles—and not getting stuck in the limitations of a single tile and its one color. Zooming out further from hours and weeks to look across years and decades, these benefits continue to emerge. You recognize that you're currently in just one piece of the bigger whole. A bad year will pass, as will a bad few. A difficult relationship, a bad phase in a relationship, a wrong job, the loss of a loved one, a global pandemic . . . there's still space on your canvas for fresh starts, for new patterns, for more life.

Looking across your years makes you realize that you don't have to spend your days in such a hurry. You have over forty years between graduating from college and retirement. With millennials staying in a job for an average of four years, this means that most people nowadays will have approximately ten different jobs during their careers. This is an important reminder for my students and the pressure they put on that first job postgraduation. They don't have to nail it right out of the gate.

This is also important for parents to keep in mind. If you have children, your youngsters will only live under your roof for approximately eighteen of your forty career years; that's less than half. And you will only need to get up with them in the middle of the night for a couple of those years. Exhausting phases will be surprisingly brief, as will the best ones.

Then, following those forty career years, you will have another twenty-five to allocate postretirement. Taking this bird's-eye view displays the many vibrant years you've already lived, while simultaneously highlighting all of those you have yet to craft.

This larger canvas invites a multitude of colors—time invested in multiple interests and priorities. Even though you can't do everything at once, you can accomplish a range of pursuits over the course of a lifetime. Remember, this view is helpful in shifting your time-spending decisions from questions of *whether* to questions of *when*. *When* might you devote more time to family, to one vocation, to another, to learning, to adventure, to yourself (whatever that means to you)? Moreover, you don't have to chunk your time in large monochrome blocks. You can be creative and interweave all of these through all of your years, simply altering the amount of each color you incorporate in each phase.

## Age-Based Shifts

Looking across your life span also allows you to appreciate its inherent phases. The concerns that feel pressing today aren't the same as those that plagued you in your teens, and they won't be the same as the challenges that keep you up at night in your twilight years. If you keep a journal, you may have noticed these shifts when comparing current entries to previous ones, or you may have picked up on this while listening to the current struggles of loved ones who are in a different life stage.

It is also evident from looking online and reading "the diaries of the digital age." Sep Kamvar and Jonathan Harris wrote a computer program that crawled the blogosphere (the predecessor to the world of social media), instantaneously pulling out all expressions of emotion. This We Feel Fine computer program captured every instance someone wrote, "I feel . . ." or "I am feeling . . ." With the bloggers' profile information, We Feel Fine could identify in real time who was feeling what.

Sep and Jonathan analyzed millions of these expressed emotions, revealing an overarching shift in what worries us as we age. Concerns of self-definition and self-doubt in adolescence give way to anxieties around accomplishment in our twenties; to settling down, bodies slowing down, and the challenges of having children in our thirties; and then on to the responsibilities of family, community, and broader impact through the second half of life.

Intrigued by this data source, I chatted with Sep in line at a barbecue, asking what it might tell us about happiness. In our subsequent research project with Jennifer Aaker, we discovered that beyond worries, age also has a profound influence on happiness. Though it's not clear from this data whether age influences *how much* happiness we feel across our lives, this research—along with subsequent studies we conducted—shows that both *what makes us feel happy* and *the way we feel happy* changes over the course of life.

Remember when Amit and I were comparing our happy weekends? In those studies, we found that differences in age influence the happiness we enjoy from ordinary and extraordinary experiences. For younger people, extraordinary experiences (life milestones, once-in-a-lifetime vacations, cultural events) generate greater happiness. However, for older people, ordinary experiences (simple shared moments with loved ones, tasty treats, noticing the beauty of nature) produce just as much happiness as the more expensive and less accessible extraordinary ones. That is, as we age, we become more likely and better able to extract happiness from mundane moments in life. As we get older, we get better at savoring simple pleasures.

The blog data additionally showed that age doesn't only influence which experiences make us happiest, it also influences *how* we experience happiness. In youth, we experience happiness more as excitement—a louder and more energized positive feeling. This is evident by people in their teens and twenties being significantly more likely to express excited happiness:

+ *"I feel happy, excited—like crazy happy!"*

+ *"I feel so excited and happy."*

+ *"I feel happy and free and excited and so stressed, but so, so glad life is what it is."*

As we get older, however, we start experiencing happiness more as a calm peacefulness—a quieter, more serene and contented feeling.

While people in their thirties are equally likely to express both versions of happiness, people in their forties and fifties and afterward are increasingly more likely to express feeling calm happiness:

+ *"I feel happy and relaxed and at peace."*

+ *"I feel so calm and happy right now."*

+ *"I feel happy and calm today after a restful, no-stress weekend."*

Excitement and calm are both positive, yet as the following graph illustrates, these two forms of happiness show up in different proportions as we traverse the decades of our lives.

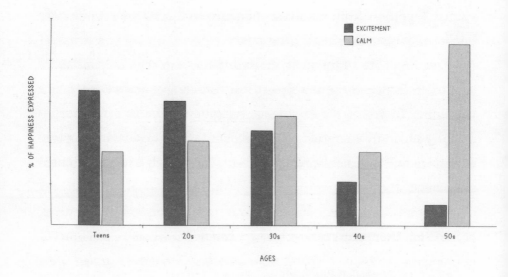

These results suggest that when a twenty-year-old and a fifty-year-old express feeling happy, they are probably feeling quite different things. Recognizing this can increase our emotional understanding of others—and *ourselves*—across ages. This helps to keep us from judging our current selves through the lens of our younger selves. Remember how happy I was following that quiet weekend with Rob and my baby Leo? A teenage version of me would probably have rolled her eyes if subjected to that set of weekend activities. However, it is not that my days had become boring and unhappy; it's that my happiness had changed. This is an important lesson: What constitutes a glorious Saturday night will honestly change. What constitutes a "happy life" will change, if it hasn't already. This isn't a bad thing. Moreover, this knowledge can help you successfully craft your future life phases and transition out of a previous one. Though happiness might look a little different, there's plenty of it available in each of life's stages.

## Importance over Urgency

Another key reason in support of taking a broader time perspective is that thinking in terms of years can be vital in informing how to spend your hours. That is, thinking about life overall highlights your values, which can then guide better immediate decisions about how to spend your time.

Indeed, going back to the people that Tayler, Joey, Hal, and I surveyed, we found that those individuals who reported taking a bird's-eye view of time dedicated more time during the week to what they felt was important, rather than what was merely urgent. This is critical, because another team's research had warned that when we feel hurried in our days, we tend to spend time on what's urgent, *regardless of its importance.*

These findings together urge you to take a broader view of time. Thinking about life overall will remind you to spend your hours on what is important to you, and not just on what seems urgent. This change in perspective could reduce the limitations you experience from being time poor; help you fight the constant distraction of your mental list of pressing to-dos; and keep your time jar from getting filled with sand.

Furthermore, this view can help to identify *what is* important to you. In previous chapters, I've advised how to identify activities that "spark joy," as well as activities that help achieve your higher-order goals. In addition to knowing which times contribute to your happiness and purpose, to live your best life you also need to recognize the moments that are consonant with your values: what ultimately matters to you. That's where these next two exercises come in. In the first, you will project forward to the end of your life and look back. In the second, you will learn from someone who has lived a full life and is looking back. By urging you to consider life as a whole, both exercises offer insight into what constitutes a meaningful and important life— for *you*.

## Your End of Life

How do you want to be remembered? At the end of your life when looking back, what do you want people to say, and which stories do you want them to share? Put simply, what do you want your legacy to be?

To push you toward your answers, I will give you the same assignment I give my students: write your eulogy. This isn't easy. Reckoning with your own mortality can be downright uncomfortable. But there is also a tremendous potential upside: being clear-eyed about the inevitability of your death is one of the most powerful ways to push you into fully living your life. Answering these questions will help clarify what ultimately matters to you: your values. Your answers can inform how you spend today, tomorrow, and all the days that follow.

## Eulogy Exercise

*H*ow will you be remembered? What effect will you have had on the world and those you loved? What goals did you achieve? What did you create? How did you contribute? What words will be used to describe you?

Following your passing, your eulogy is the speech that someone who survives you will write and deliver in your memory. For this exercise, write your own eulogy. In writing this, take another's perspective (you can choose who: e.g., a child, spouse, friend, business associate), and assume you will live into your nineties.

The eulogy opening this chapter was written by my student Nicole. Here is another nice example written by my student Justin.

*My father didn't always give me the things I wanted . . . instead he always gave me what I needed . . . and while that wasn't easy when specific "things" felt important to me—looking back now, it taught me some of the most valuable lessons in life. The "things" that are really worth having, aspiring toward, and wanting are not bought with money, but instead love, hard work, and dedication.*

*My father was an incredibly dedicated husband, dad, and friend—who constantly praised all of his children on their work— not the result that came from their work. Also, something that was a bit annoying at an early age—but something that got me through the toughest times in my life—I kept hearing my father's voice saying: "You're working so hard, you will overcome this—this challenge is here for a reason." And so, I worked and I overcame—and I constantly thought of my dad as I was doing both.*

*My father tucked me into bed every night he was in town—and every night he whispered "special words"—as we called them—into my ears. They were different for each of my siblings—so I can only speak to what they were to me. They were always about how special, caring, thoughtful, courageous, inquisitive, and perseverant of a girl I was. How much he and mommy loved me, and how proud they were of me. But even more importantly, how proud of myself I should be. And he always ended his special words with how lucky he feels to be my father and how excited he is to spend tomorrow with me. Though we won't be able to spend tomorrow together—I want to pass this same devotion and love and encouragement on to my kids. And so, not a night goes by that I don't whisper special words into their ears and tell them how special and caring and wonderful they are—how much we love them—how proud we are of them, and how proud they should be of themselves.*

*Daddy, I love you—and I want you to know how proud we all are of the father, husband, and friend that you were. You brought so much joy and happiness and dedication to each and every thing you did. You brought passion and understanding and commitment, and a way of thinking that made everyone around you that much smarter . . . wiser . . . and kinder. I love you.*

While these two eulogies offer some ideas about how to approach this assignment, your eulogy must be personal and about *you*. What do you hope will be said about you at the end of your life?

From Nicole's and Justin's eulogies, we learn the qualities each person values in themselves. It's clear what lives they aspire to lead. In fact, they are already living these lives. Sure, some of their noted life experiences (children, marriage, writing a book) have yet to occur. But how they hope to be described at the end of their lives is how I would describe each of them today: Nicole is thought-provoking. Justin is dedicated. And both of them are genuinely good and loving. Based on who they want to be, we learn who they are. From writing how they want to be remembered, their values and what they care about become evident. Nicole values open-mindedness. And Justin values hard work and his children, and he values instilling the value of hard work in his children.

Writing your eulogy will prove similarly revealing and inspiring. It will clarify the personal attributes you value most in yourself—what ultimately matters to you. This will guide you in how you engage in the world, where you dedicate your efforts, and ways you spend your time.

In my class, there's another step in this exercise (as if writing your own eulogy isn't difficult enough). Each student's eulogy is read aloud, by another student in the class. Though nerve-racking, this step is valuable for a few reasons. First, hearing your own testimonial alongside others' highlights that what you aspire to is largely unique to you. This is helpful in establishing your personal metrics for success. It is only by these dimensions (and not others' ambitions) that you should evaluate how you're doing in life. And when you observe a gap between where you are and where you aspire to be, it's only your ruler that should motivate you to change or do more.

In addition to revealing ways in which your values diverge from those of your peers, this step also allows you to see where your values converge. Recognizing shared values can help forge greater community and a sense of belonging. And as we know, this feeling of connection is a sure route to increasing happiness.

Finally, hearing your eulogy read by someone else reminds you how you exist in others' minds and hearts. What impact are you having and do you want to have? This is a good prompt to act accordingly.

## The Wisdom of Others

Writing your eulogy encourages you to project forward to the end of your life and look back. This next exercise encourages you to look to others who have inched a little closer to the end of their lives and ask *them* to look back. While our own time may be one of our most valuable resources, the time experienced by others is undeniably another. Asking people whom we admire to share their experiences, their reflections, and what they've learned along the way is a precious opportunity.

I interviewed someone whom I greatly respect and who (from my perspective) got life right. A woman ahead of her time, Jane started working in 1964 in the male-dominated profession of university publishing. Based on her forty-year career, she has a lot to be proud of. In her years working, Jane was a book editor and publishing executive. As if that wasn't enough, after she retired she began a new career as an author and published four books of her own. Yet when I asked Jane about her greatest source of pride looking back over all of her eighty-two years, without pause, she said, "My children: their character." She then explained, "I have two sons, and they are both extremely successful. But the most important thing is what kind of humans they are. One of my jobs as a mom, and now as a grandma, is to nurture the moral nature of the children. My family is accomplished. My parents rose to greatness from complete poverty as children of immigrants on the Lower East Side of New York City. So accomplishment is important. But who you are and how you treat people and how you behave—that's everything. I hope my legacy and thumbprint is on the character of my children and grandchildren."

In this next assignment, I instruct my students to do exactly this: interview someone whose life they admire.

## Learning from Admired Elders Exercise

*A*s you're figuring out how to lead a happy life, there's much to learn from someone who has already lived one. Identify an elder whose life you admire and interview this person about their experience. Ask them to reflect on their achievements, their mistakes, and the choices they made along the way. This can inform your own life choices going forward. In particular, ask about their sources of pride and regret to help guide how you might spend your time now to look back on your life with satisfaction later.

Definitely ask these two questions:

+ Looking back on your life overall, what are your greatest sources of pride?

+ Looking back on your life overall, what are your greatest sources of regret?

If there's remaining time (respecting theirs, of course), you can potentially ask these questions:

+ What were the most important decisions you made in your life?

+ Were there ever instances of conflict between your life and career? When, and how did they play out?

+ What has turned out to matter more than you expected?

+ What has turned out to matter less than you expected?

Then, during the following class, my students share what they heard in their interviews.

Most of the admired elders were a family member (e.g., a parent, a grandparent, a parent-in-law), a family friend, or a professional mentor. They represented genders equally, a variety of nationalities (e.g., American, Indian, Chinese, Korean, Colombian, British), and a variety of professions (including those who worked in the home raising a family).

Despite their varied backgrounds, there is remarkable consistency in what these people reported as their greatest source of pride in life. And, much like for Jane, the primary answer was family (67 percent). These revered elders were proudest of having strong relationships with their family members, who their children had become, having been a good parent or grandparent, and for prioritizing these relationships when it mattered. An additional 9 percent shared their pride in having managed to raise a family while also pursuing their career. So, altogether, those who mentioned their family as their greatest source of pride made up 76 percent of the interviewees.

## GREATEST PRIDE

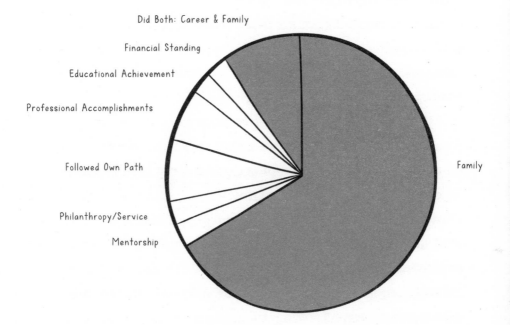

Did Both: Career & Family

Financial Standing

Educational Achievement

Professional Accomplishments

Followed Own Path

Philanthropy/Service

Mentorship

Family

With family mentioned most frequently, other sources of pride included individual achievements—educational (2.5 percent), professional (6 percent), or financial (2.5 percent)—as well as having the courage to follow one's own path (7.5 percent), mentorship (2.5 percent), and philanthropy (2.5 percent).

Despite being based on a skewed sample of particularly happy people admired by MBAs, what is illustrated in this pie chart is remarkably consistent with the conclusions from one of the most comprehensive longitudinal research studies in history. In the Harvard Study of Adult Development, researchers gathered a cohort of young men and followed them over the course of seventy-five years. Some of the participants were students at Harvard, and others were from blue-collar neighborhoods in Boston. Every few years, the researchers would survey and interview these men to see where they were, what they were doing, and how they were doing. Robert Waldinger, the current director of the study, shared the findings in his TED Talk "What Makes for a Good Life?" It turns out that the single biggest predictor of true happiness and satisfaction in life is neither wealth nor fame. It is the presence of strong, supportive relationships. It is family (or having good enough friends that they feel like family).

What about regrets? Turning to what the interviewees shared as their greatest source of regret, we arrive at the same answer. As this next pie chart shows, the most common regret was not having spent enough time with family (38 percent). Others mentioned failed relationships (7 percent), such as a marriage that ended or a broken tie with a child or sibling. And others mentioned not having fulfilled their educational or professional potential (18 percent). Still, the previous pie chart and the most frequent regret of not choosing family over these personal pursuits together posit cultivating strong relationships as a clear priority.

GREATEST REGRET

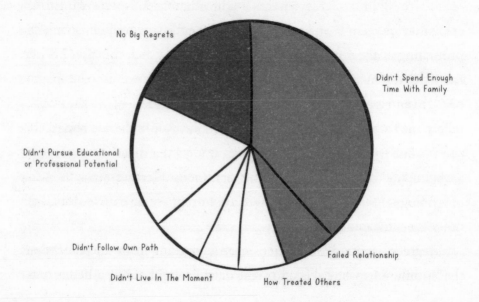

This conclusion for how to live a good life is the same as the one we've reached again and again in this book. Carve out and protect time for the people you love. And during this time, be fully there: present and undistracted. Put your phone away. And yes, relationships do take time. But they are absolutely worth the investment.

## No Regrets

Along our life journey, regret can serve as a useful navigator. It's a feeling that pipes up to let us know when we've made a mistake, guiding us on how to make a better decision next time. But with one life to live, no one wants to arrive at the end—when there is no next time—with major outstanding regrets. This is why it's so useful to leverage the hindsight of others.

When I asked Jane about her greatest regrets, she said she didn't have any. Initially, I didn't believe her. Yes, I thought she was wonderful, but she wasn't infallible. No one is. But seeing that this same answer was given by a number of my students' interviewees (18 percent), I realized there was something more here. Jane admitted to regretting others' behavior: "Do I regret the fact that, like most women in scholarly publishing at the time, I was treated like a second-class citizen? Sure. But that's not in my power. What was and is in my power is to be able to respond and react to my mistakes . . . which I do seriously." So she wasn't telling me that she never made mistakes. She did. But when she erred, she worked to fix them. She doesn't have any lingering regrets because she's already addressed them. Jane's treatment of regret fits with what psychology research has uncovered and may prove instructive for all of us looking to avoid it.

Regret is defined as negative emotion coming from the realization that a different past decision might have brought about a better outcome than what actually transpired. When researchers asked people to report their current regrets, they found there to be two types. There are regrets of action: something you should *not* have done (e.g., "I should *not* have said that," "I should *not* have accepted that job"). And there are regrets of inaction: something you *should have* done (e.g., "I *should* have said something," "I *should* have applied for that job").

Though similarly pervasive, these two regret types follow distinct time trajectories. In the short term, actions generate more regret; in the long term, inaction generates more regret. This pattern plays out because regrets of action tend to be more severe—therefore motivating people to go ahead and fix whatever they've done. For example, if you said something you shouldn't have, you know it immediately. So you apologize to rectify the situation. Or if you took a job that was clearly the wrong decision, you quit (if you can afford to). Our inclination to right these acute wrongs explains why our regrets of action are (thankfully) short-lived.

On the other hand, regrets of inaction tend to be more innocuous. Often, there isn't anything clear to fix. Unfortunately, this allows them to sneak up and last longer. If there was a professional opportunity you missed, there is rarely an event that pushes you to go ahead and take a shot at it. And it's all too easy to continue to let things go unsaid.

Something really important that is often left unsaid is "thank you." Failing to express gratitude to someone you appreciate, before it's too late, is definitely a regret you want to avoid. To give my students the needed push, I require them to write and deliver a letter of gratitude to someone in their life. Hearing about my students' experiences doing this assignment, and having done it several times myself, I can attest that this exercise can have a profound impact on both the writer and the recipient. I now want you to have this experience too.

*Gratitude Letter Exercise*

**W**rite a letter of gratitude to someone you have not properly thanked. It is up to you how you deliver this letter. You can read the letter in person or over the phone, or you can simply send the letter via email or good old-fashioned snail mail.

Getting back to the research, the documented time course of regrets provides insight into what we saw in the Greatest Regret pie chart. The dynamic of regrettable actions getting fixed and regrettable inactions sticking around explains why so many of the interviewees' great life regrets were of inaction: *not* spending more time with family, *not* reaching one's educational or professional potential, *not* following one's own path, or *not* living in the moment. But this isn't just true among the admired elders my students spoke to. Another team of researchers surveyed residents of a nursing home and found similar results. Looking back at the end of their lives, people's biggest regrets typically involved things they had *not* done and wished they had:

✦ Not spending enough time with family and friends

✦ Missing out on an educational opportunity

✦ Failing to seize the moment

✦ Missing a romantic opportunity

We should learn from our elders and take their experiences to heart. From them, we can recognize that most major life regrets involve *not* taking action—*not* spending time on what matters. We've been cautioned that we are unlikely to receive prompts that push us to correct for these mistakes. And this is why, in this chapter, I've urged you to consider the conclusion of your life journey. My intent in giving you some admittedly challenging exercises is to help you realize the ramifications of being passive about your choices. The consequences are severe: missed moments, missed joys, and regret at the end of it all. To avoid this unhappiness, go ahead and act.

I wrote this book to show you how. And I've given you the tools to start now. Don't let feelings of time poverty or lack of confidence stand in your way. Spend the time to perform acts of kindness, to exercise—and you will realize just how much you can accomplish with the time you have. Spend wisely, not wasting hours in front of a screen and instead investing them in the people and experiences that bring you joy, and in what will help you achieve your purpose (the one *you've* defined). Say thank you to the people who make your life good, and count the remaining times you have with them so that you make your shared times even better. It's never too late to live the life you aspire to be remembered for—a life without regret.

This isn't an impossibility. Some, like Jane, achieve it. You can too.

## Crafting the Time of Your Life

Regret-free lives aren't uniformly positive. Not every hour in a happy life is, or needs to be, happy. The extent to which you evaluate your life as satisfying and meaningful depends not only on what you actually choose to do but on what you choose to *focus* on: what you take from it, and the stories you tell.

## Meaning

When you look at your life overall, you want to feel happy, and you also want to see it as meaningful. Fortunately, these goals are not at odds with each other. Rhia Catapano, Jordi Quoidbach, Jennifer Aaker, and I have analyzed the happiness and meaning experienced by over 500,000 individuals across 123 countries. Our results reveal that happiness and meaning in life are very highly correlated.

However, experiencing meaning in life (i.e., viewing your life as important, purposeful, and making sense) doesn't require constantly feeling happy. In fact, negative experiences can help you find meaning—*if* you overcome them, learn from them, and develop a narrative that captures how you ended up better off. For instance, when my wedding got canceled and my dreams shattered, I picked up the pieces and recovered. And I learned an important lesson that gave me greater confidence in myself and in my happiness: I have choice. I am not reliant on inherent cheer or ideal circumstances to experience satisfaction in my life. I have agency in what I focus on and do. I am better off now having realized that I have—*we all have*—a large amount of control over how happy we feel.

Though I wish I could help spare you from experiencing any pain in life, I can't. Sadly, it is inevitable. When it happens, though, you will get through it. And having this understanding will help you reclaim your footing more quickly. I know you can do it, because you already have. The COVID pandemic was an objectively awful experience for everyone, and even more for some than for others. But you survived. You're still standing on the other side of it. Moreover, we all learned important lessons: We can stay genuinely connected despite being physically distant. Every time together is precious. We benefit from open space in our calendars to think, play, and create. We are resilient.

In getting through these trying times, it's useful to return to the metaphor of the mosaic. You can view these obstacles as tiles, which contribute to the rich texture of your collage. What's critical is how you incorporate these pieces into the pattern. You need to tie these negative events into the overarching story of your life—seeing that when tested, you were indeed able to survive and even thrive.

## Memory

In his TED Talk and book *Thinking, Fast and Slow*, Nobel Prize winner Daniel Kahneman suggests that storytelling plays a large role in our happiness. The stories we tell about our lives are based on what we remember. In turn, these stories influence what we later remember and the happiness we ultimately feel.

Let me explain. Kahneman distinguishes between two appraisals of happiness: experience and memory. Experienced happiness is being *happy in our lives*: This is how positive we feel moment-to-moment during the time. Remembered happiness is being *happy about our lives*: This is how we feel looking back and evaluating how we feel overall about the time. To illustrate, he applied this distinction to the shorter time frame of a vacation. Your experienced happiness is how you would feel during each day on the vacation. We researchers would measure your experienced happiness by having you log throughout each day how you're currently feeling (much as you did in the Time Tracking Exercise). Your remembered happiness, on the other hand, is how you would think back afterward and evaluate the vacation as a whole.

Of course, what you experience feeds into what you remember. And the activities you spend time on contribute to both forms of happiness. A fabulous dinner with good friends would, for instance, be experienced *and* remembered happily. This was evident in a study I conducted. I asked one group of people how they would spend their next hour if their goal was to maximize the happiness they experienced. I asked another group how they would spend the hour if their goal was to maximize the happiness they remembered. The results showed that the vast majority of the activities reported by both groups were the same: socialize with family and friends, enjoy a good meal, and get outdoors.

Yet even though experienced and remembered happiness are intertwined, they are distinct. Kahneman was spurred to make the delineation when his team measured, for a variety of events (from colonoscopies to vacations to movies), how positive people felt throughout and, separately, how satisfied they felt afterward. The results showed that people's moment-to-moment feelings did not simply sum up to, or even average to, their retrospective evaluations of those events. Instead, people's memories were determined by the event's peak and its ending. That is, merely adding together how you're feeling during each moment of the vacation will not perfectly predict your overall evaluation of the vacation. Your memory will be unduly colored by the most extreme moments (positive or negative) and the final moments. These findings have critical implications that extend well beyond vacations. The summing together of your every hour does not decide how satisfied you do feel (or will feel) with your life overall. The peaks and end exert a powerful influence on the stories you tell yourself about your life.

Your Time

Understanding this is essential to crafting a life that you both experience and reflect on with joy. These insights inform how to turn happier hours into a happier life.

Knowing that only particular moments will get picked up in your recollection of all the time you spend, you must ensure that your happiest moments are realized and relished as peaks. Along with the wonders of the extraordinary, don't forget about the potential joy from the ordinary.

*Notice these experiences.*

*Savor them and celebrate them.*

*Turn them into rituals.*

*Protect them in your schedule.*

*Talk about them at the dinner table.*

*And don't be distracted while you're spending this time.*

What may seem like little moments can majorly influence your satisfaction with life.

The other key insight is that endings really matter. So, make more of the endings throughout your life. As the years pass, life chapters will come to a close.

*Treat each enjoyed moment as though it's your last, and count your times left to realize it might very well be close to that.*

*Remember how you want to be remembered.*

*Say thank you.*

*End with no regrets.*

In recognizing the importance of endings, I offer you a new beginning. You have many hours, days, and years ahead of you, waiting to be lived. Spend on what brings you joy. Invest in what will help you fulfill your purpose. Don't miss out either by not dedicating the time or by not paying attention during this time. Avoid this life regret. Focus on what's good.

My research, and this book, has revealed that happiness has *agency.* Happiness is a choice. Every hour of every day. With the strategies described here, you now know *how* to make these choices—and not just in general but for you personally. I thank you for your time, and wish you many happier hours.

## CHAPTER NINE TAKEAWAYS

✦ Taking a bird's-eye view of time increases feelings of happiness, satisfaction, and meaning in life, because it motivates you to spend time on what's important, rather than merely what's urgent.

✦ This broader view reveals that what experiences make you happiest, and how you experience happiness, shift with age: from extraordinary to ordinary, and from excitement to calm.

✦ The single biggest predictor of greater overall satisfaction in life is having strong and supportive relationships (family, or friends that feel like family).

✦ Regrets of action (i.e., doing something you wish you hadn't) tend to be severe, soon addressed, and thus short-lived.

✦ Yet regrets of inaction (i.e., not doing something you wish you had) sneak up and stick around to form the greatest of life regrets. So go ahead and act now to avoid any major regrets later.

✦ Though happiness and meaning in life are closely linked, overcoming negative events can also contribute to meaning— if you're able to make sense of and learn from these negative experiences.

✦ We are most affected by and most vividly remember the peak and end moments of experiences. So craft your time to focus on and celebrate your happiest hours.

# NOTES

## Chapter One

1    **happiness changes as we grow older:** Cassie Mogilner, Sepandar D. Kamvar, and Jennifer Aaker, "The Shifting Meaning of Happiness," *Social Psychological and Personality Science* 2, no. 4 (July 2011): 395–402, DOI: 10.1177/1948550610393987.

3    **busyness as a status symbol:** Silvia Bellezza, Neeru Paharia, and Anat Keinan, "Conspicuous Consumption of Time: When Busyness and Lack of Leisure Time Become a Status Symbol," *Journal of Consumer Research* 44, no. 1 (December 2016): 118–38, DOI: 10.1093/jcr/ucw076; Anat Keinan, Silvia Bellezza, and Neeru Paharia, "The Symbolic Value of Time," *Current Opinion in Psychology* 26 (April 2019): 58–61, DOI: 10.1016/j.copsyc.2018.05.001.

3    **rushing does not feel fancy:** Maria Trupia, Cassie Mogilner, and Isabelle Engeler, "What's Meant vs. Heard When Communicating Busyness" (working paper, 2021).

4    **American Time Use Survey:** The ATUS is conducted by the U.S. Bureau of Labor Statistics, and the data can be accessed here: https://www.bls.gov/tus/#database.

4    **discretionary time and their overall happiness:** Marissa A. Sharif, Cassie Mogilner, and Hal E. Hershfield, "Having Too Little or Too Much Time Is Linked to Lower Subjective Well-

Being," *Journal of Personality and Social Psychology* 121, no. 4 (September 2021): 933–47, DOI: 10.1037/pspp0000391.

We analyzed the data of 21,736 Americans who participated in the American Time Use Survey between 2012 and 2013, the years in which our key variables were administered ($M_{age}$ = 47.92; 44.5% male; 79.3% Caucasian; 47.7% married; 43.5% have children; 33.5% with at least a bachelor's degree; 57.8% employed full-time; $M_{income}$ = $52,597.74). In answering the American Time Use Survey, respondents provide a detailed account of the activities that filled their prior twenty-four hours—indicating the time period and duration of each activity. We assessed discretionary time by calculating the amount of time people spent on discretionary activities in a day.

4    **things people want to do:** We asked a separate sample of 500 Americans to tell us which activities they view as discretionary. We presented participants with a list of 139 activities and for each activity instructed them to indicate whether it was discretionary time: "time spent on leisure activities or other pursuits where the primary function is the use of time for pleasure or some other intrinsically worthwhile purpose." We counted any activity that the vast majority (over 90%) indicated to be discretionary. The same pattern of results held when we used a more lenient threshold, in which over 75% considered the activity discretionary.

The categories of activities that at least 90% of the sample considered discretionary were relaxing and leisure (e.g., doing nothing, watching TV, listening to the radio, playing games); socializing and communicating with others (e.g., hanging out with family, hanging out with friends); arts and entertainment other than sports (e.g., attending a comedy club, attending an art gallery, attending a movie); travel related to socializing, relaxing, and leisure; personal activities (e.g., having sex, making out); attending sporting/recreational events (e.g., watching sports); playing sports with household and non-household children (e.g., riding bikes with child, strolling with child); and participating in sports, exercise, or recreation (e.g., biking, playing basketball, fishing, running, golfing, doing yoga, working out). Though a lot of research has clumped time with one's kids together as "childcare" in order to assess the happiness (or unhappiness) of parenthood, our results more precisely highlight that whether time with one's kids is considered fun and fulfilling depends on the particular way that time is spent. While playing sports with one's kids is viewed as discretionary, "looking after" them is not. And getting one's kids dressed or putting them to bed is viewed as almost as much a chore as standing in line at the DMV!

6    **not alone:** Daniel S. Hamermesh and Jungmin Lee, "Stressed Out on Four Continents: Time Crunch or Yuppie Kvetch?" *Review of Economics and Statistics* 89, no. 2 (May 2007): 374–83, DOI: 10.1162/rest.89.2.374.

6    **don't have enough time to do what they want to do:** Frank Newport, ed., *The Gallup Poll: Public Opinion 2015* (Lanham, MD: Rowman & Littlefield, 2017).

6    **always or sometimes feel rushed:** John P. Robinson, "Americans Less Rushed but No Happier: 1965–2010 Trends in Subjective Time and Happiness," *Social Indicators Research* 113, no. 3 (September 2013): 1091–104, DOI: 10.1007/s11205-012-0133-6.

6    **people lack for time:** Hielke Buddelmeyer, Daniel S. Hamermesh, and Mark Wooden, "The Stress Cost of Children on Moms and Dads," *European Economic Review* 109 (October 2018): 148–61, DOI: 10.1016/j.euroecorev.2016.12.012; Daniel S. Hamermesh, "Time Use—Economic Approaches," *Current Opinion in Psychology* 26 (April 2019): 1–4, DOI: 10.1016/j.copsyc.2018.03.010; Melanie Rudd, "Feeling Short on Time: Trends, Consequences, and Possible Remedies," *Current Opinion in Psychology* 26 (April 2019): 5–10, DOI: 10.1016/j.copsyc.2018.04.007.

6    **too little time:** Hamermesh, "Time Use," 1–4; Hamermesh and Lee, "Stressed Out on Four Continents," 374–83; Grant Bailey, "Millions of Brits Feel Overwhelmed by Life Pressures, Study Finds," *Independent*, January 19, 2018, Indy/Life, https://www.independent.co.uk/life-style/stress-work-pressures-busy-social-calenders-financial-worries-survey-a8167446.html; Lilian Ribeiro and Emerson Marinho, "Time Poverty in Brazil: Measurement and Analysis of its Determinants," *Estudos Econômicos* 42, no. 2 (June 2012): 285–306, DOI: 10.1590/S0101-41612012000200003; Elena Bardasi and Quentin Wodon, "Working Long Hours and Having No Choice: Time Poverty in Guinea," *Feminist Economics* 16, no. 3 (September 2010): 45–78, DOI: 10.1080/13545701.2010.508574; Liangshu Qi and Xiao-yuan Dong, "Gender, Low-Paid Status, and Time Poverty in Urban China," *Feminist Economics* 24, no. 2 (December 2017): 171–93, DOI: 10.1080/13545701.2017.1404621.

6    **emotionally exhausted:** Trupia, Mogilner, and Engeler, "What's Meant vs. Heard"; Tim Kasser and Kennon M. Sheldon, "Time Affluence as a Path toward Personal Happiness

and Ethical Business Practice: Empirical Evidence from Four Studies," *Journal of Business Ethics* 84, no. 2 (January 2009): 243–55, DOI: 10.1007/s10551-008-9696-1; Susan Roxburgh, "'There Just Aren't Enough Hours in the Day': The Mental Health Consequences of Time Pressure," *Journal of Health and Social Behavior* 45, no. 2 (June 2004): 115–31, DOI: 10.1177/002214650404500201; Katja Teuchmann, Peter Totterdell, and Sharon K. Parker, "Rushed, Unhappy, and Drained: An Experience Sampling Study of Relations between Time Pressure, Perceived Control, Mood, and Emotional Exhaustion in a Group of Accountants," *Journal of Occupational Health Psychology* 4, no. 1 (January 1999): 37–54, DOI: 10.1037/1076-8998.4.1.37.

7    **less happiness:** Additional analyses show that the drop in happiness we observed for having too much time depends on whether those hours are spent on discretionary activities that feel worthwhile. In particular, our results indicate that if people spend their discretionary time to cultivate social connection (e.g., hang out with friends or family) or use it productively (e.g., hobbies, exercise), they don't experience a decrease in happiness with large amounts of time.

8    **less satisfied in their lives:** In this study, we randomly assigned people to mentally simulate having either very little (15 minutes), a moderate amount (3.5 hours), or a whole lot (7.5 hours) of discretionary time every day for a period of their life. We then asked these folks to report how happy and how productive they'd feel in their situation. Replicating the upside-down U-shaped pattern we observed before, these results confirmed that having very little or a whole lot of time produces less happiness than having a moderate amount.

This study further showed that the *reason* behind there being such a thing as having too much time is a lacking sense of productivity.

8    **aversion to being idle:** Christopher K. Hsee, Adelle X. Yang, and Liao-yuan Wang, "Idleness Aversion and the Need for Justifiable Busyness," *Psychological Science* 21, no. 7 (July 2010): 926–30, DOI: 10.1177/0956797610374738; Adelle X. Yang and Christopher K. Hsee, "Idleness versus Busyness," *Current Opinion in Psychology* 26 (April 2019): 15–18, DOI: 10.1016/j.copsyc.2018.04.015.

8    **oriented toward productivity:** Anat Keinan and Ran Kivetz, "Productivity Orientation and the Consumption of Collectable Experiences," *Journal of Consumer Research* 37, no. 6 (April 2011): 935–50, DOI: 10.1086/657163.

8    **purpose in our daily lives:** Mihaly Csikszentmihalyi, "The Costs and Benefits of Consuming," *Journal of Consumer Research* 27, no. 2 (September 2000): 267–72, DOI: 10.1086/314324.

8    **sense of purpose**: This likely explains research showing that retirees who spend time volunteering are happier than those who do not. Nancy Morrow-Howell, "Volunteering in Later Life: Research Frontiers," *Journals of Gerontology: Series B* 65, no. 4 (July 2010): 461–69, DOI: 10.1093/geronb/gbq024.

9    **is not paid:** Indira Hirway, *Mainstreaming Unpaid Work: Time-Use Data in Developing Policies* (New Delhi: Oxford University Press, 2017); Eve Rodsky, *Fair Play* (New York: G. P. Putnam's Sons, 2019); Christine Alksnis, Serge Desmarais, and James Curtis, "Workforce Segregation and the Gender Wage Gap: Is 'Women's' Work Valued as Highly as 'Men's'?" *Journal of Applied Social Psychology*

38, no. 6 (May 2008): 1416–41, DOI: 10.1111/j.1559
1816.2008.00354.x.

9    **productive and purposeful:** We asked a separate sample of
500 Americans to tell us which of the discretionary activities identified in our other study were productive—where
the use of time would feel useful, accomplished, fulfilling,
helpful, purposeful, and worthwhile. These were the activities that more than 90% indicated were productive discretionary activities: hobbies, working out (including running,
aerobics, and weightlifting), and playing sports individually or with kids (including hockey, soccer, baseball, tennis/
racquetball, bowling, volleyball, rugby, horseback riding, mar-
tial arts, biking, rollerblading, wrestling, fencing, and golf).

12   **majority chose money:** Hal Hershfield, Cassie Mogilner, and Uri Barnea, "People Who Choose Time over
Money Are Happier," *Social Psychological and Personality Science* 7, no. 7 (September 2016): 697–706, DOI:
10.1177/1948550616649239. In this project we asked
thousands of adults, "Which do you want more of—time
or money?" Participants ranged in age from 18 to 82; they
ranged in income and occupations; there were single people,
married people, people with kids, and others without. Out
of the nearly 5,000 respondents, the majority (64%) chose
money over time. This greater focus on money isn't particular
to our sample. It shows up in people's Google searches and
my students' expressed aspirations. We asked an additional
question, however. This question was about happiness, and
the results were startling: regardless of how much money
our study participants were making, or how many hours
they worked per week, those who chose time over money

were significantly happier. More specifically, those whose responses showed they valued their time over their money felt happier in their daily lives and were more satisfied with their lives overall. For those who chose time, it wasn't about wanting more simply to have it. It was so that they could spend on the experiences and people that bring them happiness.

12     **time vs. money:** Cassie Mogilner, "The Pursuit of Happiness: Time, Money, and Social Connection," *Psychological Science* 21, no. 9 (August 2010): 1348–54, DOI: 10.1177/09567976 10380696; Cassie Mogilner and Jennifer Aaker, "The 'Time vs. Money Effect': Shifting Product Attitudes and Decisions through Personal Connection," *Journal of Consumer Research* 36, no. 2 (August 2009): 277–91, DOI: 10.1086/597161; Francesca Gino and Cassie Mogilner, "Time, Money, and Morality," *Psychological Science* 25, no. 2 (February 2014): 414–21, DOI: 10.1177/0956797613506438; Cassie Mogilner, "It's Time for Happiness," *Current Opinion in Psychology* 26 (April 2019): 80–84, DOI: 10.1016/j.copsyc.2018.07.002.

13     **most important pursuits:** Ed Diener et al., "National Differences in Reported Well-Being: Why Do They Occur?" *Social Indicators Research* 34 (January 1995), 7–32, DOI: 10.1111/j.0963-7214.2004.00501001.x.

13     **"tend to this end":** Blaise Pascal, *Pascal's Pensées* (New York: E. P. Dutton, 1958), 113.

13     **feel about your life overall:** Ed Diener et al., "Findings All Psychologists Should Know from the New Science on Subjective Well-Being," *Canadian Psychology* 58, no. 2 (May 2017): 87–104, DOI: 10.1037/cap0000063.

13     **and in our relationships:** Sonja Lyubomirsky, Laura King, and Ed Diener, "The Benefits of Frequent Positive Affect:

Does Happiness Lead to Success?" *Psychological Bulletin* 131, no. 6 (November 2005): 803–55, DOI: 10.1037/0033 -2909.131.6.803.

13    **challenging times:** Cassie Mogilner, "Staying Happy in Unhappy Times," *UCLA Anderson Blog,* March 24, 2020, https://www.anderson.ucla.edu/news-and-events/staying -happy-in-unhappy-times.

14    **Laurie Santos's course:** Psychology and the Good Life is the most popular undergraduate course ever taught at Yale.

14    **Designing Your Life course:** Bill Burnett and Dave Evans taught this course at Stanford's design school and wrote the book *Designing Your Life: How to Build a Well-Lived, Joyful Life* (New York: Alfred A. Knopf, 2017).

15    **your life as a result:** Every time I teach my course, I have my students assess their well-being before the first class, and again before the final class. And for every section of students, I observe a statistically significant increase in their happiness, sense of meaning, and feelings of interpersonal connection having taken the course.

## Chapter Two

19    **from the research:** Ullrich Wagner et al., "Sleep Inspires Insight," *Nature* 427, no. 6972 (January 2004): 352–55, DOI: 10.1038/nature02223.

21    **not having or being enough:** Brené Brown, *The Power of Vulnerability: Teachings of Authenticity, Connection, and Courage,* read by the author (Louisville, CO: Sounds True, 2012), Audible audio ed., 6 hr., 30 min.

21    **scarce resources:** Sendhil Mullainathan and Eldar Shafir, *Scarcity: Why Having Too Little Means So Much* (New York: Times Books, 2013).

21    **less happy:** Marissa A. Sharif, Cassie Mogilner, and Hal E. Hershfield, "Having Too Little or Too Much Time Is Linked to Lower Subjective Well-Being," *Journal of Personality and Social Psychology* 121, no. 4 (September 2021): 933–47, DOI: 10.1037/pspp0000391.

22    **physical and emotional well-being:** Patrick Callaghan, "Exercise: A Neglected Intervention in Mental Health Care?" *Journal of Psychiatric and Mental Health Nursing* 11, no. 4 (August 2004): 476–83, DOI: 10.1111/j.1365-2850.2004.00751.x; Michael Babyak et al., "Exercise Treatment for Major Depression: Maintenance of Therapeutic Benefit at Ten Months," *Psychosomatic Medicine* 62, no. 5 (2000): 633–38, DOI: 10.1097/00006842-200009000-00006; Justy Reed and Deniz S. Ones, "The Effect of Acute Aerobic Exercise on Positive Activated Affect: A Meta-Analysis," *Psychology of Sport and Exercise* 7, no. 5 (September 2006): 477–514, DOI: 10.1016/j.psychsport.2005.11.003; Lyndall Strazdins et al., "Time Scarcity: Another Health Inequality?" *Environment and Planning A: Economy and Space* 43, no. 3 (March 2011): 545–59, DOI: 10.1068/a4360.

22    **overweight:** Cathy Banwell et al., "Reflections on Expert Consensus: A Case Study of the Social Trends Contributing to Obesity," *European Journal of Public Health* 15, no. 6 (September 2005): 564–68, DOI: 10.1093/eurpub/cki034.

22    **hypertension:** Lijing L. Yan et al., "Psychosocial Factors and Risk of Hypertension: The Coronary Artery Risk Development in Young Adults (CARDIA) Study," *JAMA*

290, no. 16 (October 2003): 2138–48, DOI: 10.1001 /jama.290.16.2138.

22    **less healthy overall:** Strazdins et al., "Time Scarcity," 545–59.

23    **less likely to spend some time helping:** John M. Darley and C. Daniel Batson, "From Jerusalem to Jericho: A Study of Situational and Dispositional Variables in Helping Behavior," *Journal of Personality and Social Psychology* 27, no. 1 (July 1973): 100–108, DOI: 10.1037/H0034449.

23    **less willing to give their time:** Some 55% agreed to help in the busy condition versus 83% in the spare time condition. Zoë Chance, Cassie Mogilner, and Michael I. Norton, "Giving Time Gives You More Time," *Advances in Consumer Research* 39 (2011): 263–64.

24    **had little time:** Tom Gilovich, Margaret Kerr, and Victoria Medvec, "Effect of Temporal Perspective on Subjective Confidence," *Journal of Personality and Social Psychology* 64, no. 4 (1993): 552–60, DOI: 10.1037/0022-3514.64.4.552.

24    **promotion focus vs. prevention focus:** E. Tory Higgins, "Beyond Pleasure and Pain," *American Psychologist* 52, no. 12 (December 1997): 1280–300, DOI: 10.1037/0003 -066X.52.12.1280; Joel Brockner and E. Tory Higgins, "Regulatory Focus Theory: Implications for the Study of Emotions at Work," *Organizational Behavior and Human Decision Processes* 86, no. 1 (September 2001): 35–66, DOI: 10.1006 /obhd.2001.2972.

24    **prevention-focused:** Cassie Mogilner, Jennifer Aaker, and Ginger Pennington, "Time Will Tell: The Distant Appeal of Promotion and Imminent Appeal of Prevention," *Journal of Consumer Research* 34, no. 5 (February 2008): 670–81,

DOI: 10.1086/521901; Ginger Pennington and Neal Roese, "Regulatory Focus and Temporal Distance," *Journal of Experimental Social Psychology* 39 (March 2003): 563–76, DOI: 10.1016/S0022-1031(03)00058-1.

26    **paper to prove it**: Aaron M. Sackett et al., "You're Having Fun When Time Flies: The Hedonic Consequences of Subjective Time Progression," *Psychological Science* 21, no. 1 (January 2010): 111–17, DOI: 10.1177/0956797609354832.

27    **fear of missing out**: Erin Vogel et al., "Social Comparison, Social Media, and Self-Esteem," *Psychology of Popular Media Culture* 3, no. 4 (October 2014): 206–22, DOI: 10.1037/ppm0000047; Jenna L. Clark, Sara B. Algoe, and Melanie C. Green, "Social Network Sites and Well-Being: The Role of Social Connection," *Current Directions in Psychological Science* 27, no. 1 (February 2018): 32–37, DOI: 10.1177/0963721417730833; Hunt Allcott et al., "The Welfare Effects of Social Media," *American Economic Review* 110, no. 3 (March 2020): 629–76, DOI: 10.1257/aer.20190658.

28    **greater time poverty than dads**: Hielke Buddelmeyer, Daniel S. Hamermesh, and Mark Wooden, "The Stress Cost of Children on Moms and Dads," *European Economic Review* 109 (October 2018): 148–61, DOI: 10.1016/j.euroecorev.2016.12.012.

29    **self-efficacy**: Albert Bandura, "Self-Efficacy: Toward a Unifying Theory of Behavioral Change," *Psychological Review* 84, no. 2 (March 1977): 191, DOI: 10.1037/0033-295X.84.2.191.

29    **having more time**: Cassie Mogilner, Zoë Chance, and Michael I. Norton, "Giving Time Gives You Time," *Psycho-*

*logical Science* 23, no. 10 (October 2012): 1233–38, DOI: 10.1177/0956797612442551.

30    **increase self-esteem**: Callaghan, "Exercise," 476–83.

33    **doing kind acts**: Sonja Lyubomirsky and Kristin Layous, "How Do Simple Positive Activities Increase Well-Being?" *Current Directions in Psychological Science* 22, no. 1 (2013): 57–62, DOI: 10.1177/0963721412469809.

35    **"wasted time"**: Mogilner, Chance, and Norton, "Giving Time Gives You Time," 1233–38.

35    **ongoing obligation**: Richard Schulz, Paul Visintainer, and Gail M. Williamson, "Psychiatric and Physical Morbidity Effects of Caregiving," *Journal of Gerontology* 45, no. 5 (September 1990): 181–91, DOI: 10.1093/geronj/45.5.P181; Richard Schulz, Connie A. Tompkins, and Marie T. Rau, "A Longitudinal Study of the Psychosocial Impact of Stroke on Primary Support Persons," *Psychology and Aging* 3, no. 2 (June 1988): 131, DOI: 10.1037/0882-7974.3.2.131; Richard Schulz and Gail M. Williamson, "A Two-Year Longitudinal Study of Depression among Alzheimer's Caregivers," *Psychology and Aging* 6, no. 4 (1991): 569–78, DOI: 10.1037/0882-7974.6.4.569.

36    **can influence time affluence**: Melanie Rudd, Kathleen Vohs, and Jennifer Aaker, "Awe Expands People's Perception of Time, Alters Decision Making, and Enhances Well-Being," *Psychological Science* 23, no. 10 (2012): 1130–36, DOI: 10.1177/0956797612438731.

36    **at least for the moment**: Dacher Keltner and Jonathan Haidt, "Approaching Awe, a Moral, Spiritual, and Aesthetic Emotion," *Cognition & Emotion* 17, no. 2 (March 2003): 297–314, DOI: 10.1080/02699930302297.

36    **makes us feel happier**: George MacKerron and Susana Mour-
ato, "Happiness Is Greater in Natural Environments," *Global
Environmental Change* 23, no. 5 (October 2013): 992–1000,
DOI: 10.1016/j.gloenvcha.2013.03.010.

## Chapter Three

42    **happiness we experience**: Sonja Lyubomirsky, *The How of
Happiness: A Scientific Approach to Getting the Life You Want*
(New York: Penguin Press, 2007).

42    **general positivity**: Evidence for the effects of natural personality on one's happiness comes from studies with twins
that compare identical twins (who share 100% of their genetic makeup) and fraternal twins (who share 50% of their
genetic makeup). These studies have shown that the happiness of an identical twin (but not that of a fraternal twin)
significantly predicts the other twin's happiness—even when
the twins were raised apart. David Lykken and Auke Tellegen, "Happiness Is a Stochastic Phenomenon," *Psychological
Science* 7, no. 3 (May 1996): 186–89, DOI: 10.1111/j.1467
-9280.1996.tb00355.x; Auke Tellegen et al., "Personality
Similarity in Twins Reared Apart and Together," *Journal of
Personality and Social Psychology* 54, no. 6 (June 1988): 1031,
DOI: 10.1037/0022-3514.54.6.1031.

43    **small effects on people's subsequent happiness**: Lara B.
Aknin, Michael I. Norton, and Elizabeth W. Dunn, "From
Wealth to Well-Being? Money Matters, but Less than People Think," *Journal of Positive Psychology* 4, no. 6 (November
2009): 523–27, DOI: 10.1080/17439760903271421; Dan-

iel Kahneman and Angus Deaton, "High Income Improves Evaluation of Life but Not Emotional Well-Being," *Proceedings of the National Academy of Sciences of the United States of America* 107, no. 38 (September 2010): 16489–93, DOI: 10.1073/pnas.1011492107; Ed Diener, Brian Wolsic, and Frank Fujita, "Physical Attractiveness and Subjective Well-Being," *Journal of Personality and Social Psychology* 69, no. 1 (1995): 120–29, DOI: 10.1037/0022-3514.69.1.120; Richard E. Lucas et al., "Reexamining Adaptation and the Set Point Model of Happiness: Reactions to Changes in Marital Status," *Journal of Personality and Social Psychology* 84, no. 3 (March 2003): 527–39, DOI: 10.1037/0022-3514.84.3.527; Maike Luhmann et al., "Subjective Well-Being and Adaptation to Life Events: A Meta-Analysis on Differences between Cognitive and Affective Well-Being," *Journal of Personality and Social Psychology* 102, no. 3 (March 2012): 592–615, DOI: 10.1037/a0025948; S. K. Nelson-Coffey, "Married . . . with Children: The Science of Well-Being in Marriage and Family Life," in *Handbook of Well-Being*, eds. E. Diener, S. Oishi, and L. Tay (Salt Lake City: DEF Publishers, 2018), https://www.nobascholar.com/chapters/26.

43    **than people expect**: Daniel Gilbert, *Stumbling on Happiness* (New York: Vintage Books, 2007); Daniel T. Gilbert et al., "Immune Neglect: A Source of Durability Bias in Affective Forecasting," *Journal of Personality and Social Psychology* 75, no. 3 (1998): 617–38, DOI: 10.1037/0022-3514.75.3.617.

44    **intentional thought and behavior**: Lyubomirsky, *The How of Happiness*.

48    **excitedly energized or blissfully serene**: My research shows that happiness can be experienced in two ways—as

excitement and calm. Cassie Mogilner, Jennifer Aaker, and Sepandar D. Kamvar, "How Happiness Affects Choice," *Journal of Consumer Research* 39, no. 2 (August 2012): 429–43, DOI: 10.1086/663774; Cassie Mogilner, Sepandar D. Kamvar, and Jennifer Aaker, "The Shifting Meaning of Happiness," *Social Psychological and Personality Science* 2, no. 4 (July 2011): 395–402, DOI: 10.1177/1948550610393987.

48    **"flourishing"**: A father of positive psychology, Martin Seligman explains the components of authentic happiness being positive emotion, engagement, relationships, meaning, and accomplishment. Martin Seligman, *Authentic Happiness: Using the New Positive Psychology to Realize Your Potential for Lasting Fulfillment* (New York: Atria Books, 2002); Martin Seligman, *Flourish: A Visionary New Understanding of Happiness and Well-Being* (New York: Simon & Schuster, 2011).

49    **900 working women**: Daniel Kahneman et al., "A Survey Method for Characterizing Daily Life Experience: The Day Reconstruction Method," *Science* 306, no. 5702 (December 2004): 1776–80, DOI: 10.1126/science.1103572.

51    **including men and people who don't work**: Richard E. Lucas et al., "A Direct Comparison of the Day Reconstruction Method (DRM) and the Experience Sampling Method (ESM)," *Journal of Personality and Social Psychology* 120, no. 3 (March 2021): 816–35, DOI: 10.1177/23780231211064009.

51–52    **summiting a mountain**: George Loewenstein, "Because It Is There: The Challenge of Mountaineering . . . for Utility Theory," *KYKLOS* 52, no. 3 (August 1999): 315–44, DOI: 10.1111/j.1467-6435.1999.tb00221.x.

52    **satisfaction from our accomplishments**: Self-determination theory asserts that well-being requires fulfillment of three

fundamental psychological needs: autonomy, relatedness, and competence. The drive to feel productive and accomplished contributes to feelings of competence. Kennon M. Sheldon, Robert Cummins, and Shanmukh Kamble, "Life Balance and Well-Being: Testing a Novel Conceptual and Measurement Approach," *Journal of Personality* 78, no. 4 (August 2010): 1093–134, DOI: 10.1111/j.1467-6494.2010.00644.x; Kennon M. Sheldon and Christopher P. Niemiec, "It's Not Just the Amount that Counts: Balanced Need Satisfaction Also Affects Well-Being," *Journal of Personality and Social Psychology* 91, no. 2 (August 2006): 331–41, DOI: 10.1037/0022-3514.91.2.331.

52    **closely linked in our experiences**: My team's analysis of self-reported happiness and meaning among tens of thousands of individuals across the globe reveals that happiness and meaning are highly correlated. Rhia Catapano et al., "Financial Resources Impact the Relationship between Meaning and Happiness," *Emotion* 22 (forthcoming).

There is another line of research that looks to disentangle meaning and happiness. Though there are experiences that produce meaning but not happiness, and experiences that produce happiness but not meaning, most experiences that produce happiness are also meaningful. Roy F. Baumeister et al., "Some Key Differences between a Happy Life and a Meaningful Life," *Journal of Positive Psychology* 8, no. 6 (August 2013): 505–16, DOI: 10.1080/17439760.2013.830764; Ryan Dwyer, Elizabeth Dunn, and Hal Hershfield, "Cousins or Conjoined Twins: How Different Are Meaning and Happiness in Everyday Life?" *Comprehensive Results in Social Psychology* 2, no. 2–3 (October 2017): 199–215, DOI:

10.1080/23743603.2017.1376580; Laura A. King, Samantha J. Heintzelman, and Sarah J. Ward, "Beyond the Search for Meaning: A Contemporary Science of the Experience of Meaning in Life," *Current Directions in Psychological Science* 25, no. 4 (August 2016): 211–16, DOI: 10.1177/0963721416656354.

52    **how rewarding it felt**: Enjoyment was assessed by subtracting the average of the negative emotions (anxious, sad, frustrated, and impatient) from the average of the positive emotions (happy, relaxed). Meaning was assessed as the average of six items: feeling focused, engaged, and competent/able, and agreement to the statements "I feel the activity in this episode was worthwhile and meaningful/was useful to other people/helped me achieve important goals." Mathew P. White and Paul Dolan, "Accounting for the Richness of Daily Activities," *Psychological Science* 20, no. 8 (August 2009): 1000–1008, DOI: 10.1111/j.1467-9280.2009.02392.x.

53    **worse about themselves and worse overall**: Erin Vogel et al., "Social Comparison, Social Media, and Self-Esteem," *Psychology of Popular Media Culture* 3, no. 4 (October 2014): 206–22, DOI: 10.1037/ppm0000047; Jenna L. Clark, Sara B. Algoe, and Melanie C. Green, "Social Network Sites and Well-Being: The Role of Social Connection," *Current Directions in Psychological Science* 27, no. 1 (February 2018): 32–37, DOI: 10.1177/0963721417730833; Hunt Allcott et al., "The Welfare Effects of Social Media," *American Economic Review* 110, no. 3 (March 2020): 629–76, DOI: 10.1257/aer.20190658.

53    **between-person and within-person variability**: Lucas et al., "Direct Comparison," 816–35.

61    **very happy and very unhappy**: Ed Diener and Martin E. P.

Seligman, "Very Happy People," *Psychological Science* 13, no. 1 (January 2002): 81–84, DOI: 10.1111/1467-9280.00415.

62    **critical to human survival**: Abraham H. Maslow, "A Theory of Human Motivation," *Psychological Review* 50, no. 4 (1943): 370–96, DOI: 10.1037/h0054346. Based on his years of working with individuals as a therapist, Abraham Maslow developed this theory of what drives people, based on the needs people must meet in order to feel happy and fulfilled. The pyramid—going from physiological needs (food, water, warmth, rest) to safety needs (security, safety) to belongingness and love needs (intimate relationships, friends) to esteem needs (prestige, feelings of accomplishment) up to self-actualization (achieving one's full potential and purpose)—depicts his proposed hierarchy of needs. He argues that a lower-level need must be met before moving on to a higher pursuit. This is helpful as an underlying theory for well-being because it prioritizes the various inputs into happiness. It shows that once basic physical needs are met (food, water, health—which is where sleep comes into play—and shelter), interpersonal connection/the feeling of belonging is the most fundamental need. And only once we have strong social connection—of loving and being loved—are more individual endeavors toward personal accomplishment and then self-actualization worth pursuing. Note that this love doesn't need to be in a romantic context. Friendship and family can fulfill this need too.

62    **cope better following physiological and financial stressors**: David G. Myers, "The Funds, Friends, and Faith of Happy People," *American Psychologist* 55, no. 1 (January 2000): 56, DOI: 10.1037/0003-066X.55.1.56; Julianne Holt-Lunstad,

Timothy B. Smith, and J. Bradley Layton, "Social Relationships and Mortality Risk: A Meta-Analytic Review," *PLoS Medicine* 7, no. 7 (July 2010): DOI: 10.1371/journal.pmed.1000316; James S. House, Karl R. Landis, and Debra Umberson, "Social Relationships and Health," *Science* 24, no. 4865 (July 1988): 540–45, DOI: 10.1126/science.3399889; Gregor Gonza and Anže Burger, "Subjective Well-Being during the 2008 Economic Crisis: Identification of Mediating and Moderating Factors," *Journal of Happiness Studies* 18, no. 6 (December 2017): 1763–97, DOI: 10.1007/s10902-016-9797-y.

62    **like physical pain**: Matthew Lieberman, *Social: Why Our Brains Are Wired to Connect* (New York: Crown, 2013).

62    **satisfaction in life**: B. Bradford Brown, "A Life-Span Approach to Friendship: Age-Related Dimensions of an Ageless Relationship," *Research in the Interweave of Social Roles* 2 (1981): 23–50, DOI: 10.15288/jsad.2012.73.99; Vasudha Gupta and Charles Korte, "The Effects of a Confidant and a Peer Group on the Well-Being of Single Elders," *International Journal of Aging and Human Development* 39, no. 4 (December 1994): 293–302, DOI: 10.2190/4YYH-9XAU-WQF9-APVT; Reed Larson, "Thirty Years of Research on the Subjective Well-Being of Older Americans," *Journals of Gerontology* 33, no. 1 (January 1978): 109–25, DOI: 10.1093/geronj/33.1.109; Catherine L. Bagwell, Andrew F. Newcomb, and William M. Bukowski, "Preadolescent Friendship and Peer Rejection as Predictors of Adult Adjustment," *Child Development* 69, no. 1 (February 1998): 140–53, DOI: 10.1111/j.1467-8624.1998.tb06139.x.

62    **shared with loved ones**: Kahneman et al., "Survey Method,"
      1776–80.

64    **more connected**: Constantine Sedikides et al., "The Rela-
      tionship Closeness Induction Task," *Representative Research
      in Social Psychology* 23 (January 1999): 1–4.

65    **outside**: George MacKerron and Susana Mourato, "Happiness
      Is Greater in Natural Environments," *Global Environmental
      Change* 23, no. 5 (October 2013): 992–1000, DOI: 10.1016/
      j.gloenvcha.2013.03.010.

67    **feel unhappy**: Self-determination theory (SDT) is a macro
      theory of human motivation and personality proposed by Ed-
      ward Deci and Richard Ryan that concerns people's inherent
      growth tendencies and innate psychological needs. As part of
      the theory, they propose three basic psychological needs that
      must be satisfied to foster well-being and health, which are
      universal (i.e., apply across individuals and situations):

> * autonomy—a feeling of overall psychological liberty
> and freedom of internal will. When a person is auton-
> omously motivated, their performance, wellness, and
> engagement are heightened, rather than if a person is
> told what to do (a.k.a. control motivation).
> * competence—the ability to control the outcome
> and experience mastery. People like receiving positive
> feedback in their activities.
> * relatedness—belongingness, feeling connected to
> and caring for others.

      Richard M. Ryan and Edward L. Deci, "Self-
      Determination Theory and the Facilitation of Intrinsic Mo-
      tivation, Social Development, and Well-Being," *American*

*Psychologist* 55, no. 1 (January 2000): 68–78, DOI: 10.1037/0003-066X.55.1.68; Maarten Vansteenkiste, Richard M. Ryan, and Bart Soenens, "Basic Psychological Need Theory: Advancements, Critical Themes, and Future Directions," *Motivation and Emotion* 44, no. 1 (January 2020): 1–31, DOI: 10.1007 /s11031-019-09818-1; Kennon M. Sheldon, "Integrating Behavioral-Motive and Experiential-Requirement Perspectives on Psychological Needs: A Two Process Model," *Psychological Review* 118, no. 4 (October 2011): 552–69, DOI: 10.1037/a0024758.

68      **least happy**: In listing his least happy activities from his time tracking data, one of my students noted, "My most negative activities were 1) Boring paperwork tasks at work I have to do alone; 2) Preparing for class (not this one); 3) Running errands alone. I was alone in all of them."

68      **direct route to depression**: John T. Cacioppo and William Patrick, *Loneliness: Human Nature and the Need for Social Connection* (New York: W. W. Norton, 2008).

68      **connected and happier**: Nicholas Epley and Juliana Schroeder, "Mistakenly Seeking Solitude," *Journal of Experimental Psychology* 143, no. 5 (October 2014): 1980–99, DOI: 10.1037/a0037323.

69      **time tracking research**: Kahneman et al., "Survey Method," 1776–80.

70      **more so than wasting money**: France Leclerc, Bernd H. Schmitt, and Laurette Dube, "Waiting Time and Decision Making: Is Time Like Money?" *Journal of Consumer Research* 22, no. 1 (June 1995): 110–19, DOI: 10.1086/209439.

73      **self-esteem**: Justy Reed and Deniz S. Ones, "The Effect of Acute Aerobic Exercise on Positive Activated Affect:

A Meta-Analysis," *Psychology of Sport and Exercise* 7, no. 5 (September 2006): 477–514, DOI: 10.1016/j.psych sport.2005.11.003; Patrick Callaghan, "Exercise: A Neglected Intervention in Mental Health Care?" *Journal of Psychiatric and Mental Health Nursing* 11, no. 4 (July 2004): 476–83, DOI: 10.1111/j.1365-2850.2004.00751.x.

73    **treating depression**: Michael Babyak et al., "Exercise Treatment for Major Depression: Maintenance of Therapeutic Benefit at Ten Months," *Psychosomatic Medicine* 62, no. 5 (September 2000): 633–38, DOI: 10.1097/00006842 -200009000-00006. These researchers looked at the effect of exercise to treat depression. They had participants with major depression undergo one of three treatment regimes (Exercise: 3x week for 30 minutes; Medicine: antidepressant Zoloft; or Exercise + Medicine) for 4 months, and then measured their level of depression 6 months later.

After four months patients in all three groups who exhibited significant improvement (i.e., the proportion of remitted participants—those who no longer met diagnostic criteria for major depressive disorder) was comparable across the three treatment conditions. After ten months, however, subjects in the exercise group had significantly lower relapse rates than subjects in the medication group. Participants in the exercise group exhibited lower rates of depression (30%) than participants in the medication (52%) and combined groups (55%).

The researchers noted, "One of the positive psychological benefits of systematic exercise is the development of a sense of personal mastery and positive self-regard, which we believe is likely to play some role in the depression-reducing effects of exercise. It is conceivable that the concurrent use of medication may undermine this benefit by prioritizing an alternative, less self-confirming attribution for one's improved condition. Instead of incorporating the belief 'I was dedicated and worked hard with the exercise program; it wasn't easy, but I beat this depression,' patients might incorporate the belief that 'I took an antidepressant and got better.'"

73    **achievement among school-age kids**: Charles Hillman, Kirk I. Erickson, and Arthur F. Kramer, "Be Smart, Exercise Your Heart: Exercise Effects on Brain and Cognition," *Nature Reviews Neuroscience* 9, no. 1 (January 2008): 58–65, DOI: 10.1038/nrn2298.

74    **sleep deprivation**: David F. Dinges et al., "Cumulative Sleepiness, Mood Disturbance, and Psychomotor Vigilance Performance Decrements during a Week of Sleep Restricted to 4–5 Hours per Night," *Sleep: Journal of Sleep Research & Sleep Medicine* 20, no. 4 (April 1997): 267–77, DOI: 10.1093/sleep/20.4.267.

74    **getting enough sleep**: Matthew P. Walker et al., "Practice with Sleep Makes Perfect: Sleep-Dependent Motor Skill Learning," *Neuron* 35, no. 1 (July 2002): 205–11, DOI: 10.1016/S0896/-6273(02)00746-8; Ullrich Wagner et al., "Sleep Inspires Insight," *Nature* 427, no. 6972 (January 2004): 352–55, DOI: 10.1038/nature02223.

77    **primary resource**: Cassie Mogilner, "The Pursuit of Happiness: Time, Money, and Social Connection," *Psychological Science* 21, no. 9 (August 2010): 1348–54, DOI: 10.1177/0956797610380696.

*Chapter Four*

84    **said they don't**: Ashley Whillans et al., "Buying Time Promotes Happiness," *Proceedings of the National Academy of
Sciences of the United States of America* 114, no. 32 (August
2017): 8523–27, DOI: 10.1073/pnas.1706541114.

84    **experiential purchases:** Leaf Van Boven and Thomas
Gilovich, "To Do or to Have? That Is the Question," *Journal
of Personality and Social Psychology* 85, no. 6 (January 2004):
1193–202, DOI: 10.1037/0022-3514.85.6.1193; Thomas
Gilovich, Amit Kumar, and Lily Jampol, "A Wonderful Life:
Experiential Consumption and the Pursuit of Happiness,"
*Journal of Consumer Psychology* 25, no. 1 (September 2014):
152–65, DOI: 10.1016/j.jcps.2014.08.004.

85    **isn't the happiest one**: Marissa A. Sharif, Cassie Mogilner,
and Hal Hershfield, "Having Too Little or Too Much Time
Is Linked to Lower Subjective Well-Being," *Journal of Personality and Social Psychology* 121, no. 4 (September 2021):
933–47, DOI: 10.1037/pspp0000391.

85    **even stronger**: Elizabeth Dunn et al., "Prosocial Spending
and Buying Time: Money as a Tool for Increasing Subjective
Well-Being," *Advances in Experimental Social Psychology* 61
(2020): 67–126, DOI: 10.1016/bs.aesp.2019.09.001.

85    **relationship satisfaction**: Ashley V. Whillans, Elizabeth
W. Dunn, and Michael I. Norton, "Overcoming Barriers to
Time-Saving: Reminders of Future Busyness Encourage
Consumers to Buy Time," *Social Influence* 13, no. 2 (March
2018): 117–24, DOI: 10.1080/15534510.2018.1453866.

86    **"temptation bundling"**: Katherine Milkman, Julia Minson,
and Kevin Volpp, "Holding the Hunger Games Hostage at the

Gym: An Evaluation of Temptation Bundling," *Management Science* 60, no. 2 (February 2014): 283–99, DOI: 10.1287/mnsc.2013.1784.

87    **least happy of the day**: Daniel Kahneman et al., "A Survey Method for Characterizing Daily Life Experience: The Day Reconstruction Method," *Science* 306, no. 5702 (December 2004): 1776–80, DOI: 10.1126/science.1103572.

87    **engaged at work**: Gallup, "State of the American Workplace," 2017, https://www.gallup.com/workplace/238085/state-american-workplace-report-2017.aspx.

87    **lives to wait through**: Kahneman et al., "Survey Method," 1776–80; Gallup, "State of the American Workplace."

87    **overall life satisfaction**: Karyn Loscocco and Annie R. Roschelle, "Influences on the Quality of Work and Nonwork Life: Two Decades in Review," *Journal of Vocational Behavior* 39, no. 2 (October 1991): 182–225, DOI: 10.1016/0001-8791(91)90009-B; Amy Wrzesniewski et al., "Jobs, Careers, and Callings: People's Relations to Their Work," *Journal of Research in Personality* 31, no. 1 (March 1997): 21–33, DOI: 10.1006/jrpe.1997.2162.

88    **work with purpose**: Amy Wrzesniewski and Jane Dutton, "Having a Calling and Crafting a Job: The Case of Candice Billups," WDI Publishing, April 20, 2012, educational video, 11:48, www.tinyurl.com/CandiceBillups.

89    **satisfied on the job and with life overall**: Amy Wrzesniewski, Justin M. Berg, and Jane E. Dutton, "Managing Yourself: Turn the Job You Have into the Job You Want," *Harvard Business Review* 88, no. 6 (June 2010): 114–17; Justin M. Berg, Adam M. Grant, and Victoria Johnson, "When Callings Are

Calling: Crafting Work and Leisure in Pursuit of Unanswered Occupational Callings," *Organization Science* 21, no. 5 (October 2010): 973–94, DOI: 10.1287/orsc.1090.0497.

89    **job crafting**: Justin M. Berg, Jane E. Dutton, and Amy Wrzesniewski, "Job Crafting Exercise," Center for Positive Organizations, April 29, 2014, https://positiveorgs.bus .umich.edu/cpo-tools/job-crafting-exercise/; Justin M. Berg, Jane E. Dutton, and Amy Wrzesniewski, *What Is Job Crafting and Why Does It Matter?* (Ann Arbor: Regents of the University of Michigan, 2008).

90    **lives overall**: Wrzesniewski et al., "Jobs, Careers, and Callings," 21–33.

91    **motivated, engaged, fulfilled, and satisfied**: Adam Grant et al., "Impact and the Art of Motivation Maintenance: The Effects of Contact with Beneficiaries on Persistence Behavior," *Organizational Behavior and Human Decision Processes* 103, no. 1 (May 2007): 53–67, DOI: 10.1016/ j.obhdp.2006.05.004; Adam Grant, "Leading with Meaning: Beneficiary Contact, Prosocial Impact, and the Performance Effects of Transformational Leadership," *Academy of Management Journal* 55, no. 2 (September 2012): DOI: 10.5465/ amj.2010.0588; Christopher Michaelson et al., "Meaningful Work: Connecting Business Ethics and Organizational Studies," *Journal of Business Ethics* 121 (March 2013): 77–90, DOI: 10.1007/s10551-013-1675-5.

96    **work best friend**: Tom Rath and Jim Harter, "Your Friends and Your Social Well-Being," Gallup, August 19, 2010, https://news.gallup.com/businessjournal/127043/friends -social-wellbeing.aspx; Annamarie Mann, "Why We Need

Best Friends at Work," Gallup, January 15, 2018, https://
www.gallup.com/workplace/236213/why-need-best
-friends-work.aspx.

96    **connection and fun:** Jennifer Aaker and Naomi Bagdonas,
*Humor, Seriously: Why Humor Is a Secret Weapon in Business
and Life* (New York: Currency, 2021).

97    **very bottom of the list**: Kahneman et al., "Survey Method,"
1776–80.

97    **no shorter**: Gabriela Saldivia, "Stuck in Traffic? You're Not
Alone. New Data Show American Commute Times Are
Longer," NPR, September 20, 2018, https://www.npr.org/
2018/09/20/650061560/stuck-in-traffic-youre-not
-alone-new-data-show-american-commute-times-are
-longer; Felix Richter, "Cars Still Dominate the American
Commute," *Statista*, May 29, 2019, https://www.statista
.com/chart/18208/means-of-transportation-used-by-us
-commuters/.

98    **any time at all commuting**: "Statistics on Remote Workers
that Will Surprise You (2021)," Apollo Technical LLC, January 4, 2021, https://www.apollotechnical.com/statistics-on
-remote-workers/. A survey by Owl Labs found that during
COVID-19, close to 70% of full-time workers were working from home. Remote employees saved an average of forty
minutes daily from commuting.

98    **when things reopened**: Courtney Conley, "Why Many
Employees Are Hoping to Work from Home Even after the
Pandemic Is Over," CNBC, May 4, 2020, https://www.cnbc
.com/2020/05/04/why-many-employees-are-hoping-to
-work-from-home-even-after-the-pandemic-is-over.html.

## *Chapter Five*

107     **become less annoyed:** Leif D. Nelson and Tom Meyvis, "Interrupted Consumption: Adaptation and the Disruption of Hedonic Experience," *Journal of Marketing Research* 45, no. 6 (December 2008): 654–64.

108     **solitary confinement:** Peter Suedfeld et al., "Reactions and Attributes of Prisoners in Solitary Confinement," *Criminal Justice and Behavior* 9, no. 3 (September 1982): 303–40, DOI: 10.1177/0093854882009003004.

109     **any happier:** Philip Brickman, Dan Coates, and Ronnie Janoff-Bulman, "Lottery Winners and Accident Victims: Is Happiness Relative?" *Journal of Personality and Social Psychology* 36, no. 8 (September 1978): 917–27, DOI: 10.1037/0022 -3514.36.8.917.

109     **returned to baseline levels:** Rafael Di Tella, John H. New, and Robert MacCulloch, "Happiness Adaptation to Income and to Status in an Individual Panel," *Journal of Economic Behavior & Organization* 76, no. 3 (December 2010): 834–52, DOI: 10.1016/j.jebo.2010.09.016.

109     **just being married:** Richard E. Lucas et al., "Reexamining Adaptation and the Set Point Model of Happiness: Reactions to Changes in Marital Status," *Journal of Personality and Social Psychology* 84, no. 3 (March 2003): 527–39, DOI: 10.1037/0022 -3514.84.3.527; Maike Luhmann et al., "Subjective Well-Being and Adaptation to Life Events: A Meta-Analysis on Differences between Cognitive and Affective Well-Being," *Journal of Personality and Social Psychology* 102, no. 3 (March 2012): 592–615, DOI: 10.1037/a0025948.

109     ***impact bias:*** Daniel T. Gilbert et al., "Immune Neglect: A

Source of Durability Bias in Affective Forecasting," *Journal of Personality and Social Psychology* 75, no. 3 (September 1998): 617–38, DOI: 10.1037/0022-3514.75.3.617.

112    **empirical question together:** Amit Bhattacharjee and Cassie Mogilner, "Happiness from Ordinary and Extraordinary Experiences," *Journal of Consumer Research* 41, no. 1 (June 2014): 1–17, DOI: 10.1086/674724.

115    **"close and meaningful":** Helene Fung and Laura Carstensen, "Goals Change When Life's Fragility Is Primed: Lessons Learned from Older Adults, the September 11 Attacks, and SARS," *Social Cognition* 24, no. 3 (June 2006): 248–78, DOI: 10.1521/soco.2006.24.3.248.

117    **cherished campus spots:** Jaime Kurtz, "Looking to the Future to Appreciate the Present: The Benefits of Perceived Temporal Scarcity," *Psychological Science* 19, no. 12 (December 2008): 1238–41, DOI: 10.1111/j.1467-9280.2008.02231.x.

117    **chocolate in the sequence:** Ed O'Brien and Phoebe Ellsworth, "Saving the Last for Best: A Positivity Bias for End Experiences," *Psychological Science* 23, no. 2 (January 2012): 163–65, DOI: 10.1177/0956797611427408.

117    **enjoy the good stuff:** Tim Urban, "The Tail End," *Wait but Why* (blog), December 11, 2015, https://waitbutwhy.com/2015/12/the-tail-end.html.

127    **overall snack time more:** Ed O'Brien and Robert W. Smith, "Unconventional Consumption Methods and Enjoying Things Consumed: Recapturing the 'First-Time' Experience," *Personality and Social Psychology Bulletin* 45, no. 1 (January 2019): 67–80, DOI: 10.1177/0146167218779823.

127    **relationship satisfaction and commitment:** Ximena Garcia-Rada, Ovul Sezer, and Michael I. Norton, "Rituals and

Nuptials: The Emotional and Relational Consequences of Relationship Rituals," *Journal of the Association for Consumer Research* 4, no. 2 (April 2019): 185–97, DOI: 10.1086/702761.

128    **funerals:** Michael I. Norton and Francesca Gino, "Rituals Alleviate Grieving for Loved Ones, Lovers, and Lotteries," *Journal of Experimental Psychology: General* 143, no. 1 (February 2014): 266–72, DOI: 10.1037/a0031772.

128    **enjoy it more:** Ovul Sezer et al., "Family Rituals Improve the Holidays," *Journal of the Association for Consumer Research* 1, no. 4 (September 2016): 509–26, DOI: 10.1086/699674.

128    **eating chocolate:** Nelson and Meyvis, "Interrupted Consumption," 654–64; Leif D. Nelson, Tom Meyvis, and Jeff Galak, "Enhancing the Television-Viewing Experience through Commercial Interruptions," *Journal of Consumer Research* 36, no. 2 (August 2009): 160–72, DOI: 10.1086/597030.

129    **savored it more:** Jordi Quoidbach and Elizabeth W. Dunn, "Give It Up: A Strategy for Combating Hedonic Adaptation," *Social Psychological and Personality Science* 4, no. 5 (September 2013): 563–68, DOI: 10.1177/1948550612473489.

130    **happier and more satisfied:** Jordan Etkin and Cassie Mogilner, "Does Variety among Activities Increase Happiness?" *Journal of Consumer Research* 43, no. 2 (August 2016): 210–29, DOI: 10.1093/jcr/ucw021.

131    **happier with their spouses:** Arthur Aron et al., "Couples' Shared Participation in Novel and Arousing Activities and Experienced Relationship Quality," *Journal of Personality and Social Psychology* 78, no. 2 (March 2000): 273–84, DOI: 10.1037/0022-3514.78.2.273.

*Chapter Six*

133    **than drunk drivers**: Paul Atchley, "Fooling Ourselves: Why Do We Drive Distracted Even Though We Know It's Dangerous?" (academic seminar, Behavioral Decision Making Group Colloquium Series, UCLA Anderson School of Management, Los Angeles, CA, April 7, 2017).

134    **oriented toward productivity:** Anat Keinan and Ran Kivetz, "Productivity Orientation and the Consumption of Collectable Experiences," *Journal of Consumer Research* 37, no. 6 (April 2011): 935–50, DOI: 10.1086/657163.

135    **currently feel**: Matthew A. Killingsworth and Daniel T. Gilbert, "A Wandering Mind Is an Unhappy Mind," *Science* 330, no. 6006 (November 2010): 932, DOI: 10.1126/science.1192439.

137    **even job performance:** Jessica de Bloom, "Making Holidays Work," *Psychologist* 28, no. 8 (August 2015): 632–36; Jessica de Bloom et al., "Do We Recover from Vacation? Meta-Analysis of Vacation Effects on Health and Well-Being," *Journal of Occupational Health* 51, no. 1 (January 2009): 13–25, DOI: 10.1539/joh.K8004; Jessica de Bloom et al., "Vacation from Work: A 'Ticket to Creativity'?: The Effects of Recreational Travel on Cognitive Flexibility and Originality," *Tourism Management* 44 (October 2014): 164–71, DOI: 10.1016/j.tourman.2014.03.013.

137    **greater life satisfaction overall**: Colin West, Cassie Mogilner, and Sanford DeVoe, "Happiness from Treating the Weekend Like a Vacation," *Social Psychology and Personality Science* 12, no. 3 (April 2021): 346–56, DOI: 10.1177%2F1948550620916080.

137    **doesn't get a single one**: Alexander E. M. Hess, "On Holiday: Countries with the Most Vacation Days," *USA Today*,
June 8, 2013, https://www.usatoday.com/story/money/
business/2013/06/08/countries-most-vacation-days/
2400193/.

137    **Americans don't take them**: Abigail Johnson Hess, "Here's
How Many Paid Vacation Days the Typical American
Worker Gets," CNBC, July 6, 2018, https://www.cnbc
.com/2018/07/05/heres-how-many-paid-vacation-days
-the-typical-american-worker-gets-.html; US Travel Association, "State of American Vacation 2018," May 8, 2018,
https://projecttimeoff.com/reports/state-of-american
-vacation-2018/.

137    **reason is time**: NPR, Robert Wood Johnson Foundation,
and Harvard T. H. Chan School of Public Health, "The Workplace and Health," RWJF, July 11, 2016, http://www.rwjf
.org/content/dam/farm/reports/surveys_and_polls/
2016/rwjf430330.

138    **tested this idea**: West, Mogilner, and DeVoe, "Happiness
from Treating the Weekend," 346–56.

138    **treat the weekend like a vacation:** I observed that "treat the
weekend like a vacation" was one of the most helpful pieces
of advice I gave for how to stay happy during the unhappy
times of the COVID pandemic. The days, weeks, and seasons
bled into each other, and everyone was stuck in their homes
for work, school, and . . . everything else. It became more
important than ever to take breaks. I implemented this
advice myself to keep my spirits up.

Treating the weekend like vacation reminded us to log off
on Friday afternoons, which helped to partition weekends

from workweeks. But even more importantly, it licensed us to relax for a couple of days. It encouraged us to give ourselves a break from working so hard and anxiously to "get through it." It urged us to take a breath and be in the moment, so that we'd enjoy Sunday morning pancake breakfasts and each other more. With flights canceled, museums closed, gates of theme parks locked, we could still relish those summer "vacation" days: the kids slept in the tent pitched in the backyard, marshmallows got roasted for s'mores over the barbecue, and slow hours were spent listening to music, playing card games, and sipping rosé midday—just like a vacation.

140    **"in the present"**: Kirk W. Brown and Richard M. Ryan, "The Benefits of Being Present: Mindfulness and Its Role in Psychological Well-Being," *Journal of Personality and Social Psychology* 84, no. 4 (April 2003): 822, DOI: 10.1037/0022-3514.84.4.822.

141    **and interpersonal relationships**: Kirk W. Brown, Richard M. Ryan, and J. David Creswell, "Mindfulness: Theoretical Foundations and Evidence for its Salutary Effects," *Psychological Inquiry* 18, no. 4 (December 2007): 211–37, DOI: 10.1080/10478400701598298.

141    **increasing feelings of connection**: Hedy Kober, "How Can Mindfulness Help Us," TEDx Talk, May 13, 2017, YouTube video, 17:48, https://www.youtube.com/watch?v=4hKfXyZGeJY; Judson A. Brewer et al., "Meditation Experience Is Associated with Differences in Default Mode Network Activity and Connectivity," *Proceedings of the National Academy of Sciences of the United States of America* 108, no. 50 (October 2011): 20254–59, DOI: 10.1073/

pnas.1112029108; Barbara L. Fredrickson et al., "Open Hearts Build Lives: Positive Emotions, Induced through Loving-Kindness Meditation, Build Consequential Personal Resources," *Journal of Personality and Social Psychology* 95, no. 5 (November 2008): 1045–62, DOI: 10.1037/a0013262; Michael D. Mrazek et al., "Mindfulness Training Improves Working Memory Capacity and GRE Performance while Reducing Mind Wandering," *Psychological Science* 24, no. 5 (May 2013): 776–81, DOI: 10.1177/0956797612459659; Britta K. Hölzel et al., "Mindfulness Practice Leads to Increases in Regional Brain Gray Matter Density," *Psychiatry Research: Neuroimaging* 191, no. 1 (January 2011): 36–43, DOI: 10.1016/j.pscychresns.2010.08.006; Cendri A. Hutcherson, Emma M. Seppala, and James J. Gross, "Loving-Kindness Meditation Increases Social Connectedness," *Emotion* 8, no. 5 (November 2008): 720, DOI: 10.1037/a0013237; Brown, Ryan, and Creswell, "Mindfulness," 211–37.

141    **anxiety:** A feeling of worry or nervousness about future events and uncertain outcomes.

141    **anxiety disorder:** When anxiety is experienced persistently and becomes debilitating, interfering with one's daily activities.

141    **in the US:** National Alliance on Mental Illness, "Mental Health by the Numbers," September 2019, https://www .nami.org/mhstats.

141    **around the world:** Hannah Ritchie and Max Roser, "Mental Health," Our World in Data, April 2018, https://ourworldin data.org/mental-health.

141    **as men:** Olivia Remes et al., "A Systematic Review of

Reviews on the Prevalence of Anxiety Disorders in Adult Populations," *Brain and Behavior* 6, no. 7 (June 2016): 1–33, DOI: 10.1002/brb3.497.

141  **during the COVID pandemic**: Jean M. Twenge and Thomas E. Joiner, "US Census Bureau–Assessed Prevalence of Anxiety and Depressive Symptoms in 2019 and during the 2020 COVID-19 Pandemic," *Depression and Anxiety* 37, no. 10 (October 2020): 954–56, DOI: 10.1002/da.23077; Min Luo et al., "The Psychological and Mental Impact of Coronavirus Disease 2019 (COVID-19) on Medical Staff and General Public: A Systematic Review and Meta-Analysis," *Psychiatry Research* 291, no. 113190 (September 2020): DOI: 10.1016/j.psychres.2020.113190.

142  **in multiple languages**: UCLA Mindful Awareness Research Center, "Free Guided Meditations," UCLA Health, https://www.uclahealth.org/marc/audio. Diana Winston, director of the center, has videos explaining what mindfulness is and provides guided meditations at https://www.uclahealth.org/marc/getting-started.

145  **during work:** Mihaly Csikszentmihalyi and Judith LeFevre, "Optimal Experience in Work and Leisure," *Journal of Personality and Social Psychology* 56, no. 5 (June 1989): 815–22, DOI: 10.1037/0022-3514.56.5.815. This article finds that the majority of flow experiences are reported when working instead of during leisure.

145  **yet unimportant ones**: Meng Zhu, Yang Yang, and Christopher Hsee, "The Mere Urgency Effect," *Journal of Consumer Research* 45, no. 3 (October 2018): 673–90, DOI: 10.1093/jcr/ucy008.

145–46    **on any one task**: Bradley R. Staats and Francesca Gino, "Specialization and Variety in Repetitive Tasks: Evidence from a Japanese Bank," *Management Science* 58, no. 6 (June 2012): 1141–59, DOI: 10.1287/mnsc.1110.1482.

146    **gone to bed**: Chapter 3 covers additional insights shared by Dr. Alon Y. Avidan, director of UCLA's Sleep Disorders Center, on the virtues of sleep.

147    **doing one at a time**: Shalena Srna, Rom Y. Schrift, and Gal Zauberman, "The Illusion of Multitasking and Its Positive Effect on Performance," *Psychological Science* 29, no. 12 (October 2018): 1942–55, DOI: 10.1177/0956797618801013.

147    **laptops open**: Helene Hembrooke and Geri Gay, "The Laptop and the Lecture: The Effects of Multitasking in Learning Environments," *Journal of Computing in Higher Education* 15, no. 1 (September 2003): 46–64, DOI: 10.1007/BF02940852; Laura L. Bowman et al., "Can Students Really Multitask? An Experimental Study of Instant Messaging while Reading," *Computers & Education* 54, no. 4 (2010): 927–31, DOI: 10.1016/j.compedu.2009.09.024.

148    **twice as often**: Asurion, "Americans Check Their Phones 96 Times a Day," November 21, 2019, https://www.asurion.com/about/press-releases/americans-check-their-phones-96-times-a-day/.

148    **dinner dates and church**: Harris Interactive, "2013 Mobile Consumer Habits Study," Jumio, 2013, http://pages.jumio.com/rs/jumio/images/Jumio%20-%20Mobile%20Consumer%20Habits%20Study-2.pdf.

149    **more distracted**: Ryan Dwyer, Kostadin Kushlev, and Elizabeth Dunn, "Smartphone Use Undermines Enjoyment of

Face-to-Face Social Interaction," *Journal of Experimental Social Psychology* 78 (September 2018): 233–39, DOI: 10.1016/j.jesp.2017.10.007.

151    **enjoyable and connecting**: Nicholas Epley and Juliana Schroeder, "Mistakenly Seeking Solitude," *Journal of Experimental Psychology* 143, no. 5 (October 2014): 1980–99, DOI: 10.1037/a0037323.

152    **during darker economic times**: Hal E. Hershfield and Adam L. Alter, "On the Naturalistic Relationship between Mood and Entertainment Choice," *Journal of Experimental Psychology: Applied* 25, no. 3 (May 2019): 458–76, DOI: 10.1037/xap0000220.

152    **depression and domestic violence went up**: Catherine K. Ettman et al., "Prevalence of Depression Symptoms in US Adults before and during the COVID-19 Pandemic," *JAMA Network Open* 3, no. 9 (September 2020): DOI: 10.1001/jamanetworkopen.2020.19686; Stacy Francis, "Op-Ed: Uptick in Domestic Violence amid COVID-19 Isolation," CNBC, October 30, 2020, https://www.cnbc.com/2020/10/30/uptick-in-domestic-violence-amid-covid-19-isolation.html.

## Chapter Seven

157    **short film by Meir Kay**: Meir Kalmanson, "A Valuable Lesson for a Happier Life," May 4, 2016, YouTube video, 3:05, https://youtu.be/SqGRnlXplx0.

159    **tiny screens**: Sherin Shibu, "Which Generation Is Most Dependent on Smartphones? (Hint: They're Young.)," *News*

*and Trends* (blog), November 20, 2020, https://www
.entrepreneur.com/article/360098.

160    **TV every day:** Nielsen Media Research, "Nielsen Total
Audience Report: September 2019," September 2019,
https://www.nielsen.com/us/en/insights/report/2019/
the-nielsen-total-audience-report-september-2019/.

161    **tendency to overcommit:** Gal Zauberman and John G.
Lynch Jr., "Resource Slack and Propensity to Discount
Delayed Investments of Time versus Money," *Journal of
Experimental Psychology* 134, no. 1 (March 2005): 23–37,
DOI: 10.1037/0096-3445.134.1.23.

162    **worse at this than men:** Alia E. Dastagir, "The One Word
Women Need to Be Saying More Often," *USA Today*,
April 25, 2021, https://www.usatoday.com/story/life/health
-wellness/2021/04/20/why-its-so-hard-for-women-to-say
-no/7302181002/.

162    **say yes more often:** Sara McLaughlin Mitchell and Vicki L.
Hesli, "Women Don't Ask? Women Don't Say No? Bargain-
ing and Service in the Political Science Profession," *PS: Political Science & Politics* 46, no. 2 (April 2013): 355–69, DOI:
10.1017/S1049096513000073. Women faculty are significantly more likely to serve on department-level committees,
school-level committees, and committees for their field than
are male faculty, but they are significantly less likely to be
asked to chair these committees. Meanwhile, male faculty are
more likely to be asked and to serve as department chairs or
as an academic program director.

166    **how to declutter your house:** Marie Kondo, *The Life-
Changing Magic of Tidying Up: The Japanese Art of Declutter-
ing and Organizing* (Berkeley, CA: Ten Speed Press, 2014).

171    **overly self-controlled:** Ran Kivetz and Anat Keinan, "Repenting Hyperopia: An Analysis of Self-Control Regrets," *Journal of Consumer Research* 33, no. 2 (September 2006): 273–82, DOI: 10.1086/506308.

*Chapter Eight*

185    **dinners as his lifeline:** Barack Obama and Bruce Springsteen, "Fatherhood," March 29, 2021, in *Renegades: Born in the USA*, produced by Spotify, podcast audio, https://open .spotify.com/episode/6yFtWJDdwZdUDrH5M0lVZf.

186    **satisfied with their lives overall:** Martin Seligman et al., "Positive Psychology Progress: Empirical Validation of Interventions," *American Psychologist* 60, no. 5 (July 2005): 410–21, DOI: 10.1037/0003-066X.60.5.410; Robert A. Emmons and Michael E. McCullough, "Counting Blessings versus Burdens: An Experimental Investigation of Gratitude and Subjective Well-Being in Daily Life," *Journal of Personality and Social Psychology* 84, no. 2 (February 2003): 377, DOI:10.1037/0022-3514.84.2.377.

195    **moms even more than dads:** Hielke Buddelmeyer, Daniel S. Hamermesh, and Mark Wooden, "The Stress Cost of Children on Moms and Dads," *European Economic Review* 109 (October 2018): 148–61, DOI: 10.1016/j.euro ecorev.2016.12.012.

195    **than fathers:** Laura M. Giurge, Ashley V. Whillans, and Colin West, "Why Time Poverty Matters for Individuals, Organisations and Nations," *Nature Human Behaviour* 4, no. 10 (October 2020): 993–1003, DOI: 10.1038/s41562

-020-0920-z; Jerry A. Jacobs and Kathleen Gerson, *The Time Divide: Work, Family, and Gender Inequality* (Cambridge: Harvard University Press, 2004); Marybeth J. Mattingly and Liana C. Sayer, "Under Pressure: Gender Differences in the Relationship between Free Time and Feeling Rushed," *Journal of Marriage and Family* 68, no. 1 (February 2006): 205–21, DOI: 10.1111/j.1741-3737.2006.00242.x; Daniel S. Hamermesh and Jungmin Lee, "Stressed Out on Four Continents: Time Crunch or Yuppie Kvetch?" *Review of Economics and Statistics* 89, no. 2 (May 2007): 374–83, DOI: 10.1162/rest.89.2.374.

196    **stuck home from school**: David Leonhardt, "Not Enough to Sort of Open," *New York Times,* May 3, 2021.

196    **significantly less happy**: Laura M. Giurge, Ashley V. Whillans, and Ayse Yemiscigil, "A Multicountry Perspective on Gender Differences in Time Use during COVID-19," *Proceedings of the National Academy of Sciences of the United States of America* 118, no. 12 (March 2021): DOI: 10.1073/pnas.2018494118.

196    **as Sheryl Sandberg describes it**: Sheryl Sandberg, *Lean In: Women, Work, and the Will to Lead* (New York: Alfred A. Knopf, 2013).

196    **divide domestic work between couples**: Eve Rodsky, *Fair Play: A Game-Changing Solution for When You Have Too Much to Do (and More Life to Live)* (New York: G. P. Putnam's Sons, 2019). Eve makes a compelling case for all of us who have too much to do yet aspire toward more from life. She advises that having a clear division of household labor effectively lessens individual resentment and increases happiness in one's relationship and overall. Rob and I have found that this can be achieved through smart scheduling.

202    **enjoy watching the show more:** Leif D. Nelson, Tom Meyvis, and Jeff Galak, "Enhancing the Television-Viewing Experience through Commercial Interruptions," *Journal of Consumer Research* 36, no. 2 (August 2009): 160–72, DOI: 10.1086/597030.

202    **end up less happy:** Jordan Etkin and Cassie Mogilner, "Does Variety among Activities Increase Happiness?" *Journal of Consumer Research* 43, no. 2 (August 2016): 210–29, DOI: 10.1093/jcr/ucw021.

203    **dread and intensely feel:** As I mentioned in chapter 7, responding to email feels like a chore to me. I dread opening my inbox wondering what requests await me and knowing I will get sucked in and lose hours that I could have spent better otherwise. If I were to intermittently check my email throughout the day, it would cloud my entire week with anticipated and carried-over anxiety. Instead, I set aside two hours toward the end of each workday to, all at once, tackle my email and the administrative work that falls from these emails.

I consolidate my meetings into particular afternoons. I don't dislike meetings, but I know they require a different form of mental energy. I've noticed that transitioning between quiet thinking and social interactions takes time; therefore, by scheduling meetings back-to-back, I reduce the time I waste transitioning, and also protect my individual work time to be more productive.

Not because I don't enjoy teaching, but because presenting requires a significant amount of preparation (not to mention the time it takes to blow out my hair and pull together a nice outfit), I try to consolidate my time in front of audiences within the week. This way, I can leverage across my presentations the time I spend rehearsing and the adrenaline that inevitably kicks in before stepping in front of the class.

205 **anew every time:** Leaf Van Boven and Thomas Gilovich, "To Do or to Have? That Is the Question," *Journal of Personality and Social Psychology* 85, no. 6 (January 2004): 1193–1202, DOI: 10.1037/0022-3514.85.6.1193; Thomas Gilovich, Amit Kumar, and Lily Jampol, "A Wonderful Life: Experiential Consumption and the Pursuit of Happiness," *Journal of Consumer Psychology* 25, no. 1 (September 2014): 152–65, DOI: 10.1016/j.jcps.2014.08.004; Cindy Chan and Cassie Mogilner, "Experiential Gifts Foster Stronger Social Relationships than Material Gifts," *Journal of Consumer Research* 43, no. 6 (April 2017): 913–31, DOI: 10.1093/jcr/ucw067.

## Chapter Nine

213 **Poem:** Henry van Dyke, "Katrina's Sun-dial," in *Music and Other Poems* (New York: Charles Scribner's Sons, 1904), 105.

216 **how they think about their time:** Cassie Mogilner, Hal Hershfield, and Jennifer Aaker, "Rethinking Time: Implications for Well-Being," *Consumer Psychology Review* 1, no. 1 (January 2018): 41–53, DOI: 10.1002/arcp.1003; Tayler Bergstrom et al. (working paper, 2021). Agreeing with these four items is associated with greater flourishing, meaning in life, life satisfaction, and positive affect, and less negative affect. These results hold controlling for demographic variables, including how old the person is and their parental status.

218    **"diaries of the digital age":** Jennifer Aaker, "Jennifer Aaker: The Happiness Narrative," Future of StoryTelling, August 31, 2015, Vimeo video, 4:59, https://vimeo.com/137841197.

218    **in real time who was feeling what:** Sep Kamvar and Jonathan Harris, *We Feel Fine: An Almanac of Human Emotion* (New York: Scribner, 2009), http://www.wefeelfine.org/.

219    **changes over the course of life:** Cassie Mogilner, Sepandar D. Kamvar, and Jennifer Aaker, "The Shifting Meaning of Happiness," *Social Psychological and Personality Science* 2, no. 4 (July 2011): 395–402, DOI: 10.1177/1948550610393987; Cassie Mogilner, Jennifer Aaker, and Sepandar D. Kamvar, "How Happiness Affects Choice," *Journal of Consumer Research* 39, no. 2 (August 2012): 429–43, DOI: 10.1086/663774.

219    **ordinary and extraordinary experiences:** Amit Bhattacharjee and Cassie Mogilner, "Happiness from Ordinary and Extraordinary Experiences," *Journal of Consumer Research* 41, no. 1 (June 2014): 1–17, DOI: 10.1086/674724.

221    **what was merely urgent:** Bergstrom et al. (working paper). We told participants, "Sometimes we do tasks because they are important to us (i.e., the consequences are big), and sometimes we do tasks because they are urgent (i.e., they must be completed soon). Tasks can be important and urgent, or neither important nor urgent, but there are also tasks that are urgent but not important, and tasks that are important but not urgent." They were then asked on a scale of 1 (never) to 7 (all the time), "In the past week, to what extent did you dedicate your time to tasks that are important?" and "In the past week, to what extent did you dedicate your time to tasks that are urgent?" We found that agreeing to the four items in the bird's-eye-view scale predicts time spent on important tasks

when controlling for time spent on urgent tasks. The scale did not predict time spent on urgent tasks when controlling for time spent on important tasks. This suggests that people with high BEV spend more time on important, but not urgent, tasks.

221     **regardless of its importance:** Meng Zhu, Yang Yang, and Christopher Hsee, "The Mere Urgency Effect," *Journal of Consumer Research* 45, no. 3 (October 2018): 673–90, DOI: 10.1093/jcr/ucy008.

229     **most comprehensive longitudinal research studies in history:** Robert Waldinger, "What Makes a Good Life? Lessons from the Longest Study on Happiness," TEDx BeaconStreet, November 2015, TED video, 12:38, https://www.ted.com/talks/robert_waldinger_what_makes_a_good_life_lessons_from_the_longest_study_on_happiness?language=en.

232     **two types:** Mike Morrison and Neale Roese, "Regrets of the Typical American: Findings from a Nationally Representative Sample," *Social Psychological and Personality Science* 2, no. 6 (November 2011): 576–83, DOI: 10.1177/1948550611401756.

233     **had not done and wished they had:** Thomas Gilovich and Victoria Husted Medvec, "The Experience of Regret: What, When, and Why," *Psychological Review* 102, no. 2 (May 1995): 379–95, DOI:10.1037/0033-295X.102.2.379.

235     **happiness and meaning in life are very highly correlated:** Rhia Catapano et al., "Financial Resources Impact the Relationship between Meaning and Happiness," *Emotion* 22 (forthcoming).

235     **doesn't require constantly feeling happy:** Laura A. King, Samantha J. Heintzelman, and Sarah J. Ward, "Beyond

the Search for Meaning: A Contemporary Science of the Experience of Meaning in Life," *Current Directions in Psychological Science* 25 no. 4 (August 2016): 211–16, DOI: 10.1177/0963721416656354.

235    **ended up better off:** Kathleen Vohs, Jennifer Aaker, and Rhia Catapano, "It's Not Going to Be that Fun: Negative Experiences Can Add Meaning to Life," *Current Opinion in Psychology* 26 (April 2019): 11–14, DOI: 10.1016/j.copsyc.2018.04.014.

237    **a study I conducted:** Cassie Mogilner and Michael Norton, "Preferences for Experienced versus Remembered Happiness," *Journal of Positive Psychology* 14, no. 2 (April 2018): 244–51, DOI: 10.1080/17439760.2018.1460688.

As part of this project, I conducted this study in which I asked six hundred adults, "If you had the goal of *experiencing* happiness or of *looking back* immediately [in 1 year/in 10 years] and feeling happy, how would you spend the next hour?" They were then presented with 22 activities from Kahneman et al.'s Day Reconstruction Survey and asked to rate on a 7-point scale the extent to which they would spend their time doing the following. A factor analysis on how people would spend their time revealed 6 factors for happy ways to spend time: passive leisure (TV, internet, reading), active leisure (exercise, sports, outdoors), socializing with friends or colleagues, engaging with romantic partner, spending time with family, and working vs. relaxing (this was a bipolar dimension). Experienced vs. remembered happiness only impacted the tendency to work vs. relax. All of the other factors were equally likely for experienced vs. remembered happiness. That is to say that the one difference that emerged was that memory maximizers were more likely than experience maximizers to mention doing work; whereas experience maximizers mentioned being more likely to relax.

237    **peak and its ending:** Ed Diener, Derrick Wirtz, and Shigehiro Oishi, "End Effects of Rated Life Quality: The James Dean Effect," *American Psychological Society* 12, no. 2 (March 2001): 124–48, DOI: 10.1111/1467-9280.00321; Barbara L. Fredrickson and Daniel Kahneman, "Duration Neglect in Retrospective Evaluations of Affective Episodes," *Journal of Personality and Social Psychology* 65, no. 1 (July 1993): 45–55, DOI: 10.1037/0022-3514.65.1.45; Daniel Kahneman et al., "When More Pain Is Preferred to Less: Adding a Better End," *Psychological Science* 4, no. 6 (November 1993): 401–405, DOI: 10.1111/j.1467-9280.1993.tb00589.x; Donald A. Redelmeier and Daniel Kahneman, "Patients' Memories of Painful Medical Treatments: Real-Time and Retrospective Evaluations of Two Minimally Invasive Procedures," *Pain* 66, no. 1 (July 1996): 3–8, DOI: 10.1016/0304-3959(96)02994-6; Derrick Wirtz et al., "What to Do on Spring Break?: The Role of Predicted, On-Line, and Remembered Experience in Future Choice," *Psychological Science* 14, no. 5 (September 2003): 520–24, DOI: 10.1111/1467-9280.03455.

# ACKNOWLEDGMENTS

A giant thank-you to my book team, without whom *Happier Hour* would not exist. Margo Fleming, you are the most perfect and wonderful agent I could have ever wished for. Despite my reservations, you cheered me into writing a book and have continued to be my much-appreciated cheerleader along the way. Thank you for understanding me and helping spread happiness. To my astute and insightful editor, Karyn Marcus—thank you for seeing and sharing in my vision, and for guiding me so wisely in turning it into a reality. Jane Isay, your coaching during the writing process was crucial and an absolute treat. I've learned so much from you, not just in how to tell a story but in how to live a good life. You're an inspiration for all of us working moms; thank you for your mentorship and friendship. To my caring and expert publicity team, Aileen Boyle, Jill Siegel, and Sally Marvin—thank you for everything you've done to help *Happier Hour* reach more people so that more people can be happier . . . and for not making me spend time on social media. To my multitalented design guru and nanny, Hannah Sanders—thank you for creating the graphics to so perfectly illustrate the lessons in this book and for taking such wonderful care of Leo and Lita so I could spend time writing. Because of you, I felt okay closing my office door, continuing to hear laughter ring through the house. To my fastidious research assistant, Joanna Zobak—thank you for being my careful reader and for compiling the references.

I am deeply grateful to all of my research collaborators. You've made the process of creating knowledge about happiness much, much happier. I admire each of you for your intellect and dedication, and thank you for making my work hours way more fun. In order of projects mentioned in the book, I sincerely thank you, Jennifer Aaker, Sep Kamvar, Hal Hershfield, Marissa Sharif, Maria Trupia, Isabelle Engeler, Uri Barnea, Francesca Gino, Zoë Chance, Mike Norton, Rhia Catapano, Jordi Quoidbach, Cindy Chan, Amit Bhattacharjee, Jordan Etkin, Colin West, Sanford DeVoe, Tayler Bergstrom, and Joey Reiff.

I am so appreciative of all the UCLA Anderson students who have taken my course. Thank you for so openly sharing in your personal journeys toward greater satisfaction and connection. A special thank-you to those of you who shared your stories for the book—Justin Sternberg, Nicole Schwartz, and Gaby Koenig—and to those of you whose stories have stuck in my mind and heart, allowing me to share on your behalf. And to my guest speakers, I greatly thank Dr. Alon Avidan and Sara Tucker for teaching us about the significant emotional benefits from getting good sleep and practicing meditation, and Jeff Buenrostro for teaching us how to cultivate happiness within organizations.

To my incredible, inspiring, and supportive friends—you consistently confirm the loads of research that identify having good friends as key for immediate and lasting happiness. You have bettered my time, filling it with laughter, adventure, and understanding. I additionally thank those of you who were so generous by giving some of your time to share your experiences for these pages. Thank you for your friendship Ashley Kaper, Shaolee Sen, Colette Bernard, Katy Milkman, Cullen Blake, Ian McGuire, Julie McGuire, Alison Mackenzie, Dan Levin, Ali Weinberger, Elsa Collins, Alana Kagan, Matt Kagan, Sue Tran, Charles Hsieh, Kim Tripp, Owen Tripp, Kristy Friedrichs, Jason Friedrichs, My Le Nguyen, Chris Adams, Matt Spetzler, Jackie Spetzler, Deanna Kehoe, Bianca

Russell, Andy Russell, Dianna Sternberg, Karla Sayles, Linda Guerrero, Brett Berkowitz, Anna Gross, and David Gross. Thank you, Eve Rodsky and Sarah Mlynowski, for your guidance and friendship in navigating the book process. And thank you, Matt Sayles, Alex Weinberger, and Riley Ehrlich for sharing your professional purpose. It's clear that you each have found your calling, and it's an inspiration for all of us. And thank you, Scott Fitzwater, for explaining your craft of making mosaics.

And to my family—thank you for all the good times we have shared over the years and for giving some up over these last couple so that I could finish this book. I thank my brother and best friend, Sam Mogilner, for keeping me laughing from our childhood through now. I thank my sister-in-law, Christina Gould, for joining in the laughter and for always being there for both of us. I thank my mom, Vickie Mogilner, for teaching us the importance of turning all moments (no matter how ordinary) into celebrations. I thank my parents-in-law, Irene and Lock Holmes, and my sisters- and brother-in-law, Ann Holmes, Amelia Luna, and Aaron Luna for their continued support. And I thank my niece, Lolly Mogilner, and nephews, P. J. Mogilner and Renzo Luna, for keeping things silly.

Most of all, my heart bursts with gratitude for my husband and kids. Rob, Leo, and Lita, you are wonderful. I can't thank you enough for making the hours of my life so fun and meaningful. Rob, thank you for choosing happiness with me every day, and for inspiring me by all you do, and for supporting me in all that I do. Leo, your giant smile, belly laugh, and humor perpetually bring me joy. Thank you for reminding me every day to pause and smell the roses. Lita, your delight with the world makes each of our days brighter. I will forever treasure our "Thursday Morning Coffee Dates," no matter the day of the week.

# INDEX